Declaration of Independence

Seven Freemason Iconographies

by Dan Mento

A NOTE ON HISTORICAL SPECULATION

` This book presents a highly speculative and interpretative analysis of "The Declaration of Independence." The theories regarding hidden drawings and their esoteric meanings are the author's unique conceptualizations, built upon a framework of historical inquiry and imaginative exploration. Readers are invited to engage with this work as speculative nonfiction, where historical context and innovative interpretation intersect.

Before delving into the complexities of this story, I want to express my respect for both the "Declaration of Independence" and the Fraternity of Freemasonry. My intention is not to disparage either, but rather to engage in a hypothetical exploration of the hidden graphical process and methods employed by the Freemasons in the "Declaration of Independence."

ISBN: 978-0-9996397-6-4 (Paperback)

Preface

Reader's Notice on Method, Pace, and Interpretation

What appears in the following chapters as a rapid sequence of visual identifications did not arise quickly, intuitively, or all at once. The work presented here unfolded over nearly a decade of repeated examination, mechanical testing, rejection, and return. Most observations described in a few paragraphs reflect months or years of uncertainty, abandonment, and reevaluation before being permitted to remain.

The order of presentation reflects structural logic, not the chronology or speed of discovery. Images, alignments, and correspondences are grouped according to geometric dependencies and procedural clarity, rather than by the order in which they were first noticed. This compression is a necessity of communication, not a reflection of how conclusions were reached.

Throughout this study, countless apparent patterns were examined. Many shapes initially suggested familiar figures or symbolic forms but failed to hold up under rotation, mirroring, scaling, or repetition. Only those configurations that survived multiple constrained transformations, maintained proportional coherence, and reappeared consistently under the same mechanical rules were retained. No interpretation was pursued unless the underlying geometry remained stable without symbolic assistance.

The reader should understand that recognition precedes identification in this work. A form is first treated as geometry: points, alignments, proportions, and transformations. Only after such a form proves mechanically persistent is it compared, carefully and provisionally, to symbolic or historical imagery. These comparisons are descriptive rather than declarative. They are offered to aid visual understanding, not to assert intent, belief, or authorship.

This book does not ask the reader to accept any symbolic interpretation as fact. It asks only that the reader observe whether a constrained graphical method produces repeatable, non-random structure within the text of the *Declaration of Independence*. Interpretation, when present, is explicitly marked as such and is always secondary to method.

The path described here is not one of sudden insight but of long familiarity, of seeing, setting aside, returning, and seeing again. What follows should therefore be read not as a revelation, but as a record of a disciplined visual process applied patiently over a decade of work.

A straight line can be drawn through any two points.

Euclid's First Postulate
Euclid's Elements

Provocation

What follows is constrained by rule, repetition, and exclusion.
Its meaning, if any, comes later.

The figures presented here are not offered as proof, but as provocation: evidence that something structured may be present before any explanation is attempted.

This is not an invitation to believe, but a challenge to observe the method.

Chapter One

Whispers from the Founders

This study began as a practical experiment rather than a historical argument. I wanted to know whether the engrossed copy of the *Declaration of Independence* could be treated as a graphical plane, much like a drafting surface, and whether any non-random structure would emerge if it were analyzed under a strict set of mechanical constraints. The engrossed copy of the *Declaration of Independence* has been analyzed to yield seven intricately designed drawings with symbolic themes. The *Declaration's* text block can be interpreted as a graphical plane. On this "plane," the visual center point of each occurrence of the letters Y, W, V, B, G, P, and M is used as an independent graphical point. By connecting these specific letter points, seven distinct principal drawings emerge, revealing structured geometric relationships. Every instance of each letter is used, with none omitted and none added, a deliberate constraint that strongly suggests the precise placement may have contributed to defining the geometry of each design. Although the text was written by a scribe, this study examines whether the layout was dictated by a primary architect to ensure that these geometric constraints remained intact. Each of the seven

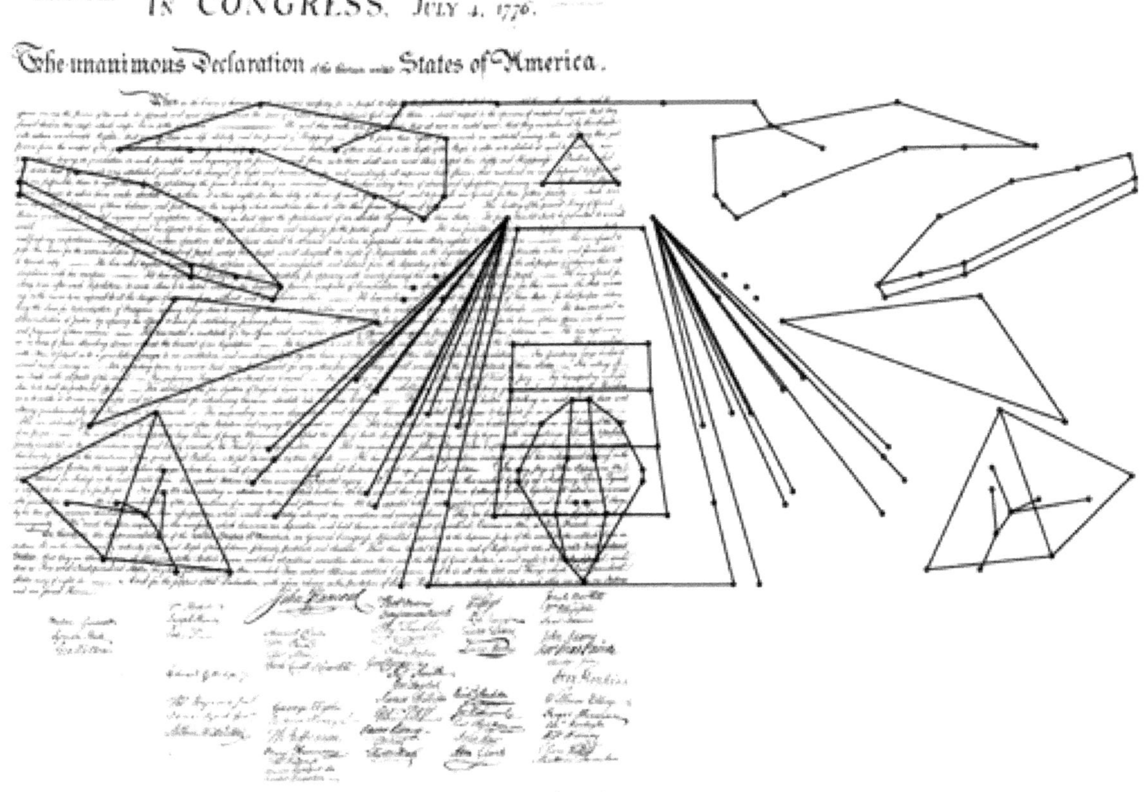

Fig. 1

resulting drawings presents a masterful composition made up of numerous smaller, seemingly illustrative elements. For example, the drawing I have derived from exclusively connecting the letter Vs (Fig. 1) creates a rich tapestry that could be seen as featuring more than twenty images, including the Eye of Providence, the unfinished pyramid, and a Freemason ascending the three steps: Entered Apprentice, Fellow Craft, and Master Mason.

This chapter focuses on the mechanical and graphical process by which images are derived. Interpretive identifications are introduced provisionally and examined in greater depth in later chapters. The parallel lines of the *Declaration* text block form a graduated graphical plane, with the mirror line serving as the starting point for all images. The mirror line serves as a variable axis; its placement is determined by the unique spatial distribution of the selected letter (W, V, Y, etc.).

The position of the image relative to the edge of the *Declaration* determines where the mirror line is placed. The mirror line can be positioned at either the left or right edge of the document, depending on the layout required for the selected letter. The image appears either in the correct reading orientation or inverted relative to the *Declaration's* text. The mirror line typically aligns with the edge of the text block. At times, the mirror line is positioned a few centimeters in from the edge, with the letter's graphical points and their mirrored points alternating on either side of the mirror line, making the solution more difficult. When placing the graphics points/dots, the dot is anchored to the optical center-point of the corpus 'body' of the letter, excluding ascenders, descenders, and ornamental strokes, and determined consistently by visual balance rather than typographic measurement.

All letters of the alphabet were first processed uniformly as point sets. Only after mirrored stabilization tests consistently failed for most letters were W, V, Y, M, B, G, and P retained for further analysis. What sets the W, V, Y, M, B, G, and P letters apart from the rest of the alphabet? The selected letter counts in the *Declaration* are W-97, V-74, Y-81, M-144, B-95, G-130, and P-138. The range of 81-144 strikes a manageable balance between word-letter maneuverability within the text block and the contrast between deliberate shapes and spaces. Below the number 74, the absence of dots reduces detail, increasing ambiguity and blurring the image. Above 144, the dot density becomes unmanageable. All letters of the alphabet were processed as dot patterns and thoroughly analyzed for edge-mirrored complex geometric imagery, but failed to produce stable shapes, such as triangles, septagrams, trapezoids, hexagrams, and rhombuses, before proceeding with the selected W, V, Y, M, B, G, and P. Where the two dot pattern halves meet, a mirror line is formed. The two halves are continuously slid until the dot patterns at the mirror line form multiple independent geometric relationships that stabilize simultaneously. Like a combination lock, the image only 'clicks' into focus at a specific alignment; move it by a fraction to the left or right, and it dissolves back into a random jumble of letters. The visual imagery supports the geometrically stabilizing mirrored balance: in the case of the letter V image (Fig. 1), the coffin, loop, three steps, and altar.

The diagram (Fig. 2) illustrates the mechanical basis of the plotting method used throughout this study. The dashed horizontal guides correspond to fixed textual positions within the engrossed *Declaration* and are employed strictly as spatial reference markers, not as semantic or interpretive selections. Each solid dot represents the optical center of a single occurrence of the selected letter, recorded directly from the manuscript without omission, substitution, or adjustment. Open dots indicate the mirrored counterparts generated through a single-axis reflection applied only after all original points were plotted. The connecting lines do not impose form but reveal relationships that emerge only at a specific mirror alignment; when the alignment is altered, proportionality collapses, and the geometry loses coherence. This figure, therefore, documents not an illustrative overlay but the constrained conditions under which ordered structure can be resolved from the text block itself. Any further movement breaks the coherence.

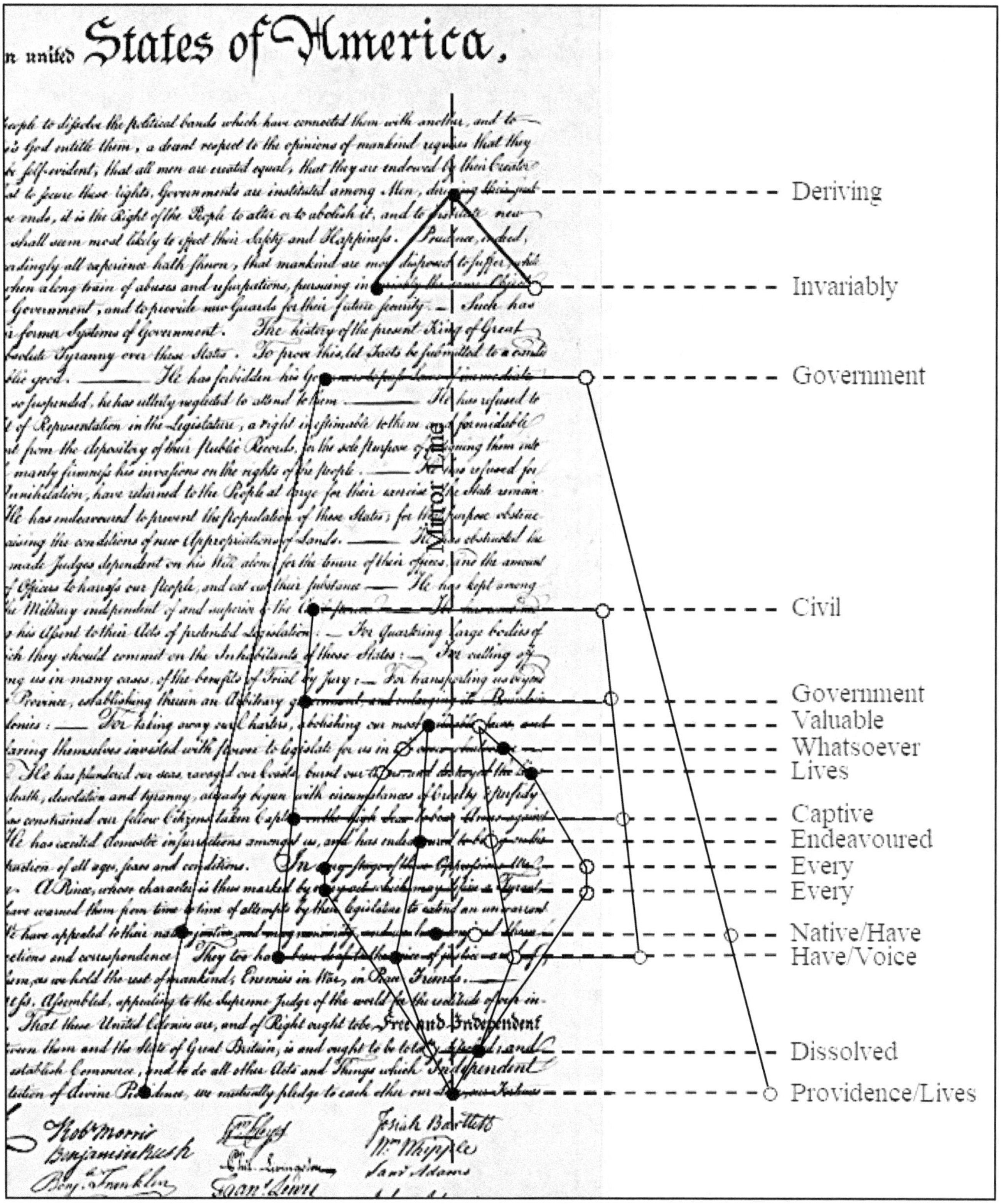

States of America,

Mirror Line

Deriving
Invariably
Government
Civil
Government
Valuable
Whatsoever
Lives
Captive
Endeavoured
Every
Every
Native/Have
Have/Voice
Dissolved
Providence/Lives

Fig. 2

The Challenge of Proving Intent

An attempt was made to mathematically analyze the placement of individual letters within the *Declaration of Independence* to determine if they were positioned randomly or by design. To do this, we used standard spatial tests, the same tools scientists use to study how stars are scattered in a galaxy or how trees grow in a forest. These include Ripley's K-Function and the Nearest Neighbor Index (NNI), which measure whether dots are "clumped" or "spread out" more than one would expect by pure chance.

However, applying these "off-the-shelf" math tests to a 250-year-old handwritten document proved unreliable. In a perfectly random system (known in math as a Poisson Point Process), every dot is independent. But the *Declaration* is not a blank slate; it is a grid of 18th-century handwriting. The "noise" of the document, the natural tilt of the pen, the varying lengths of dashes, and the gaps between words distort the raw data.

Standard algorithms often fail because they misinterpret these deliberate manual variations as mere 'noise' or 'over-dispersion', statistical messiness that masks the underlying precision. For example, when we perform a Quadrat Analysis, dividing the document into a grid to count letters, the math often yields a chaotic jumble. This is because the order isn't found in the dots' density, but in their relationship to an invisible center.

The "Whispers from the Founders" are encoded through a method called Mirrored Stabilization. Think of it as a "latent order", a hidden blueprint that is currently invisible. In technical terms, the Spatial Entropy (the level of disorder) is too high for a computer to recognize a pattern in the raw dots alone.

The signal achieves statistical significance only when the point set is subjected to a single-axis reflection, suggesting the 'key' is symmetry-based rather than frequency-based. This act of reflection reduces the chaos, allowing a structured geometric signal to emerge from the noise. Because the pattern depends on this specific mirrored alignment rather than a uniform scattering of letters, the geometry remains hidden from conventional frequency tests, waiting for the correct axial "key" to unlock it.

Hatmaker's Sign

Thomas Jefferson was frustrated by the changes the Continental Congress made to the rough draft of the *Declaration*. Ben Franklin noticed Jefferson's agitated state during a debate over editing the Rough Draft of the *Declaration of Independence*. Jefferson recalled how Franklin tried to calm him by telling a story about a hatmaker who was having a sign made for his new shop. Jefferson's reaction is not evidence of hidden structure. It is, at most, compatible with the possibility that revisions disrupted a system sensitive to spacing and segmentation.

Franklin told Jefferson of a hatter who began with a detailed sign, name, trade, service, terms, and, after successive "improvements" by friends, saw each functional word removed until nothing remained but the name and a painted hat. This anecdote is included to contextualize period attitudes toward revision; any connection to structural or graphical considerations is purely hypothetical.

Jefferson Hypothesis

The following hypothesis is not required to accept the graphical findings already presented, but is offered as one possible contextual explanation should those findings withstand scrutiny. Thomas Jefferson's reaction to the changes made to the *Declaration* by the Continental Congress was noticeable to Franklin. I was puzzled about why Jefferson became so emotional over the additional corrections to the Rough Draft. Ben Franklin noticed Jefferson's agitation during a debate over editing the document. He tried to calm him by telling a story about a hatmaker who was having a sign made for his new shop. The anecdote was meant to ease Jefferson's frustration, reminding him that even careful work could require adjustments and that patience was sometimes necessary, even for someone drafting words destined to change the course of history.

Yet the anecdote does not fully account for the scale of Jefferson's reaction. I offer a speculative reconstruction of that pivotal moment:

Jefferson's visible frustration during the revision process has traditionally been interpreted as artistic or rhetorical concern. A purely mechanical, speculative perspective is that revisions may have disrupted a carefully organized textual structure, as evaluated in this study. Jefferson, as a master draftsman, possessed the technical skill to conceive of a document in which lettering and spatial geometry could coexist.

Franklin, known as a skilled printer, would have been familiar with how textual alignment could be mechanically preserved using movable type. This context is provided to illustrate feasibility rather than documented involvement in this process. Franklin's hatmaker anecdote, recorded as a calming gesture, functionally reframes the editing process as a benign adjustment rather than a structural disruption.

The authorship of the *Declaration of Independence*, a cornerstone of American history, has sparked controversy. Thomas Jefferson asserted his authorship of the *Declaration* in the 1790s, drawing criticism from John Adams, who believed it was a collective effort by the Committee of Five. Some historians argue that Jefferson's *Declaration of Independence* was influenced by the works of John Locke, George Mason, and Thomas Paine. Thomas Jefferson is still widely acknowledged as the author. This debate adds a layer of intrigue and engagement to the crafting of the *Declaration*. This discussion is included to provide historical context; no interpretive claims about geometric findings rely on these authorship debates.

Historical Scrutiny and Exhaustion

The *Declaration of Independence* was a formal statement asserting the United States' independence from Great Britain. It served as a political document to justify the revolution, rally support, and gain international recognition. The *Declaration* exists in several essential forms, including the Committee of Five Rough Draft, the letter-pressed Dunlap Broadside, and Timothy Matlack's handwritten engrossed copy on parchment. In 1820, Secretary of State John Quincy Adams commissioned Washington engraver William J. Stone to create a copperplate-engraved facsimile of Matlack's handwritten engrossed copy for printing.

The idea of hidden geometric or symbolic content has prompted significant scrutiny from linguists, scholars, and historians. They have examined its authorship, penmanship, grammar, content, signatures, punctuation, including the use of dashes, and the handprint on the back. Lectures, debates, and numerous written works have examined its validity.

Speculative interpretations, sometimes suggesting Masonic connections, have inspired popular fiction, such as the National Treasure films, reflecting public fascination with the potential for hidden structures. Experts have conducted extensive historical textual analyses of the *Declaration*, significantly strengthening the knowledge base. These dedicated scholars have taken the study of the *Declaration* to new heights. They have investigated the use of punctuation, such as periods, commas, and notably varied-sized dashes, throughout the text.

One historically grounded interpretation is that the differently sized dash, also known as a horizontal rule or calligraphic dash, served to create pauses in reading, consistent with colonial-era punctuation practices. While reading the *Declaration of Independence*, if a reader encounters a short dash, they pause briefly; if they come across a long dash, they take a longer moment to ponder and reflect on the preceding passage. The notion that the dash in textual analysis creates a pause is reasonable and was used during the colonial era to emphasize the text and highlight significant points or phrases within sentences (Allen).

If dashes create reading pauses, they can also, hypothetically, be treated, in a graphical analysis, as markers delineating structural divisions in text. Recognizing that the varying-length dash was used grammatically in textual analysis gave the dash a clear purpose. However, the different relative lengths of the dashes, dependent on the alignment of key letters, in a graphical analysis (in which textual elements are treated visually as point data), were the catalyst for my solution. The varying-length dashes allowed me to treat each text segment, the portion of a sentence between two dashes, as a movable unit. By shifting these segments along an imagined WVY-BGP-M grid, the individual letters within them could be precisely aligned to serve as points. Connecting these points revealed structured geometric patterns within the text, as per the method used in this study. This process is documented in full-scale detail in Chapter Four.

Working hypothesis

Any observed non-random alignment of this complexity would imply that a preparatory scaffold, whether conceptual, diagrammatic, or procedural, could have facilitated it. The following discussion presents a hypothetical framework that could account for the alignment observed under this method. This proposal does not assert the historical fact of such a document, only that some preparatory scaffold would have been necessary if the observed alignment is non-random. The proposed image outline for the *Declaration* would have been carefully crafted, merging letters with images. It would have required a significant amount of time to create. This outline would have established the framework for a more rapidly produced combined text-image version of the *Declaration*, from the initial letterpress printing through the completion of the engrossed copy. The role of Timothy Matlack as the scribe is critical here; the hypothesis suggests he may have followed a precise spatial template provided to him to ensure the 'latent order' was preserved in the final parchment. The short time between the letterpress and hand-scribed engrossed copy would have made it impractical to develop an original embedded text-to-image model. Instead, the image outline would have laid the groundwork, requiring only textual corrections to the *Declaration* of the Continental Congress; the new text would then be aligned with the imagery using the variable-length dash to jog the image into position.

If such a layout existed, revisions made during Congressional review could have affected the alignment of text segments as observed in this analysis. Without using the various dashed, segmented bodies of text and the underlying imagery, it would not have been able to preserve any of the images. In this hypothetical model, each segmented text block could be considered independently adjustable to correspond with an underlying geometric framework. Compiling each segmented body of text separately allowed for flexibility in wording and spacing, essentially constructing a wall of words by stacking each aligned textual entry on top of the next. Dashes of varying lengths were used to fill the gaps between segments and to serve as registration marks indicating where one segment began and ended.

A1Z26 Cipher

How could I prove that this coordinate-point theory was used throughout the *Declaration*? I could hardly read the engrossed *Declaration* and had no chance of identifying any letter patterns. I needed a plaintext version of the *Declaration*, and with a few keystrokes, I obtained one from the National Archives. I opened a Microsoft Word document and adjusted the paper size to roughly match the original *Declaration* text block, measuring 15 inches high by 20 inches wide.

I pasted the plaintext *Declaration of Independence* and adjusted its font size to fit the Word document. As I focused on the identical letters throughout the *Declaration*, looking for geometric patterns, I found my eyes becoming entangled with the symbolism of each letter. I needed to remove the letter symbolism from the plaintext *Declaration* to check for any letter geometry within the document. To neutralize linguistic recognition, I used an online tool for simple letter-to-number substitution, known as the A1Z26 cipher. The encryption tool I chose was the A1Z26 substitution cipher, which replaces the letter "A" with the number "1," "B" with "2," "C" with "3," "D" with "4," and so on. This step does not generate images, reveal symbols, or encode meaning. Any monoalphabetic substitution preserving spatial order would produce identical results.

This substitution was employed strictly as a control measure to neutralize linguistic recognition while preserving spatial position and sequence. I entered the entire plaintext

Declaration into the A1Z26 generator, transforming the text block into a numbered format, with dashes now represented by large spaces between numbers. These spaces preserved the dash-defined segmentation already identified as structurally significant, without introducing new markers or adjustments. I copied the number block from the A1Z26 generator and pasted it into the Word document. Then, I zoomed out to view the entire page. With letter symbolism removed, spatial repetition, vertical alignment, and clustering could be evaluated without interference from linguistic meaning.

Reader Orientation for Graphical Analysis

Before proceeding to the numerical substitutions, plotted point sets, and geometric outcomes examined in the following chapter, it is necessary to pause and establish how the material that follows is meant to be read. The analyses presented in this book depend not on interpretive freedom, symbolic intuition, or selective emphasis, but on a strictly constrained sequence of mechanical operations applied uniformly to the text block of the engrossed *Declaration*.

Because these operations involve treating written language as spatial data rather than as rhetoric, the results can appear counterintuitive without prior orientation. The following process provides a concise procedural overview of the observational framework used throughout the study. It is not an argument, nor a summary of conclusions, but a reader's guide to method, intended to clarify what is being done, what is not being claimed, and the limits within which all subsequent figures and interpretations must be evaluated.

How to View the *Declaration* in This Study

For the purposes of this analysis, the *Declaration* of Independence is treated not as a linear text but as a fixed graphical field.

1. **The Field**: The engrossed *Declaration*'s justified text block forms a rectangle approximately 15 inches high by 20 inches wide. All observations are confined strictly to this area. All physical reconstructions are performed at a 1:1 scale to eliminate proportional distortion.
2. **Orientation**: The left margin functions as a fixed vertical reference line (Y-axis). The forty-four lines of text run horizontally in parallel, forming a stable spatial grid.

3. **Numerical Neutralization (A1Z26)**: To eliminate linguistic bias and "symbolic entanglement," the text is converted into a numbered format (A=1, B=2, etc.). This preserves the exact spatial sequence and positional data while neutralizing the reader's instinct to "read" the prose. This allows geometric analysis to focus on spatial relationships rather than semantic content.
4. **Segmentation (The "Jog")**: Varying-length dashes and sporadic blank spaces are treated as mechanical spacers (registration marks). These allow horizontal segments of text to be "jogged" by shifting them laterally without altering vertical line order or disrupting the rhetorical flow of the sentences.
5. **Anchor Letters**: Specific letters (W, V, Y, B, G, P, M) are selected as anchor points for further analysis based on frequency and distribution sufficient to yield visually interpretable patterns.
6. **Point Plotting**: Each instance of a selected letter is marked at its optical center within the field. No connecting lines are drawn at this stage. The resulting pattern appears as an "incomplete" or "halved" projection.
7. **Mirror Stabilization**: The plotted dots are reflected across a vertical axis. The position of this axis, whether at the document's edge or offset within the text block, is determined by "sliding" the mirror halves until multiple independent geometric relationships stabilize simultaneously.
8. **Composite Formation**: Original and mirrored points are displayed together, resulting in a balanced configuration. The lines observed in these figures represent "revealed relationships" that emerge only when the points reach maximum stabilization.
9. **Stacking and Transformation**: Completed point sets may be layered (stacked), rotated 180°, or reflected using standard geometric operations consistent with mechanical drafting practices (Orthographic and Isometric projection).
10. **Constraints**: No points are added, removed, or manually repositioned. The method permits only selection, marking, and transformation. The process is agnostic to the linguistic content of the segments; symmetry is revealed rather than constructed.
11. **Interpretive Overlay**: "Interpretive overlay" refers to the descriptive labeling of recognizable forms (e.g., "The Eye of Providence" or "The Lion"). Such overlays are not treated as evidentiary claims or indicators of authorial intent, but as perceptual

descriptors applied only after all mechanical and geometric constraints have been satisfied.

Throughout this study, references to Jefferson or Franklin describe historically documented skills and practices that establish mechanical feasibility, not assertions of conscious intent unless explicitly stated.

Chapter Two

The Number 22

In this context, the number 22 refers to the A1Z26 numerical equivalent of the letter V, used here solely as an indexing device rather than as a symbolic value. The letter representing V, or the number 22, displayed the same consistent geometry. At that point, the repeated appearance of stable geometry suggested that the earlier results were not isolated artifacts. I was analyzing the *Declaration's* non-random geometry, and my compulsive urge to finish what I had started was kicking in. I needed to complete the geometry. I took the original, digitally engrossed copy of the *Declaration* and placed it in the background of the Word document. Then, I layered the plain text *Declaration* over the original engrossed document, spacing the plain text words to align with the scripted ones. This overlay was performed to test positional correspondence, not to recreate handwriting or stylistic features. The alignment of the plain text was nearly precise with that of the scripted *Declaration*. I entered the letter V into the Word document's search bar and hit Enter. This action highlighted the letter 'V' in yellow. My eyes darted back and forth over the document, revealing geometry. However, like the dashes in the scripted *Declaration*, something was missing. The plotted points suggested systematic incompleteness rather than noise.

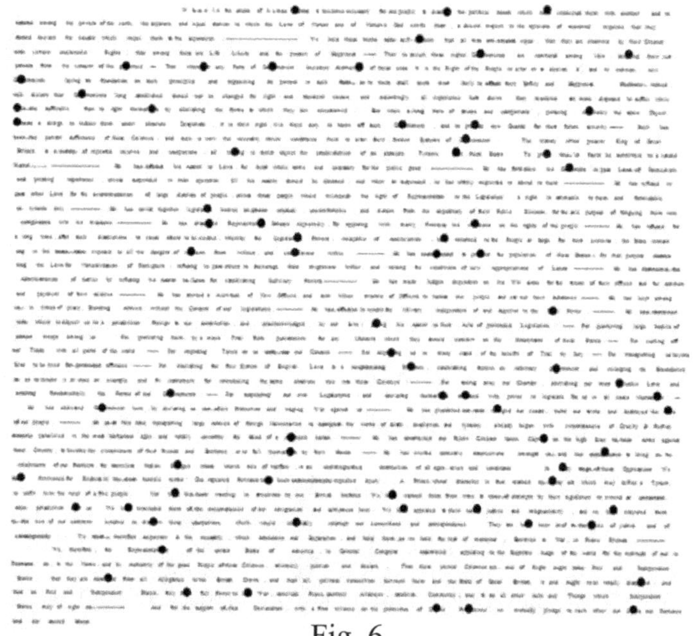

Fig. 6

There was an imbalance or awkwardness in the document. The geometry can be resolved as if the document were constructed from a partial projection, without asserting conscious design. The *Declaration of Independence* is imagined as a half-image (Fig. 6). This possibility was treated as a provisional hypothesis, tested through geometric completion rather than assumed to be the intent. This reminded me of how modern digital compression works, allowing large images to fit into smaller spaces. The letter "V" in the *Declaration* seemed to work the same way, only as a half-image. I started placing small black dots over each highlighted letter V, one at a time. When I finished marking the dots, I grouped them, copied the set, and mirrored it to connect the two sides. That gave me a coherent geometric configuration, balanced and symmetrical. I clicked the File menu, then clicked Print. With the printed copy in hand, I started sketching out the shapes I had visualized.

Pareidolia

The scientific term for perceiving recognizable images in chaotic patterns is pareidolia. Pareidolia operates in the absence of external constraint, relying solely on perceptual projection. It helps explain how our minds try to organize random marks into recognizable shapes. Most often, we see the outlines of human faces in landscapes and clouds; pareidolia highlights a fascinating aspect of our perception. A notable example of pareidolia is the NASA photo known as "The Face on Mars" (Fig. 7).

When I looked closely at the *Declaration's* layout, I began to notice shapes that seemed built into the design. Seeing those possible images led me to read a few academic papers about how people find patterns in random data, the same kind of thinking that often leads to conspiracy theories. Two papers stood out: "Connecting the Dots" and "Finding Meaning in the Clouds." Both discussed how people perceive connections in things that aren't actually related. This leads to a suspicion of individuals who are more likely to see patterns in random data and find meaning in nonsensical conspiracies. These articles serve as a standard grounding rod, where introspection and logic should have concluded my quest. Instead, they clarified the criteria for evaluating the results. That said, I paused and carefully compared

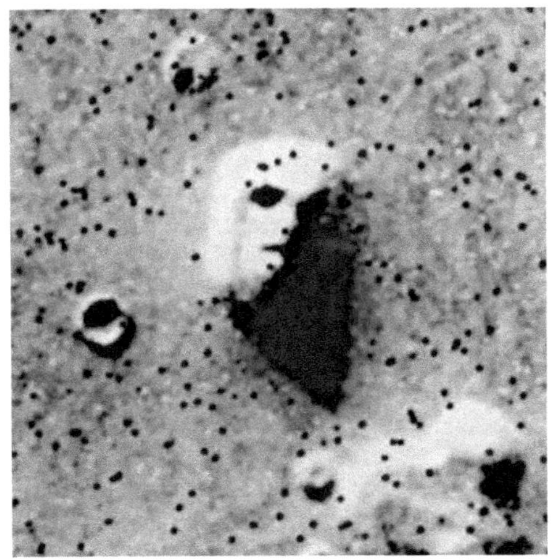

(NASA/JPL)
Fig.7

the images I created to the description of pareidolia. My conclusion is that pareidolia operates without external constraint, whereas the drafting-based visualization applied here operates only within fixed, repeatable constraints. The distinction lies not in whether images can be seen, but in whether they persist under fixed, repeatable operations.

Visualization

Two hundred and fifty years have passed since the *Declaration of Independence* was signed. If any hidden geometric structure truly exists within it, that structure lies dormant for generations. Dormancy, in this sense, refers to perceptual invisibility rather than absence.

I speculate that this recognition arose from a convergence of experience rather than from any singular insight. While writing my first book, I immersed myself deeply in the history, symbolism, and practices of Freemasonry. That study provided a conceptual framework, familiarity with symbolic systems, geometric thinking, and the tradition of encoding meaning within constrained forms. When this framework interacted with professional training in mechanical drafting, spatial visualization, and letterpress printing, it created the conditions for examining specific patterns in the *Declaration* through a different lens.

I taught mechanical drafting for nearly thirty years.

Orthographic Multiview

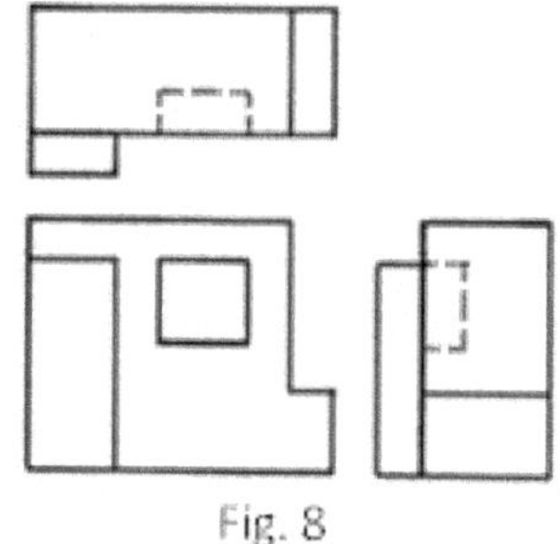

Fig. 8

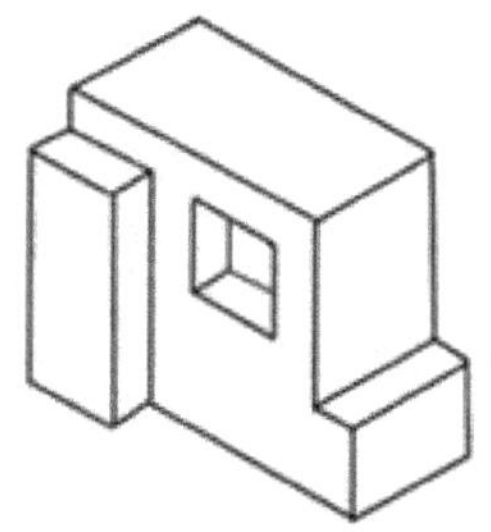

Isometric Projection

Fig. 9

Central to that discipline is the skill of visualization, not imagination, but structured mental transformation. Students are trained to interpret Orthographic Multiview drawings (Fig. 8), mentally reconstruct a three-dimensional object, then rotate, deconstruct, and translate it back into accurate two-dimensional representations. Conversely, they learn to infer multiple flat projections from a single isometric view (Fig. 9). This form of spatial reasoning is foundational in engineering and technical graphics, where meaning emerges not from a single view but from the relationship between constrained, partial representations.

In drafting education, visualization is procedural. It depends on recognizing fixed axes, invariant distances, symmetry, and alignment. A drawing is not interpreted freely; it is reconstructed according to strict geometric rules. Missing views are not invented; they are logically completed based on projection, proportionality, and constraints. Over decades of teaching, this process became second nature to me.

Figure 10 illustrates how this training was applied to my examination of the *Declaration*. The black dots represent the recorded positions of a specific letter—V—within the text. Alone, these plotted points appeared incomplete and asymmetrical, suggesting not randomness but an unresolved structure. Based on principles routinely used in drafting, I applied a mirror operation along a fixed vertical axis, not at the edge of the document, but offset within the text block. This step was neither intuitive nor symbolic; it was a universally standard geometric completion technique used to resolve partial projections. Such operations are routinely applied without interpretive intent in engineering and technical drafting.

The mirrored white dots represent the mentally visualized counterparts generated by this operation. When combined, the black and white points formed a balanced, proportionate configuration. Only after this procedural completion did a coherent geometric configuration emerge. The same mirrored-line method was then applied consistently to the other identified

letters. Importantly, the alternation of dot placement across the mirror line further obscures the structure, requiring both detection and transformation before any coherent form can appear.

n united States of America.

eople to dissolve the political bands which have connected them with another, and to
e's God entitle them, a decent respect to the opinions of mankind requires that they
be self-evident, that all men are created equal, that they are endowed by their Creator
at to secure these rights, Governments are instituted among Men, deriving their just
se ends, it is the Right of the People to alter or to abolish it, and to institute new
shall seem most likely to effect their Safety and Happiness. Prudence, indeed,
ordingly all experience hath shewn, that mankind are more disposed to suffer, while
hen a long train of abuses and usurpations, pursuing invariably the same Object
Government, and to provide new Guards for their future security. — Such has
former Systems of Government. The history of the present King of Great
bsolute Tyranny over these States. To prove this, let Facts be submitted to a candid
blic good. —— He has forbidden his Governors to pass Laws of immediate
so suspended, he has utterly neglected to attend to them. —— He has refused to
t of Representation in the Legislature, a right inestimable to them and formidable
nt from the depository of their Public Records, for the sole purpose of fatiguing them into
manly firmness his invasions on the rights of the people. —— He has refused for
Annihilation, have returned to the People at large for their exercise; the State remain
He has endeavoured to prevent the population of these States; for that purpose obstruc
aising the conditions of new Appropriations of Lands. —— He has obstructed the
made Judges dependent on his Will alone for the tenure of their offices, and the amount
f Officers to harrass our people, and eat out their substance. —— He has kept among
he Military independent of and superior to the Civil power. —— He has combined
his Assent to their Acts of pretended Legislation: — For Quartering large bodies of
ich they should commit on the Inhabitants of these States: — For cutting off
ng us in many cases, of the benefits of Trial by Jury: — For transporting us beyond
Province, establishing therein an Arbitrary government, and enlarging its Boundarie
lonies: —— For taking away our Charters, abolishing our most valuable Laws, and
aring themselves invested with power to legislate for us in all cases whatsoever. —
He has plundered our seas, ravaged our Coasts, burnt our towns, and destroyed the Li
death, desolation and tyranny, already begun with circumstances of Cruelty & perfidy
as constrained our fellow Citizens taken Captive on the high Seas to bear Arms against
He has excited domestic insurrections amongst us, and has endeavoured to bring on the
ruction of all ages, sexes and conditions. In every stage of these Oppressions We
r. A Prince, whose character is thus marked by every act which may define a Tyrant,
ave warned them from time to time of attempts by their legislature to extend an unwarrant
We have appealed to their native justice and magnanimity, and we have conjured them
ctions and correspondence. They too have been deaf to the voice of justice and of
em, as we hold the rest of mankind, Enemies in War, in Peace Friends. ——
ess, Assembled, appealing to the Supreme Judge of the world for the rectitude of our in
. That these United Colonies are, and of Right ought to be Free and Independent
ween them and the State of Great Britain, is and ought to be totally dissolved; and
establish Commerce, and to do all other Acts and Things which Independent
tection of divine Providence, we mutually pledge to each other our Lives, our Fortunes

Robt Morris
Benjamin Rush
Benj. Franklin
Wm Floyd
Phil. Livingston
Fran. Lewis
Josiah Bartlett
Wm Whipple
Saml Adams

Fig. 10

This process does not, by itself, establish authorial intent or prove the existence of deliberate encoding. All references that follow to historical figures or practices are offered solely to illustrate mechanical feasibility and perceptual access, not to support claims of authorship or intention. It establishes only whether a structured order can be mechanically resolved. What it explains is how someone trained to synthesize incomplete geometric data, across drafting, printing, and symbolic study, might recognize ordered structure where others see only dispersion. The claim, therefore, is not that such geometry must exist because it can be visualized. Still, that visualization, when governed by constraint and method, can reveal whether non-random structure is present at all. In this sense, the discovery is less about intuition than about perception shaped by long practice. It is the outcome of seeing text not solely as language, but also as spatial data, capable of alignment, segmentation, transformation, and reconstruction, much as Jefferson's known training in drafting and geometry establishes that he possessed the skills required to engage with text as spatial structure, a point raised solely to demonstrate feasibility rather than historical action.

This distinction is relevant when considering the presence of older geometric, ritual, and allegorical structures within the founding documents of the United States, and it will become increasingly important as those structures are examined in later chapters.

The following comparison is offered as an analogy, not as documentary evidence. Jefferson's personal methodology provides a useful analogy for the *Declaration's* hidden structure. In his later work, *The Life and Morals of Jesus of Nazareth* (the "Jefferson Bible"), he employed a literal "cut-and-paste" technique, excising specific passages from the *Gospels of Matthew, Mark, Luke,* and *John* to assemble a refined, ethical narrative. This process of isolating particular data (the Four Evangelists) provides an analogy for the WVY-BGP-M grid identified in the *Declaration*.

Just as Jefferson instructed his nephew to 'fix reason firmly in her seat' and 'question with boldness,' his later treatment of the *New Testament* demonstrates a willingness to reorganize text without regard to traditional sanctity, without implying that the same method was applied to the *Declaration*. It's mechanically plausible to treat the *Declaration's* text block as a graphical plane, independent of documented authorial intent, so that specific letters could be isolated and "stacked" to form a higher, composite image.

Strategic Wording and Punctuation

In The Stylistic Artistry of the *Declaration of Independence*, Stephen E. Lucas argues that the *Declaration* is a meticulously engineered document in which form and function operate at a microscopic level. Lucas demonstrates that Jefferson was a "diligent student of rhythm, accent, timing, and cadence." This analysis is cited here to establish Jefferson's demonstrated sensitivity to micro-level textual control. Composing for the ear as much as for the eye, an approach Jefferson himself confirmed through his technical analysis of accentuation in *Thoughts on English Prosody*. From this perspective, punctuation marks such as dashes were not incidental but functioned to regulate rhythm, pacing, and rhetorical pause.

Lucas further notes that the prose of the *Declaration* is defined by a "felicitous blend" of short and long words, precisely arranged to achieve harmony, cadence, and eloquence. Vocabulary choice and phrase length are shown to be carefully balanced, suggesting that Jefferson exercised extraordinary control over adjacent words and clauses. Under this reading, every pause, interruption, or structural break, particularly those indicated by dashes, serves a calculated rhetorical purpose: to manage breath, emphasize ideas, and support the formal delivery of long, periodic sentences.

What Lucas identifies as rhetorical precision may also enable a structural reading of Jefferson's meticulous word choice, independent of later mechanical execution. If the document were composed not only for sound and sense but also for spatial order within the text block, then the same control over word length, placement, and punctuation would have been essential for maintaining internal alignment. In this view, the dash functions not merely as a rhetorical pause but as a mechanical spacer, capable of subtly adjusting the position of specific letters within a line without disrupting readability or cadence.

Such a dual-purpose approach is consistent with the possibility that Jefferson's diction appears unusually exact even by 18th-century standards. The careful blending of short and long words, noted by Lucas, would serve both the auditory demands of eloquent prose and the physical requirements of maintaining fixed letter positions within the text block. A dash, while perceived by the reader as a pause in thought, could simultaneously provide the minute spatial correction needed to preserve alignment from line to line.

Seen this way, Jefferson's artistry operates on two parallel planes: one audible and rhetorical, the other visual and structural. Lucas's observations about rhythm, cadence, vocabulary balance, and punctuation remain fully intact. At the same time, the possibility of a secondary structural function operating alongside rhetorical intent remains mechanically plausible. It emerges that the same disciplined control over the document was also evident in Jefferson's unusually exact diction, which would have been a necessary precondition for any mechanically constrained spatial coherence to persist, regardless of whether such coherence was intentionally pursued. This level of control would be a necessary precondition for any non-obvious spatial coherence to persist within the Declaration's layout. The document's remarkable precision, the very quality that has drawn scholarly attention for generations, may therefore reflect not only Jefferson's concern for eloquence but also an exacting compositional method in which word choice, punctuation, and spacing were inseparable (Lucas). Such inseparability is a necessary precondition for mechanically constrained spatial coherence to persist throughout the document.

Benjamin Franklin, the Dash, and Eighteenth-Century Print Practice

One of the most persistent typographic features of the engrossed *Declaration* of Independence is the use of long dashes. While the dash was not unusual in eighteenth-century writing, its consistent placement and function within the *Declaration* raise questions that extend beyond grammar alone. In the context of this study, where the *Declaration* is treated not merely as prose but as a structured graphical plane, the dash emerges as a possible mechanical device rather than a purely rhetorical one. This framing does not assume that the dash was introduced for a graphical purpose, only that its physical properties permit such a role within a mechanically constrained analysis.

This line of inquiry was prompted by a comparison between the *Declaration's* dashes (Fig. 11) and those found in Benjamin Franklin's personal correspondence (Franklin), (Fig. 12), (Fig. 13), and (Fig. 14). Digital scans from the Library of Congress's *Benjamin Franklin Papers* reveal a handwritten letter in which Franklin employs dashes in a manner strikingly similar in form and spacing to those in the *Declaration*. These manuscripts, preserved in the public domain by the Manuscript Division of the Library of Congress, demonstrate Franklin's familiarity with the dash as a visual and functional element of written text. Familiarity alone establishes feasibility, not authorship, design intent, or participation in the *Declaration's* final graphical arrangement.

It must be stated plainly: the presence of similar dashes in Franklin's handwriting does not prove that Franklin inserted the dashes in the *Declaration* for encoding purposes, nor does it confirm his direct involvement in the document's final graphical construction. What it does provide, however, is an important contextual connection, evidence that Franklin was accustomed to using the dash and understood it as a flexible, space-bearing tool within both handwritten and printed environments.

By contrast, the surviving handwritten correspondence of Thomas Jefferson, John Adams, Roger Sherman, Robert R. Livingston, and Timothy Matlack uses the dash infrequently as a spatial element. Outside the Committee of Five, comparable late-eighteenth-century manuscripts also show sparse dash usage. For example, the *Articles of Confederation* contain no dash punctuation; George Washington's First Inaugural Address (April 30, 1789) contains isolated instances distributed across several pages; Alexander Hamilton's *Statement of My Property and Debts* contains only a handful of dashes across two pages; and the Fairfax and Boucher letters to Washington exhibit similarly limited usage. In each case, the dash functions as occasional punctuation rather than as a recurring spatial structuring device. By comparison, the Timothy Matlack-engrossed *Declaration of Independence* exhibits a substantially higher density of dash-gaps, suggesting a more deliberate spatial role within that document.

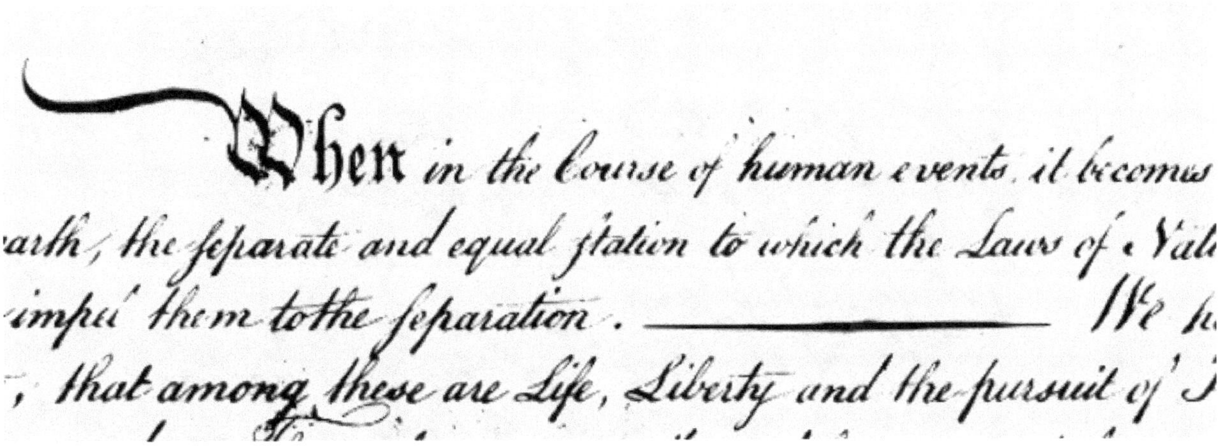

When in the Course of human events, it becomes
earth, the separate and equal station to which the Laws of
impel them to the separation. ——
, that among these are Life, Liberty and the pursuit of

Fig. 11

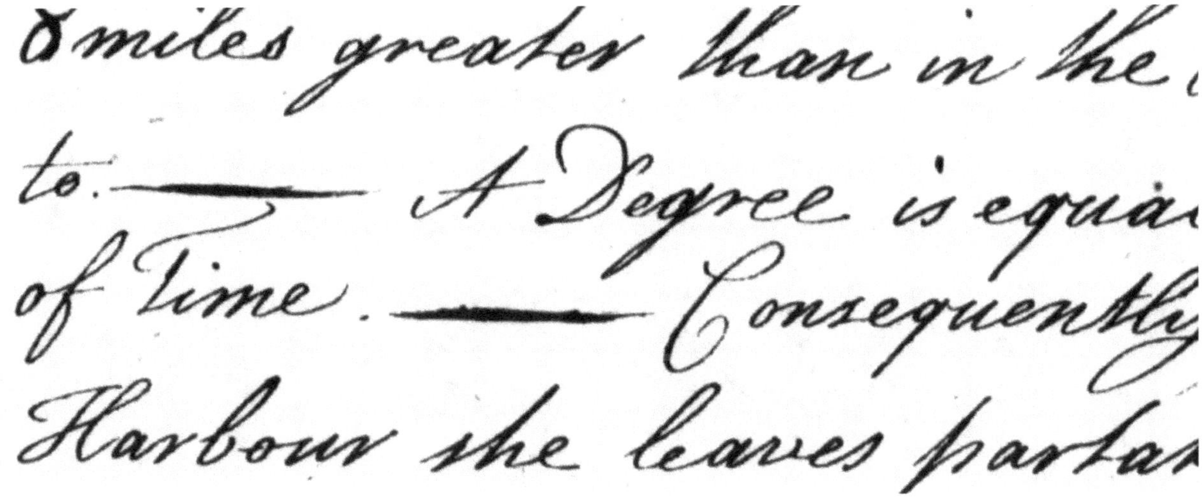

miles greater than in the
to. —— A Degree is equal
of Time. —— Consequently
Harbour she leaves

Fig. 12

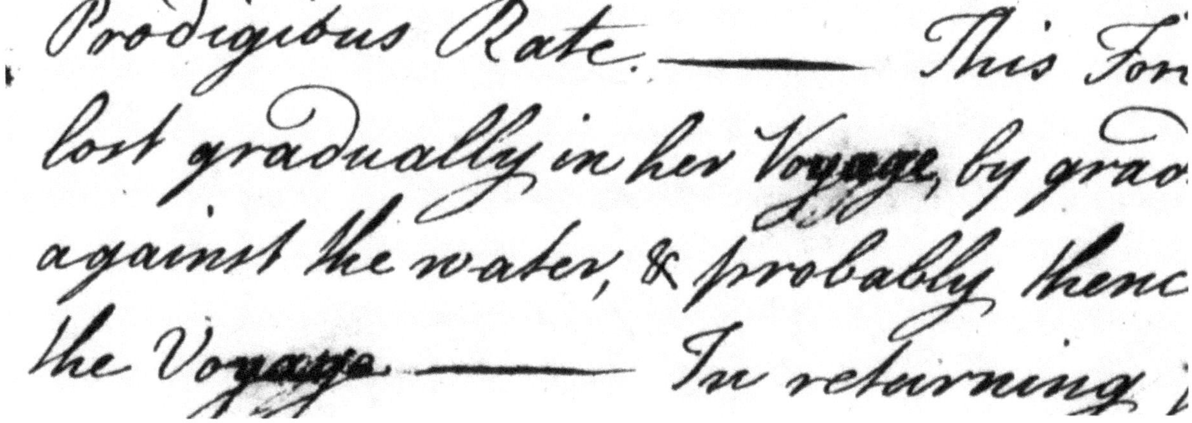

Prodigious Rate. —— This
lost gradually in her Voyage, by
against the water, & probably
the Voyage —— In returning

Fig. 13

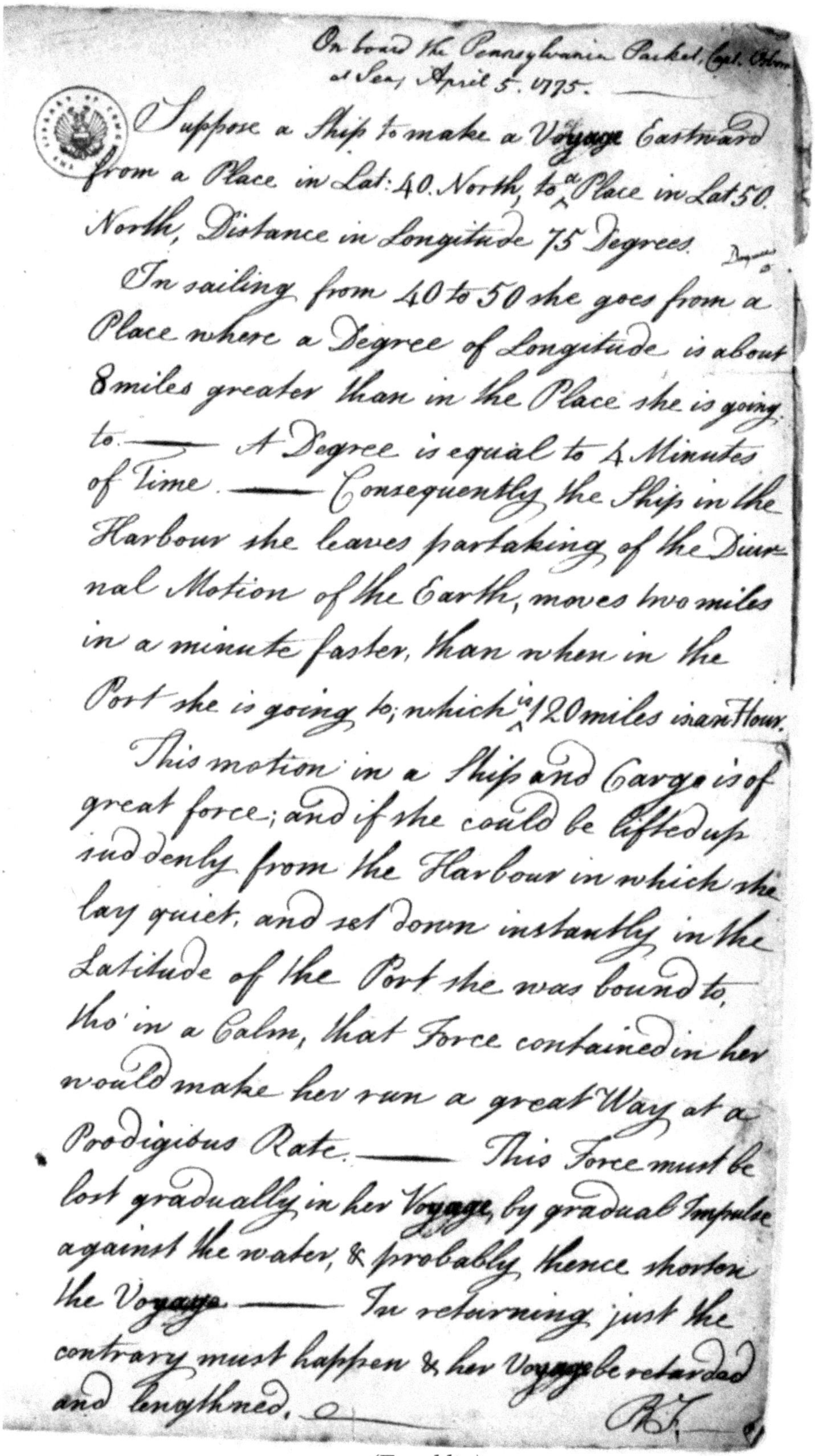

On board the Pennsylvania Packet, Capt. Osborn
at Sea, April 5. 1775.

Suppose a Ship to make a Voyage Eastward from a Place in Lat: 40. North, to a Place in Lat 50. North, Distance in Longitude 75 Degrees.

In sailing from 40 to 50 she goes from a Place where a Degree of Longitude is about 8 miles greater than in the Place she is going to. —— A Degree is equal to 4 Minutes of Time. —— Consequently the Ship in the Harbour she leaves partaking of the Diurnal Motion of the Earth, moves two miles in a minute faster, than when in the Port she is going to; which is 120 miles in an Hour.

This motion in a Ship and Cargo is of great force; and if she could be lifted up suddenly from the Harbour in which she lay quiet, and set down instantly in the Latitude of the Port she was bound to, tho' in a Calm, that Force contained in her would make her run a great Way at a Prodigious Rate. —— This Force must be lost gradually in her Voyage, by gradual Impulse against the water, & probably thence shorten the Voyage. —— In returning just the contrary must happen & her Voyage be retarded and lengthned. ——

B.F.

(Franklin)

Fig. 14

This observation becomes more significant when viewed through the lens of Franklin's professional life as a printer. Keith Arbour's *Benjamin Franklin's First Government Printing* documents Franklin's technical mastery of movable type and page justification. One illustrative example is Franklin's 1729 mortgage register printing, where insufficient blank space was left after the printed word "he," forcing later handwritten corrections by scriveners. Because the line had already been typeset, adding space would have required reworking the entire line, a mechanical inconvenience Franklin clearly understood (Arbour).

This incident highlights a crucial principle of eighteenth-century printing: space itself was a managed and deliberate element. Blank space, spacing blocks, and justification were not aesthetic afterthoughts but mechanical constraints that demanded forethought. Within this environment, punctuation marks that occupied horizontal space, such as dashes, functioned as adjustable material elements rather than as fixed semantic units. Franklin's experience navigating these constraints suggests an acute awareness of how text could be shifted, aligned, and stabilized across a page.

It is within this mechanical framework that the dash in the *Declaration* becomes relevant. Unlike commas or periods, the dash actively occupies horizontal space. It can replace words, pause sentences, or, most importantly for this study, serve as a spacer that maintains alignment without altering surrounding text. If one imagines the *Declaration*'s text block as a justified plane, the dash becomes a stabilizing device that could preserve alignment while allowing textual flexibility.

The Dash as a Mechanical Spacer

This possibility led to a working hypothesis: *What if the Declaration's text block were treated as a graphical coordinate system?* This hypothesis concerns mechanical survivability under revision, not the motives or intentions of any historical actor. In this hypothetical model, the rigid left margin serves as the Y-axis, while the horizontal flow of lines serves as the X-axis. Under such a framework, consistent anchor points are required to maintain positional integrity across the page. The dashes, used to regulate spacing without introducing additional letters, could serve precisely this function.

For this model to hold, one condition must be met: the aligned points must correspond to the same letter throughout the text block. This assumption is not rhetorical but testable. If alignment fails, if different letters occupy the same horizontal position, the hypothesis collapses. Conversely, consistent alignment supports mechanical plausibility, though not intent. Importantly, this framing does not require the dash to be a cipher symbol in itself. Instead, it functions as a mechanical facilitator, enabling the preservation of letter positions across a justified page. Franklin's demonstrated expertise with spacing, justification, and the practical consequences of insufficient blank space lends credibility to the idea that he understood, perhaps better than anyone of his generation, how textual geometry could be preserved or disrupted. This observation is offered solely to establish technical literacy within the period, not to imply direct intervention or design.

The handwritten letters from the Library of Congress reinforce this plausibility. They show that Franklin habitually used dashes in a way that mirrors the *Declaration*'s visual rhythm. This does not imply secrecy or encryption; rather, it situates the dash within Franklin's known graphic vocabulary. The dash was a familiar tool, not an exotic one.

It is also worth noting that the dash's prevalence in eighteenth-century writing makes it an ideal candidate for a mechanical role that would attract little attention. Its use would not appear anomalous to contemporary readers, scribes, or printers. Thus, even if employed for alignment purposes, it would not stand out as suspicious or novel.

In keeping with the methodological discipline applied throughout this study, the dash hypothesis is offered as contextual support rather than confirmation. It demonstrates that Franklin possessed both the technical skill and the customary familiarity necessary to understand how dashes could serve a purpose beyond mere punctuation. It also reinforces the broader premise that the *Declaration's* text may be evaluated not only as language but as a structured visual field subject to mechanical constraints.

When viewed alongside Franklin's printing background, the *Declaration's* disciplined justification, and the recurring geometric alignments explored in earlier chapters, the dash becomes another connective element in a larger system. Alone, it proves nothing. This strengthens the case for mechanical plausibility within eighteenth-century print constraints, without establishing deliberate encoding. As with the other observations presented in this work, the role of the dash remains an open question, subject to verification, refutation, or refinement. Its value lies not in what it claims to prove, but in what it allows us to test. In that sense, the dash is less a symbol than a hinge, quietly holding the text in place while inviting closer examination of the structure it supports. If consistent letter alignment cannot be demonstrated after dash-based segmentation, this hypothesis fails.

The Dash and the *Declaration*

Image (Fig. 16) depicts fragments of the *Declaration*, with the segments stacked, illustrating how the dash shifts the letters of a sentence into position, strategically placing W, V, Y, B, G, P, and M to create a coordinate-point drawing. This figure is schematic and illustrative, intended to demonstrate mechanical possibility rather than to reproduce the historical process verbatim. The practice of printers using spacers in movable type and arranging a passage on a composing stick originated with the first Gutenberg printers. Benjamin Franklin, a master printer, applied this technique to his letterpress work.

The hand-scribed dashes of varying lengths within the engrossed version of the *Declaration* (Fig. 15) could also serve as a type of printer's registration mark when compiling the independent segments within this analytical model. For instance, the *Declaration* consists of segments of text; some are single sentences while others are paragraphs, separated by varying-length dashes. Only the words containing the letters W, V, Y, B, G, P, and M were retained (Fig.16). In contrast, filler words without these letters were removed. These filler words also allow the compositional process to make minor adjustments to better position words containing the letters W, V, Y, B, G, P, and M. The *Declaration*'s segmented form allows the author to align independent bodies of text by weaving the segments together with varying lengths of dashes (Fig.15). Here, "author" refers to the compositional process itself rather than to a documented, conscious intention. Throughout this study, agency is attributed to procedure and constraint unless explicitly stated otherwise.

Fig. 15

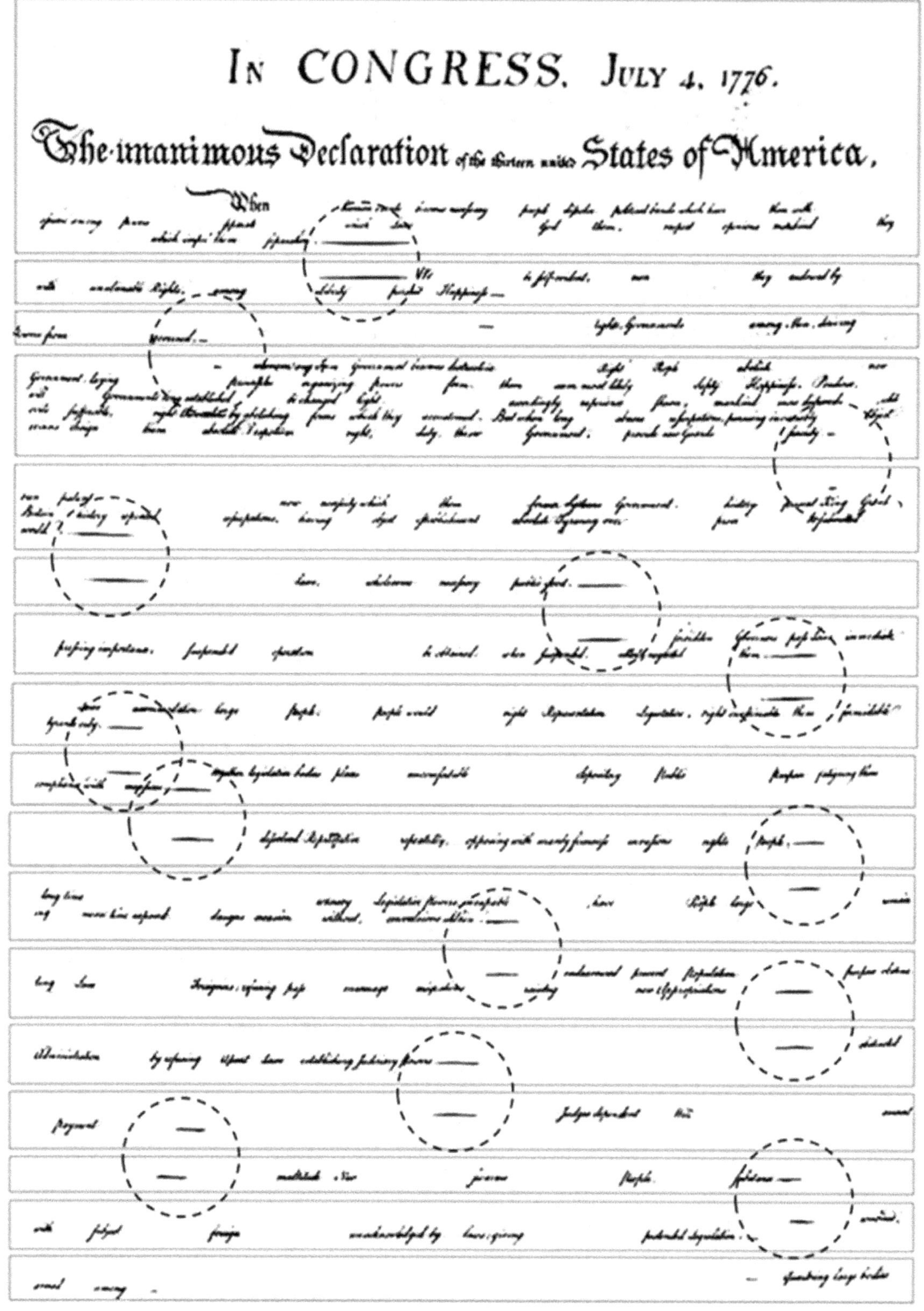

IN CONGRESS. JULY 4. 1776.

The unanimous Declaration of the thirteen united States of America,

When

Fig. 16

Jogging into Alignment

My undergraduate degree required several graphics technology classes, often referred to as the print shop.

This subject covered various printing processes, darkroom work, and, of course, movable type. The movable type process utilizes small blocks with a raised letter or punctuation mark on one end. The letters are stored in a California Job Case, a large tray divided into numerous compartments that hold different letters of the alphabet, punctuation marks, and spacers. The type is positioned on a composing stick, letter by letter. Often, a string of text requires spacers to be placed between certain letters to justify the words in the sentence, ensuring that the paragraph has even edges. Typesetters also use spacers between letters to create openings for advertisements or images within a body of text. My graphics technology professor described adjusting a sentence with spacers as "jogging the letters of a sentence into alignment." The phrase reflects standard trade jargon rather than a metaphor. It is included here to describe an established mechanical practice, not to suggest that such terminology was used in the eighteenth century."

As I scanned the *Declaration* for clues about a graphical process, my eyes focused on the purposefully apparently varied lengths of the dashes. If Matlack was indeed the scribe of the *Declaration,* this attribution remains probable rather than conclusively established. The aesthetic contrast between the elegance of the penmanship and the variable lengths of the dashes was apparent. Each dash has a unique length: some features greater spacing at the front, others have extra spacing at the end, and some sentences include extra spacing without a dash.

What if the text block were considered a graphical plane? This framing is hypothetical and is evaluated solely for mechanical plausibility. The rigid left margin of the text block would represent the Y-axis, while the parallel sentences would symbolize the X-axis. If this is correct, this framing requires identifying consistent graphical anchor points. Given that the dashes serve to align words, the working assumption is that the points remain the same letter throughout the text block. This assumption is testable and falsifiable through inconsistent alignment. Failure to demonstrate consistent letter correspondence across segments would invalidate the dash-based alignment model presented here.

Before addressing the question of intent, it is necessary to examine the physical layout of the engrossed document itself.

The Measured Dash-Gaps of the Engrossed Declaration

The geometric investigation of the Declaration of Independence naturally extends beyond letterforms to the document's spatial architecture. If proportion governs the plotted figures within the text, it is reasonable to examine whether proportion also governs the intervals that structure its rhetoric. The dash-gaps separating clauses and sentences are not incidental pauses; they are physical distances deliberately inscribed into the parchment.

The present measurements were taken from a 1:1 facsimile of the Stevens copy, preserving the original scale of the engrossed document. Using calipers, the following notable dash-gap lengths were recorded in millimeters (±1 mm potential human measurement variance):

7.07, 64.23, 6.92, 6.27, 6, 14.09, 12.62, 6.06, 5.21, 13.26, 13.89, 17.89, 19.03, 13.84, 56.23, 41.42, 38.62, 6.51, 33.15, 5.58, 5.58, 34, 27.44, 31.39, 6.69, 5.19, 30.59, 35.18, 28.44, 21.71, 27.56, 28.11, 19.51, 15.2, 18.81, 20.82, 21.33, 16.93, 19.33, 27.68, 17.25, 3.99, 11.2, 31.01, 27.91, 27.48, 5.8, 19.14, 4.44, 20.63, 8.29, 9.06, 14.67, 6.99, 9.99, 10.2, 11.84, 14.9, 7.22, 32.93, 24.54, 11.95, 5.98, 37.55.

When examined collectively, these measurements display tiered clustering:

- Minor intervals (~5–7 mm)
- Intermediate separations (~9–15 mm)
- Major sentence pauses (~17–22 mm)
- Structural breaks (~27–35 mm)
- Sectional divisions (~38–64 mm)

Such stratification is not characteristic of casual spacing. It instead suggests conceptual segmentation during layout planning. The engraver appears to have employed multiple magnitudes of interval to distinguish rhetorical weight and structural transition. The document's physical spacing mirrors its argumentative progression. The proportional question, however, requires restraint.

For a tolerance of 0 mm, no exact-integer-multiple modular system can be demonstrated. Using 5.58 mm (a repeated small-gap value) as a base unit, only the base itself appears precisely. Larger intervals approach integer multiples but do not match exactly.

Under ±1 mm tolerance, approximate modular relationships become visible. Several intervals correspond closely to 2×, 3×, 5×, and even 10× multiples of the small-gap cluster

(~5.5–6 mm). This suggests the possibility of a working spatial unit guiding layout decisions. Yet these relationships remain approximate, not mathematically fixed.

The distinction is critical. The dash-gaps provide strong evidence of measured, tiered spatial control. They do not, at strict tolerance, prove harmonic or numerological encoding. What they establish is disciplined variation consistent with intentional design.

The Declaration's rhetoric is structured. Its spacing appears structured as well. Whether that spatial order carries allegorical significance beyond compositional balance remains a matter of interpretation. What can be affirmed with confidence is that the physical architecture of the text reflects deliberation. The document presents itself not only as a political argument but as a carefully proportioned artifact.

Tracing Paper

Oiled, translucent paper (papier huilé or carta lucida) was an essential tool for Enlightenment-era draftsmen and thinkers, achieving its clarity by allowing oil to saturate the paper, producing a transparent effect. This permanent alteration was invaluable for creating precise, duplicatable designs. Thomas Jefferson, a skilled architect, would have relied on this translucent paper to trace, copy, and overlay architectural plans, ensuring the geometric accuracy of designs for projects like Monticello and the University of Virginia. This establishes familiarity with the tool, not evidence of its use in composing the *Declaration*. This discussion establishes only that layered graphical concealment techniques existed during the period, not that they were commonly applied to public documents. Concurrently, Benjamin Franklin, a printer focused on communication and espionage, saw the paper's potential not only for drafting but also for steganography, using its layered properties to conceal secret diplomatic or intelligence messages by requiring the precise superimposition of two drawings to reveal a third, hidden image. The layered properties of translucent paper demonstrate a known technical capability for concealment techniques of the period; no claim is made that Franklin employed such methods in relation to the *Declaration*. This possibility is introduced to demonstrate technical feasibility rather than historical documentation.

Graphical Analysis

The National Archives and Records Administration examiners found that no guidelines or pinholes were used to align the sentences in parallel. Their absence limits reconstruction of the process but does not preclude non-invasive alignment methods. The distinctive parallel lines of the *Declaration* appear to have originated from the skilled hand of the suspected scribe, Timothy Matlack. Adding to the mystery surrounding the *Declaration*, Matlack is the most likely candidate to have penned it. Furthermore, in a graphical context, the left margin of the text body is precisely ruled perpendicular to the parallel lines. Logically, the alignment of the parallel lines and the vertical positioning of the left margin could have been marked easily using a traditional drafting board and T-square. However, no such marks indicate that either was employed. Aligning and scaffolding selected recurring letters within the text block of the document would currently be speculative; the author's method likely used a non-marring technique, possibly a paper overlay with predetermined WVYBGP and M points marked, with the edge of the overlay serving as a guide to ensure parallel construction with the lines in the document as it was written. This proposal remains speculative and is offered only as one mechanically plausible scenario.

Preliminary Visual Outcomes

What follows is not offered as proof of intent, but as a preview of the visual outcomes produced by a single constrained method. These outcomes are described here not to persuade, but to orient the reader before the machinery is fully revealed. Interpretive identifications are provisional and will be discussed in greater detail in later chapters. The descriptions that follow do not constitute claims of original intent.

The seven letter-based drawings are divided into two groups: WVY and BGP, with the letter M standing alone, arranged as WVY-M-BGP. This describes the mechanical process by which images emerge. When the WVY images are stacked on a lightbox, the transparent drawings produce a fourth composite image that can be interpreted by viewers as anthropomorphic forms, later compared in this study to figures such as Horus or Jesus for descriptive purposes. In this context, "Horus–Jesus" refers to separate deities, each with its own trinities: Father, Son, and Holy Spirit, and Osiris, Isis, and Horus. In terms of Revelation, the WVY represents a man. It does not suggest a blending of deities but instead depicts three distinct entities represented by the WVY images. The terminology used here is comparative and descriptive, not theological.

This fourth WVY composite is then rotated 180 degrees, forming a fifth image from that perspective. Rotation is applied as a standard geometric transformation, not as an interpretive act.

This image depicts an ox, also from *Revelation*, and its meaning is associated with the Egyptian god Apis. Future chapters describe the W image as a lion-Father-Osiris, the Y image as a dove-eagle-Isis, and the letter V image as representing the Eye of Providence. When combined, WVY produces a composite anthropomorphic form, later compared to Jesus or Horus as descriptive analogies. When rotated, it becomes an ox-Apis. These four images—lion, eagle, ox, and man—symbolize the Four Living Creatures from "Revelation 4:7": Lion (Mark), Ox (Luke), Man (Matthew), and Eagle (John).

The same principle applies to the letters BGP; each letter represents an independent image. When the BGP images are layered together, they form a Mesopotamian leopard that represents Nimrod. These identifications reflect visual resemblance rather than asserted historical encoding.

When rotated 180 degrees, it transforms into a hooded, androgynous Light Bringer with alchemical feminine and masculine facial triangles. The combined BGP leopard and light-bringer are displayed (Fig. 17). The drawing of the letter M includes many smaller images, with the central depiction of Hermes Trismegistus seated on a throne being somewhat ambiguous. Ambiguity here is acknowledged rather than resolved.

When the letter M drawing is rotated 180 degrees, Hermes Trismegistus transforms into the Egyptian god Anubis, giving rise to the syncretic figure of the Greco-Egyptian Hermeanubis.

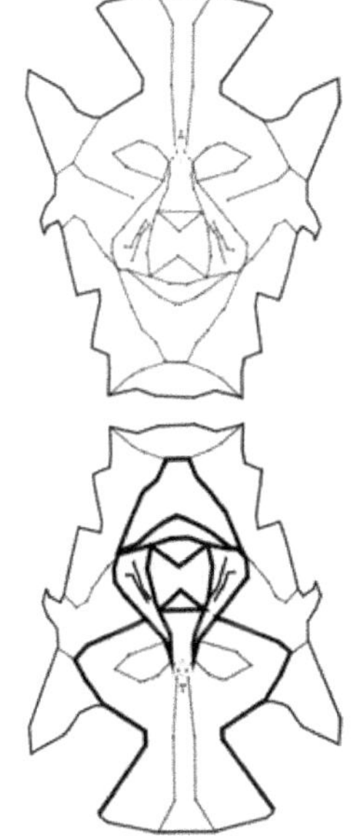

Fig. 17

Jefferson and Euclid's Elements

Thomas Jefferson harbored a deep and lasting affinity for *Euclid's Elements*, an involvement that significantly shaped his intellectual landscape. This affinity is documented through education, library holdings, and correspondence rather than explicit statements of influence on the *Declaration*. He studied Euclid during his formative years at the College of William and Mary, where he was mentored by Professor William Small, who introduced him to natural philosophy and mathematics. Jefferson retained an interest in mathematics, particularly geometry, throughout his life, owning at least two copies of *Euclid's Elements* in his library (The Library of Congress). Ownership alone does not establish use, but it does indicate sustained engagement.

Euclid's Elements exposed him to the power of axiomatic systems built upon seemingly self-evident truths. This immersion in Euclidean logic, a system where complex theorems are rigorously deduced from fundamental postulates, profoundly influenced Jefferson's approach to political philosophy. The connection lies in the notion that just as Euclid's theorems are derived from self-evident truths, Jefferson believed that certain truths about human rights are self-evident and should form the foundation of a just political system. This parallel has been widely noted in Jefferson scholarship but remains interpretive rather than declarative.

Consequently, when drafting the *Declaration of Independence*, he seems to have deliberately adopted a similar axiomatic framework, stating certain truths about human rights as 'self-evident,' akin to Euclid's foundational principles that require no further proof. The phrase "seems to have" reflects inference rather than documentary confirmation.

Thomas Jefferson's extensive knowledge of Euclidean geometry and his skills as a draftsman and writer establish that he possessed the technical capacity to engage with text as structured form. Whether such capacity was exercised in composing the *Declaration* remains hypothetical and is examined here only as mechanical plausibility rather than historical conclusion.

The mechanics of blending images and words to create a tapestry of doctrine and imagery align with Jefferson's skill set. Alignment of skills does not imply sole authorship or independent execution. Benjamin Franklin's documented leadership within Freemasonry and familiarity with symbolic traditions establish a context in which such ideas would have been intelligible, without implying supervision, direction, or confirmation of intent. This role is proposed as advisory and facilitative rather than directive.

Continental Congress and the Committee of Five

Between 1774 and 1788, fifteen individuals served as Presidents of the Continental Congress before George Washington took office as the first President of the United States. The Presidents of the Continental Congress included three who served during the drafting and publication of the *Declaration*.

- Peyton Randolph (1774-1775): A Freemason (Denslow).
- Henry Middleton (1774): A Freemason (Denslow).
- John Hancock (1775-1777): A Freemason (Denslow).

These affiliations are noted to establish cultural context rather than to assert coordinated intent.

Peyton Randolph, Henry Middleton, and John Hancock served as presidents of the Continental Congress from 1774 to 1777, overseeing the drafting, submission, and approval of the *Declaration of Independence*. On June 7, 1776, Richard Henry Lee, a Freemason member of Hiram Lodge No. 59 in Westmoreland County, Virginia, introduced the *Lee Resolution*. The resolution's introduction demonstrates Masonic presence rather than doctrinal influence. "The resolution had three parts: a *Declaration of Independence*, a call to form foreign alliances, and a plan for confederation" (The U.S. National Archives and Records).

Historically, the Committee of Five, comprised of Jefferson, Adams, Franklin, Sherman, and Livingston, drafted the *Declaration of Independence*. Thomas Jefferson served as the primary author and may have been a Freemason. John Adams, who was not a Freemason, participated in the Sons of Liberty, strongly advocated for independence, and made significant contributions to drafting the document. Benjamin Franklin, a distinguished statesman, scientist, and Freemason, provided valuable insights and revisions. Roger Sherman, a prominent lawyer and politician, played a vital role in shaping the document's legal framework. Although it is unclear whether Roger Sherman was a Freemason, his descendants believe he was. This ambiguity reflects broader limitations in eighteenth-century membership records.

They donated his Masonic apron to Yale University, which is now part of its historical collection. The magazine *Connecticut Freemason* has a different perspective. "Roger Sherman was often claimed to have been a Mason; he was not, although his two sons were Masons. The claim that his apron is in the archives at Yale University is believed to be the apron of Deputy Grand Master David Daggett, who was a distant relative" (Littlefield).

Robert Livingston, a Freemason, was a wealthy landowner and politician from New York who had a lesser role in the drafting process. The question of who was or wasn't a Freemason suggests that some of these framers were familiar with Freemasonry's practices, rituals, secrecy, and lodge system throughout the colonies. These affiliations are presented to establish cultural proximity rather than to coordinate authorship or a shared symbolic program.

Indication of Freemasonry

The figures produced through the constrained plotting method described in this study resemble pictorial conventions found in Masonic tracing boards, reflecting a syncretic view of ancient religions. Similarity in visual language does not establish origin.

Only circumstantial evidence suggests that Jefferson may have been a Mason, including references to his relatives and associates. Jefferson's son-in-law, Thomas Mann Randolph, and his eldest grandson, Thomas Jefferson Randolph, were members of Door to Virtue Lodge No. 44 (Moore).

Jefferson admired and associated with Freemasons in both America and Europe, including figures such as George Washington, Benjamin Franklin, James Monroe, Voltaire, and Lafayette. Some Masonic literature claims Jefferson was a Freemason, while other sources dispute this notion. Jefferson, not a Freemason, was a Masonic sympathizer and intellectual ally. This distinction is central to the argument that follows. His friendships with Freemasons establish familiarity with symbolic vocabularies later used as comparative references in this analysis.

However, like most organizations, Freemasonry has a written constitution that outlines the laws governing its practices and provides guidelines for member conduct. The Constitutions of the Free-Masons by James Anderson clearly states: "No Labourer shall be employ'd in the proper Work of Masonry; nor shall Free Masons work with those that are not free, without an urgent Necessity; nor shall they teach Labourers and unaccepted Masons as they should teach a Brother or Fellow" (Anderson). This provision is cited only to demonstrate theoretical permissibility within Masonic practice, not to suggest that the *Declaration* constituted a Masonic work or that such permission was invoked. The Masonic Constitutions outline the exceptions to the exclusivity that Masons impose on the outside world. The phrase "without an urgent Necessity," or the need for a specialized skill, would allow for the employment of a non-Mason, such as Jefferson, to work on a Masonic project. This allowance establishes theoretical permissibility rather than historical documentation.

This provision establishes feasibility, not historical certainty. In the case of the *Declaration* images, it would not have mattered whether Jefferson was a Freemason; he possessed the unique skills necessary to embed the illustrations into the hand-scribed version of the *Declaration*. He was known to the Masons and had an interest in and understanding of encryption, having invented the Jefferson Wheel, a tool for encoding. This establishes familiarity with cipher mechanics rather than evidence of their application to the *Declaration*. Additionally, he was a friend of the Freemason Benjamin Franklin, who held a leadership position that would have enabled Jefferson's participation in drafting the *Declaration*.

Some will argue that the content of this book does not reflect today's Freemasonry. They would be correct. In the eighteenth century, English Freemasonry divided into two broad currents often described as the "Moderns" and the "Ancients." These distinctions are scholarly constructs applied retrospectively.

The Moderns, organized in London in 1717, emphasized standardization, social respectability, and a rationalized approach to ritual. The Ancients, formally organized in 1751, claimed to preserve older ceremonial, biblical, and symbolic elements that they believed the Moderns had altered or removed.

This older approach proved especially influential in Ireland, Scotland, and the American colonies, where lodges developed greater independence and retained traditional forms. Although Benjamin Franklin was initiated before the Ancients were formally constituted in England, his writings, practices, and symbolic sensibilities align more closely with what later came to be identified as Ancient Masonry. This alignment is inferred from symbolic preferences rather than formal affiliation.

The findings I present suggest a possible duality. One interpretive hypothesis explored in later chapters considers whether constrained visual structures produced by the graphical plane method resemble syncretic religious symbolism, without asserting intentional embedding or coordinated authorship. This hypothesis is introduced provisionally and remains subject to falsification.

How could the nation's fiercest proponent of civil liberty participate in such an act? The answer might lie in Jefferson's deep conviction that the state has no authority over personal belief. Any private symbolic interests Jefferson may have held would not, by his own reasoning, conflict with the public function of the document. His involvement in creating this hidden layer was permissible under the very philosophy he articulated in *Notes on the State of Virginia*: "But it does me no injury for my neighbour to say there are twenty gods, or no god. It neither picks my pocket nor breaks my leg. If it be said, his testimony in a court of justice cannot be relied on, reject it then, and be the stigma on him" (Peterson).

If such geometry and symbolism were intentionally embedded, they would, by this definition, constitute private religious statements that posed no civil injury. They did not "pick the pocket or break the leg" of any citizen. It is this fundamental separation, between the mystical philosophy of the framers and the public law of the new republic, that defines the document's dual nature and is the key to understanding the chapters that follow.

Chapter Three
Proposed Graphical Methodology

This is one mechanically plausible method, consistent with known tools and constraints, to invisibly embed the seven drawings (W, V, Y, B, G, P, M) into the engrossed *Declaration*; a process of Blind Stylus Incising could have been employed, using the letters themselves as anchor points. The term is descriptive rather than historical and is used here to distinguish the process from inked, punctured, or graphite-based marking. It is presented as one viable pathway rather than the only possible mechanism. This hypothetical workflow, the scribed text, and margins provided the scaffolding needed to align the grid. This metaphor refers strictly to spatial alignment, not to semantic structure.

What follows is a reconstructed workflow inferred from material constraints rather than a documented procedure.

- The scribe placed translucent templates of oiled rag paper in the form of a flap, reflecting the arrangement of the seven letters (dots) within sentence sections positioned between two dashes.
- These flaps were precisely positioned over the *Declaration* using a registration mask similar to the grille cipher, allowing the scribe to lift and lower the flap to mark letters of words precisely. The term "registration mask" refers to a non-invasive alignment aid, not a permanent guide or marking device.
- Finally, a blind stylus (a dull, pointed instrument) was used to firmly press down only on the precise location of each anchor letter onto the *Declaration* parchment. Pressure depth is assumed to be minimal to avoid parchment rupture.

This pressure created a fine, localized indentation on the parchment, leaving no trace of ink, chalk, pencil, or pinhole, yet forming an invisible network of dot-impressions visible only under specific lighting. The existence of such impressions is proposed as mechanically feasible rather than empirically verified. The resulting drawings exist not as pigment or connecting lines, but as microscopic indentations (dots) where the letters sit, providing a reference layer from which the reconstructed image can be derived.

The Cursive and the Code

The cursive lettering flows beautifully with graceful curves and elegant strokes. While generally admired, the seemingly inconsistent dashes are not flaws but an essential part of the underlying structural system.

The dash, used as a dramatic pause in reading, also serves a dual purpose; it acts as the key to a graphical code that integrates embedded images into the body of the *Declaration's* text. Its function as a key is inferred from repeated positional behavior rather than explicit instruction.

Within this proposed system, the dash functions as a potential organizing key to understanding the underlying code's structure. My undergraduate degree serves as a lens, not a qualification, equipping me with a range of skills. This background informs the observational method, not the historical authority.

Mechanical drafting and letterpress printing are two skills directly related to interpreting the *Declaration* through a graphical perspective. Thomas Jefferson trained in the exact T-square and drafting-board techniques that I did, and Franklin was an expert in movable-type printing, which I also have experience with. These two skills, drafting and typesetting, are closely connected to the awkward dash and follow a unique form that aligns with the functional graphical process. Shared training does not imply shared execution.

Drafting and letterpress printing have enabled me to re-examine the *Declaration* through the lens of techniques such as steganography, in which the text's very ordinariness conceals a hidden message. The best cipher is one that no one suspects is a cipher. Who would think that the *Declaration of Independence* contains a hidden message? Steganography can be achieved in various ways, making detection challenging without specific knowledge or tools. In the case of the *Declaration*, typographic variations in font, spacing, or character glyphs, such as dashes, can encode the hidden message. The human eye is not always sensitive enough to notice subtle changes in text or images, making the use of insertion and typographic variations a practical approach.

Disarrangement in steganography refers to a technique where the hidden message is intentionally scrambled or rearranged within the cover medium. The secret imagery in the *Declaration* text block is halved, reducing the likelihood of raising suspicion by introducing this complexity. The message is only understandable once mirrored. Mirroring is presented as an analytical reconstruction, not a claim about original reader intent.

The following measurements and letter counts are provided to establish scale, density, and opportunity rather than to imply encoded meaning by frequency alone. The *Declaration*'s text block measures approximately 15 inches high by 20 inches wide. It consists of forty-four lines of parallel text containing 1,323 words. The text block features 477 A's, **95 B's**, 184 C's, 252 D's, 859 E's, 180 F's, **130 G's**, 349 H's, 449 I's, 16 J's, 14 K's, 228 L's, **144 M's**, 483 N's, 513 O's, **138 P's**, 6 Q's, 425 R's, 478 S's, 640 T's, 209 U's, **74 V's**, **97 W's**, 9 X's, **81 Y's**, and 4 Zs.

The Process

The pictures I pulled from the letter V were complete and detailed; the drawings were proportionate to one another, and all were contextually related. Context here refers strictly to geometric compatibility. At this stage, 'related' refers only to internal proportionality and structural compatibility, not to symbolic interpretation.

If I were to dive into this rabbit hole, I would do it on a full-scale, 1:1 basis, consistent with full-scale drafting practices available to Franklin or Jefferson. This scale eliminates proportional distortion introduced by digital resizing.

I went to the National Archives online store and ordered a full-size reproduction of the *Declaration of Independence* on faux parchment. Then, I purchased a large light box, 1/8-inch sticky dots, various Sharpies, metal rulers, poster paper, a magnetic whiteboard with ceramic magnets, an eight-inch illuminated magnifying lens with a base, and surgical tweezers. These materials replicate observational conditions, not historical tools.

While I waited for the supplies to arrive, I returned to my layered version of the *Declaration* and began examining the later letters in the alphabet. I discovered geometric patterns in both the letters W and Y. The non-random geometry of W and Y resembled the geometric dot structure of the letter V. Discovery here refers to observed alignment, not inferred symbolism. I returned to the National Archives store, ordered two additional copies of the *Declaration*, and continued to wait.

A few days later, the supplies showed up. I unrolled the *Declaration* from its plastic tube and laid it flat on my magnetic whiteboard, holding the corners down with small ceramic magnets. Using an eight-inch lighted magnifier and a pair of tweezers, I started placing seventy-four 1/8-inch sticky dots on every letter V. Seeing it full-size made everything I'd seen on the computer much clearer. When I finished dotting the V's, I set the *Declaration* on the light box. I placed a sheet of white poster paper on top, about twice the size of the *Declaration's* text area.

To keep everything lined up, I taped the corners of both sheets with painter's tape. With the lightbox on full brightness, the tiny dots showed right through the poster paper. Then, I used a medium black Sharpie to mark each spot, transferring all 74 dots from the *Declaration* to the poster paper. After marking the dots, I folded the poster paper along its centerline, splitting the image into two halves. With the lightbox on, I used the Sharpie to mirror each dot onto the opposite side. When I unfolded the poster paper, it measured twice the size of the *Declaration's* text block. The geometry and symmetry lined up perfectly, one-to-one in scale, just as I imagined it might have looked when it was first drawn. "Perfectly" denotes consistent positional correspondence within observable tolerance.

Chapter Four

The Letter V

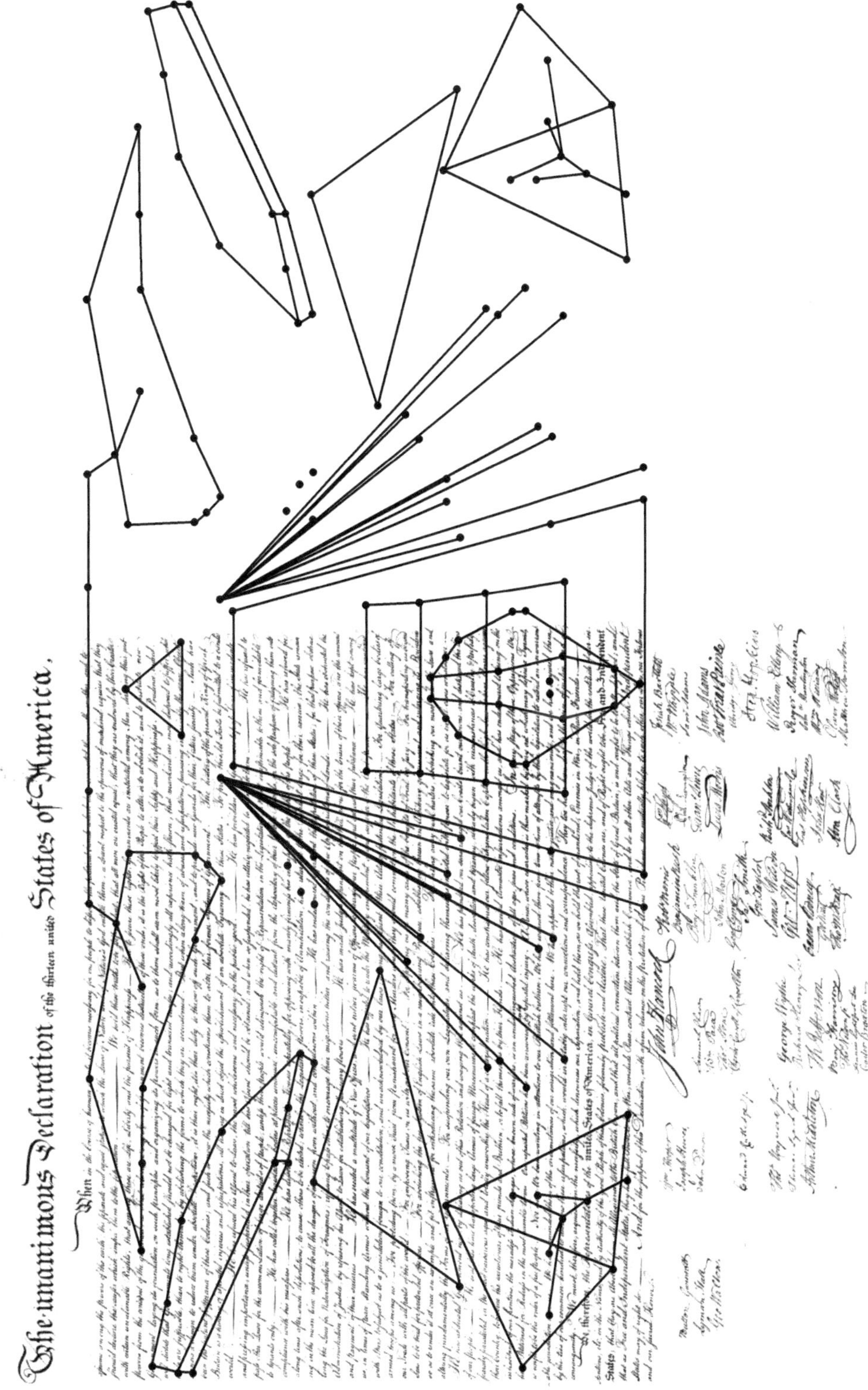

Fig. 18

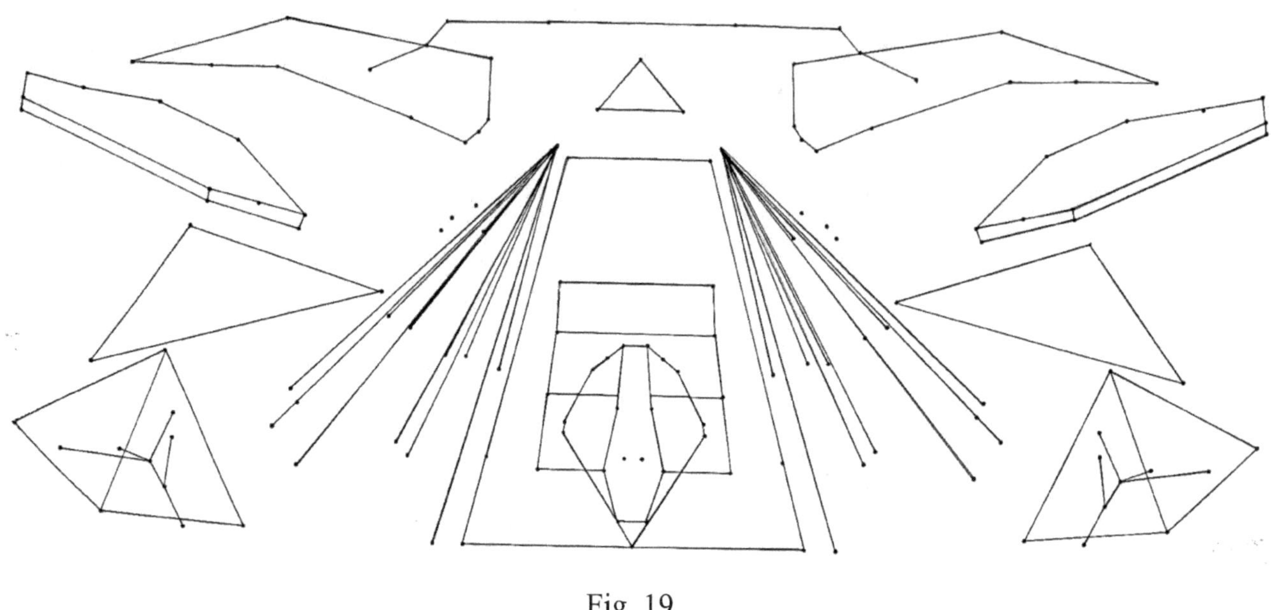

Fig. 19

The first letter I noticed showing precise geometry in the *Declaration* was V. This observation was based solely on positional alignment and repetition, prior to any symbolic interpretation. I later realized its design represented the Eye of Providence and an unfinished pyramid. This interpretation emerged only after the geometric structure was fully resolved (Fig. 18).

The image (Fig. 19), based on the letter V, features an unfinished pyramid in the central panel of a three-panel triptych. The term "triptych" is used descriptively to denote bilateral symmetry around a central axis. The unfinished pyramid symbolizes ongoing progress. This symbolism aligns with later iconographic usage but is not asserted here as definitive intent. The base of the unfinished pyramid contains a large Egyptian oval loop, symbolizing the loop of an Egyptian Ankh. The identification is based on visual correspondence rather than textual annotation. This oval loop represents the concept of an eternal afterlife. It rests upon three steps, signifying the three stages of life: youth, manhood, and old age. The steps also represent the three degrees of Masonry: Apprentice, Fellowcraft, and Master Mason. A traditional Masonic two-dimensional coffin rests atop the three steps. It illustrates the earthly human spirit transitioning through life's three degrees and stages, from inevitable death to a new life. This reading parallels established Masonic symbolism rather than serving as independent proof. The Masonic coffin does not directly represent the human spirit but symbolizes the transformative journey of self-improvement. It signifies the death of the old self, the acknowledgment of mortality, and the potential for rebirth and spiritual growth. The coffin form emerges from geometric completion rather than from illustrative intent. Above the unfinished pyramid is a floating triangular capstone identified as the Eye of Providence. The capstone symbolizes the all-seeing eye of God.

The three points of the floating triangular capstone symbolize the Godhead, also known as the Trinity. Above it rests an image of a two-dimensional ancient religious altar used for burning sacrifices to God. An actual three-dimensional altar has horns protruding from each of its four corners. Since the altar's letter V image is two-dimensional, only two horns are portrayed. The scale of the altar appears disproportionate compared to the smaller pyramid, triangle, and three-dimensional coffin. The enlarged altar horns will serve a dual purpose when layered with the letter W and Y drawings. Scale variation becomes relevant only when the image is layered with other letter constructions.

The triptych's two mirrored outer panel images feature smaller hermetic symbols. Three dots on either side of the unfinished pyramid's apex represent three stars. Alnitak, Alnilam, and Mintaka together form Orion's Belt in the Orion constellation, symbolically representing the three great pyramids of Giza. This constellation is also associated with the mighty hunter, often identified in tradition as the biblical Nimrod, a renowned hunter and the great-grandson of Noah. The astronomical reference is used here as a visual analogue, not as a claim of celestial mapping. Adjacent to the Orion constellation is the word "prove," marking the origin point for thirteen descending points that cascade downward, creating thirteen divine rays of glory, also known as light rays. The number thirteen is noted for recurrence rather than for singular symbolic determination.

At the bottom of the mirrored triptych panel is an image of a four-sided pyramid, precisely proportional to a pyramid figure composed of two conjoined triangles, as described in the first book of *Euclid's Elements*, Proposition 5. The reference is geometric rather than textual. Seven dots are placed inside the four-sided Euclidean pyramid. Connecting these seven points forms a Masonic sprig of acacia, often depicted near or on Masonic coffin illustrations that symbolize immortality. The identification rests on proportional similarity rather than explicit depiction.

The photograph on the next page (Fig. 20) displays a stone carving from the sarcophagus of Ramses, currently housed in the Louvre in Paris, France. It depicts a hieroglyph of the

Goddess Isis, centered between two four-sided pyramids, with a similar carving of the Goddess Nephthys on the opposite side. Another version of this Isis-Nephthys hieroglyph, flanked by pyramids, is showcased at Mit Rahina, an open-air museum in ancient Memphis. Both hieroglyphs feature Isis at the center, with four-sided pyramids on either side, creating a triptych reminiscent of the unfinished pyramid on the *Declaration of Independence*, surrounded by four-sided pyramids. These images are provided for comparative context rather than as evidence of transmission.

(Tangopaso)

Fig. 20

The points on the acacia sprig serve a dual purpose. Using a draftsman's compass on these points reveals their careful arrangement, which represents the first three propositions from Book 1 of *Euclid's Elements*. The procedure follows standard drafting practice. Additionally, two points from the Euclidean pyramid, combined with three points from the acacia sprig, form the surface development of a three-dimensional pyramid. By employing a draftsman's compass and the methods outlined in Euclid's first proposition, the four additional points connect to create four joined equilateral triangle panels. When these triangles are cut and folded, they produce a three-dimensional surface development model of a four-sided pyramid. Surface development is a mechanical operation independent of symbolic interpretation. A surface development drawing is a two-dimensional illustration that, when folded, assembles into a three-dimensional shape.

Above the letter V image of the Euclidean pyramid, there is a scalene obtuse triangle that, when geometrically developed, represents the Phi Pythagorean triangle. The identification is geometric rather than numerological. Positioned above the triangle is a three-dimensional coffin, rising from the pyramid, feet first, symbolizing the spirit in the afterlife.

Two-Dimensional Coffin

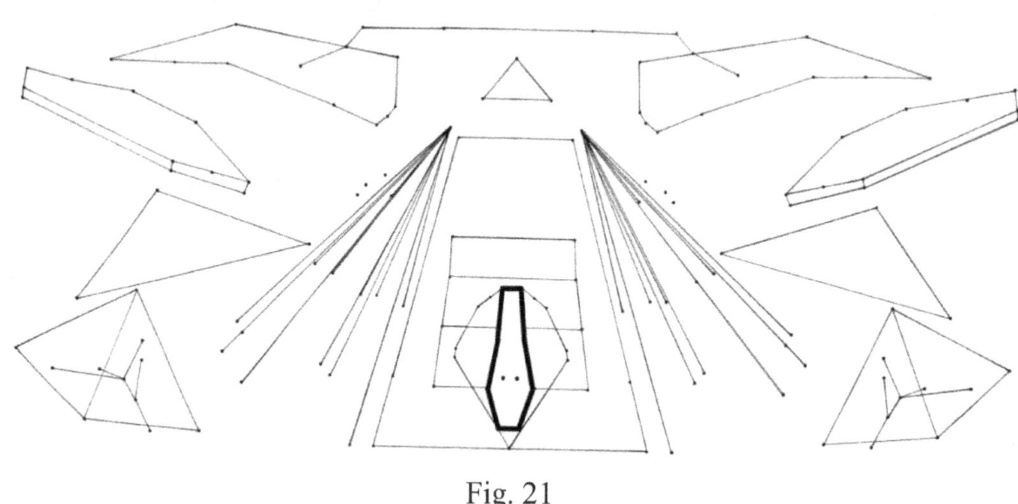

Fig. 21

(A Member of the Craft)
Fig. 22

The first image I visualized and put to paper was a traditional Masonic coffin constructed from V (Fig. 21), derived from the words valuable, endeavored, have, voice, and dissolved (Fig. 23). "Endeavored" is more common in modern texts, while "endeavoured" is the preferred spelling in older English. Letter sourcing establishes positional origin rather than semantic emphasis.

Notice the acacia that adorns the two 1780 Masonic coffins in the pictures (Fig. 22). Acacia symbolizes the immortality of the soul. The *Declaration* coffin features two dots at its widest points. These dots on the Masonic coffin are represented as five-pointed stars or the number five, symbolizing "The Five Points of Fellowship." The number five appears here as correspondence, not confirmation. The number five is

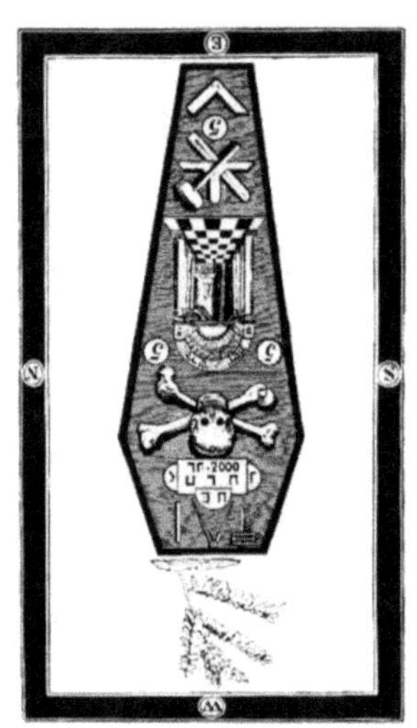

(A Member of the Craft)
Fig. 22

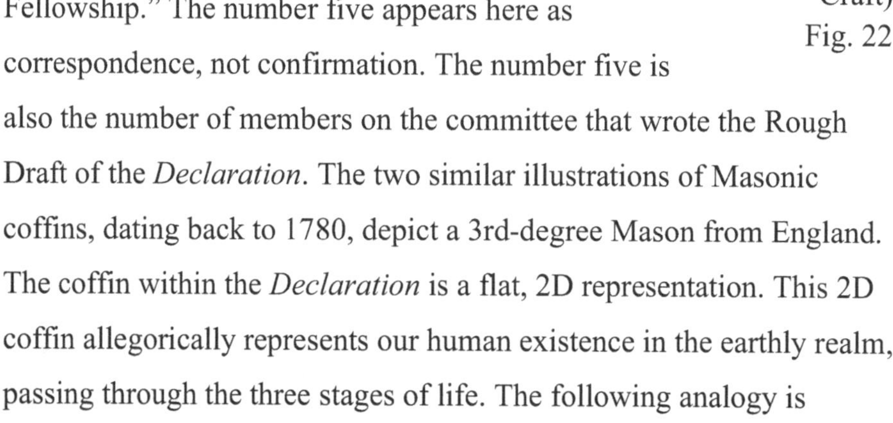

also the number of members on the committee that wrote the Rough Draft of the *Declaration*. The two similar illustrations of Masonic coffins, dating back to 1780, depict a 3rd-degree Mason from England. The coffin within the *Declaration* is a flat, 2D representation. This 2D coffin allegorically represents our human existence in the earthly realm, passing through the three stages of life. The following analogy is illustrative rather than evidentiary. Metaphorically, our earthly existence is compared to a caterpillar foraging for food, moving solely along the x-axis and y-axis, leading a 2D life. Once the caterpillar encases itself in a chrysalis, akin to a coffin or sarcophagus, it symbolically dies and is reincarnated as a butterfly. The reincarnated butterfly can now traverse the x, y, and z axes. The image of a 3D coffin leaving the temple in the *Declaration* symbolizes both the enlightenment and the afterlife of the human spirit, which can journey into the spiritual realm. The symbolism of the Masonic coffin represents the Mason's soul as they progress through the three steps: Entered Apprentice, Fellowcraft, and Master Mason. Note the orientation of the coffin's foot end on the *Declaration*. When a coffin is moved, it is transported feet first, entering and leaving the temple or church feet first, and placed into the grave in the same manner. The drawing of the unfinished pyramid in the *Declaration* depicts a coffin entering feet-first and exiting. The only exception is for the temple or church leader, who may enter headfirst to guide their flock into the temple. The hexagonal shape of the coffin is inspired by the ancient Egyptian sarcophagus, designed to fit the contours of a pharaoh's body. Similarly, the hexagonal-shaped coffin is designed to follow the shape of the human body. Modern funerals typically feature rectangular caskets. This shift from coffin to casket was a gradual process, primarily occurring in the 19th century, aimed at mitigating the impact of the burial ceremony on mourners, as a casket appears less like a human body. The hexagonal Masonic coffin shape is prevalent throughout Freemasonry’s tracing boards and symbolic artwork. The image on the adjoining page is derived from the *Declaration of Independence*. Each dot is placed on top of the letter V in a word and mirrored across the mirror line, completing the coffin drawing.

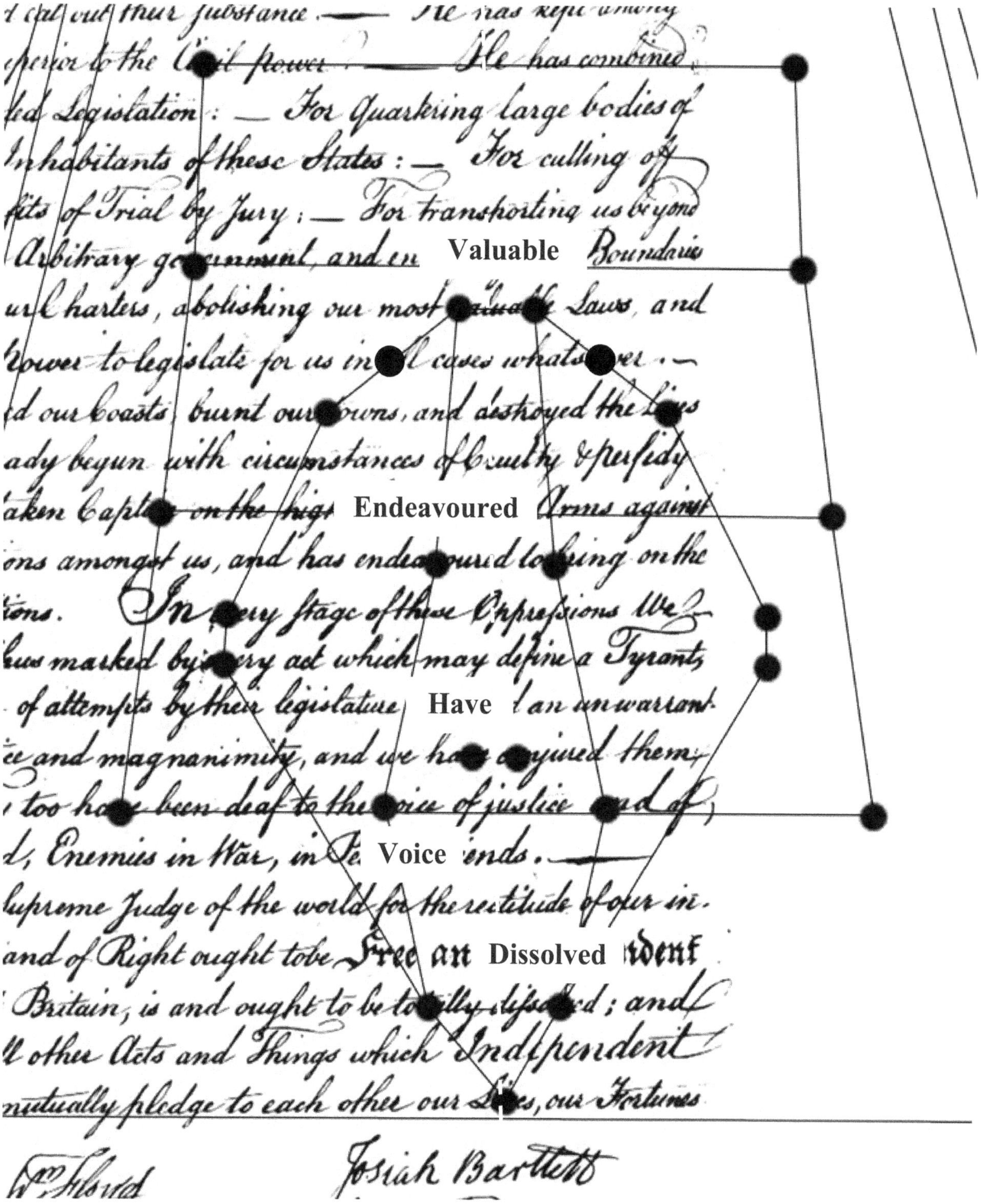

Valuable

Endeavoured

Have

Voice

Dissolved

Fig. 23

The Three Steps

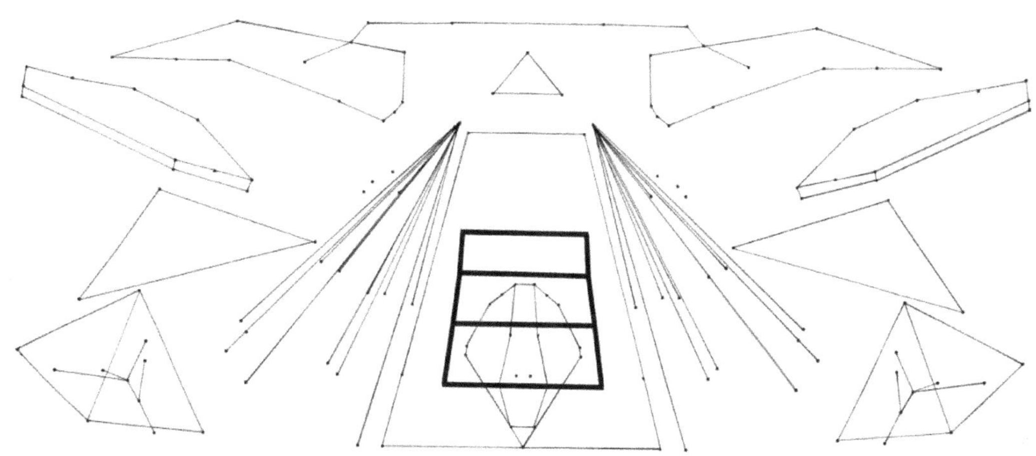

Fig. 24

The second image I recognized after the coffin was the three steps (Fig. 24). The letter V from civil, government, captive, and have forms the left side of the three steps (Fig. 25).

The four V points are reflected across the mirror line, and the lines connecting these two sets of four points form a tapered arrangement of three steps. Reflection is applied as a standard geometric completion. These three steps represent the three degrees of Freemasonry: the Apprentice, the Fellowcraft, and the Master Mason.

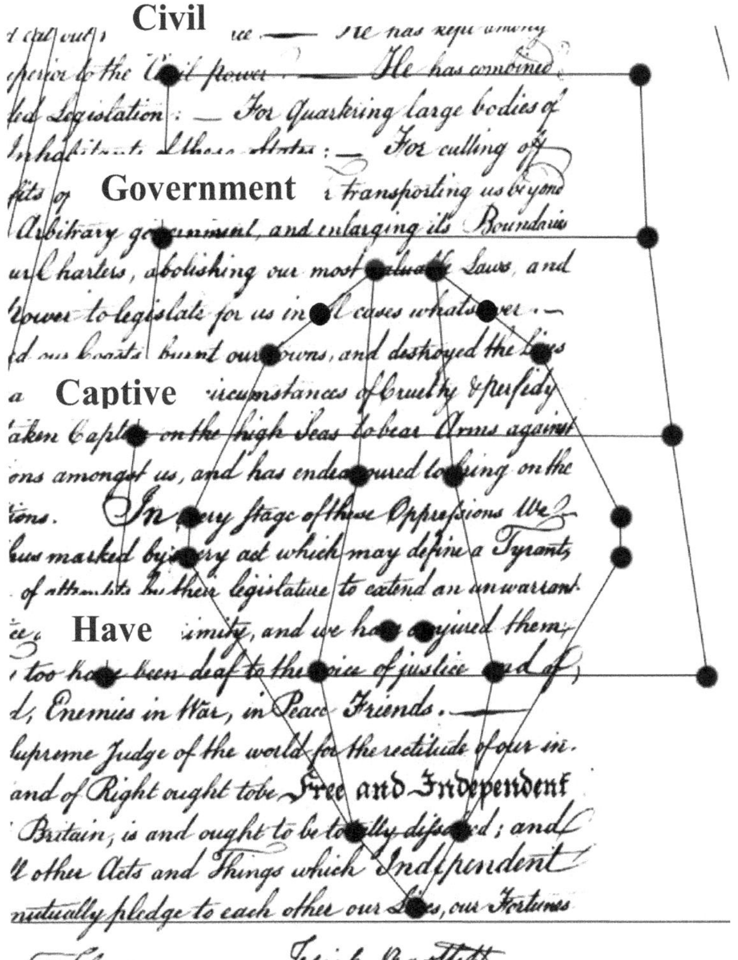

Fig. 25

"In former times and in some of the high degrees, a bier or coffin was placed in front of the altar as a well-known symbol. In passing over this to reach the altar, those various positions of the feet were necessarily taken, constituting the proper mode of advancing (Fig 26). Respect was thus necessarily paid to the memory of a worthy artist as well as to the holy altar. The three principal supports in Masonry, namely: wisdom, strength, and beauty; they also allude to the three stages in human life: youth, manhood, and age; they further allude to the three degrees in Masonry: Entered Apprentice, Fellow Craft, and Master Mason" (Duncan).

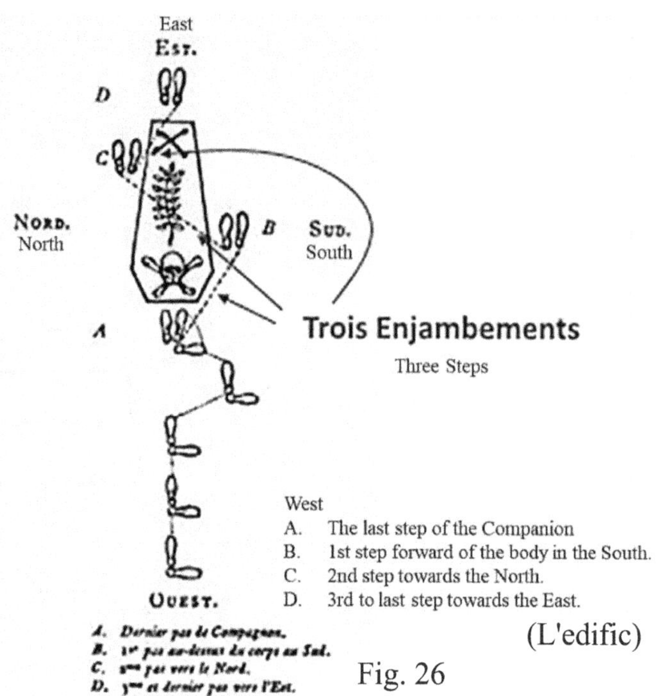

(L'edific)

Fig. 26

This citation demonstrates symbolic continuity rather than documentary linkage. The side diagram of the trapezoid drawing illustrates the outline of the three steps, resembling the tapered step image layout of the *Declaration.* If the trapezoid to the right (Fig. 27) and the coffin above (Fig. 26) were paired, the image would convey the symbolism of the *Declaration's* three steps (Duncan).

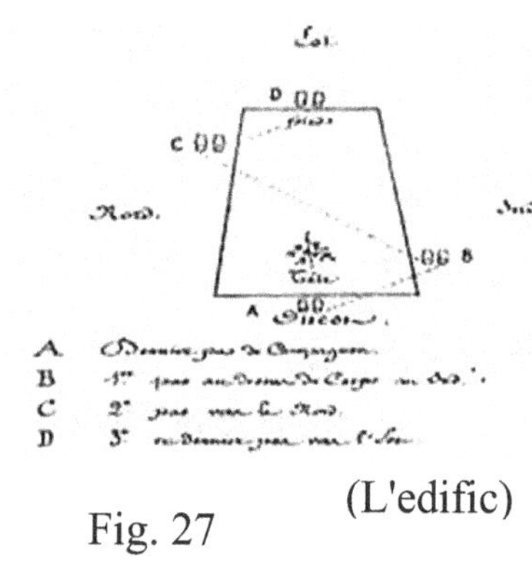

(L'edific)

Fig. 27

The image of the three steps to the right (Fig. 28) is taken from Jacob Ernst's *The Craftsman and Templars Textbook*. Chapter Four of the textbook presents a single-step picture of the First-Degree Entered Apprentice. Chapter Five features a picture of two steps representing the Fellowcraft degree, while Chapter Six shows a picture of three steps symbolizing the Master's degree (Ernst).

THE THREE STEPS

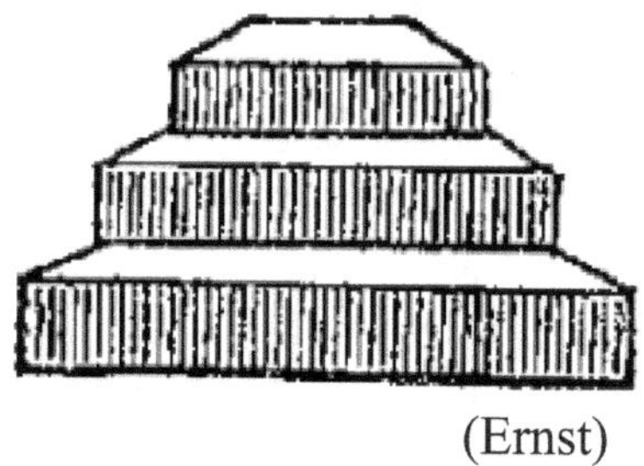

(Ernst)

Fig. 28

Egyptian Ankh Loop

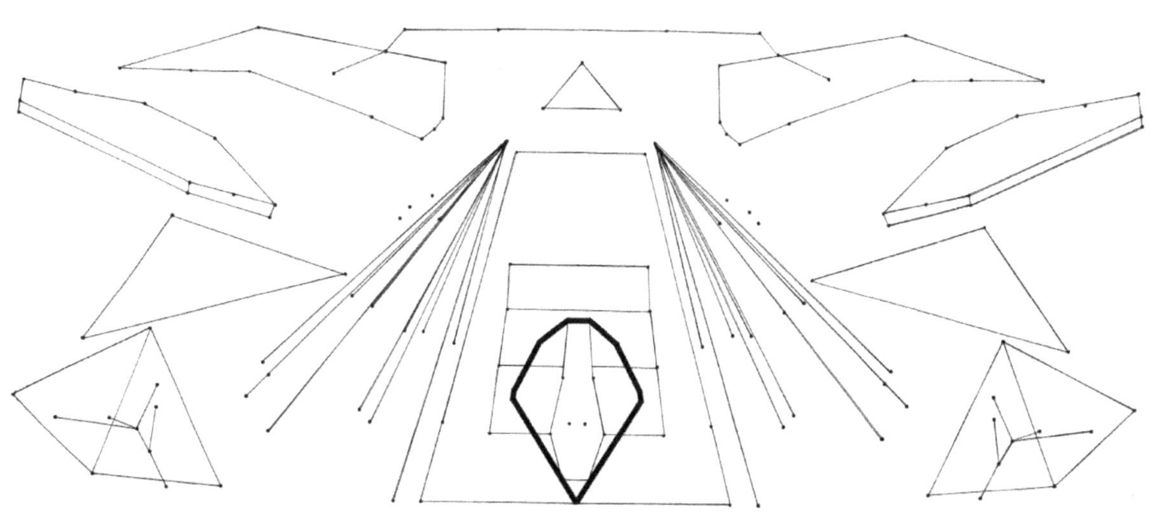

Fig. 29

Surrounding the Masonic coffin is the loop of the Egyptian Ankh, also known as the "Crux Ansata," which is Latin for a cross with a handle. The *Declaration* Ankh is created from the letter V found in the words lives, dissolved, every, every, lives, whatsoever, and valuable (Fig. 31). Each letter V forms a point when mirrored across the mirror line. Connecting these points with lines produces the Crux Ansata, or Ankh Cross, a symbol of resurrection, life, and immortality (Cloland).

(Cooper)
Fig. 30

"The Ankh: In the center of the two interlaced Triangles, we see the Ankh (or the Crux Ansata) (Fig. 30). This is composed of a circle on the top of the Tau Cross, a symbol well recognized in Freemasonry. The Tau Cross, also known as the Triple Tau, is one of the most significant symbols in Royal Arch Masonry. The Ankh is an Ancient Egyptian symbol of great antiquity that portrays the resurrection of the spirit and can also be expressed as the triumph of life over death, of spirit over matter, or as good over evil" (Robson).

The Ankh Cross, an ancient Egyptian symbol, is often depicted in art held by gods and associated with life and the divine. Its shape, resembling a Tau cross with a loop, signifies a duality between earthly and spiritual existence. In Egyptian symbolism, it is linked to reincarnation and can be seen as a union of masculine and feminine principles. Although it is not a primary Masonic symbol, the Ankh functions as a bridge symbol, a pre-Masonic precursor and Hermetic element rather than a formal lodge emblem. It is used in Templar-related orders, symbolizing rebirth and gender balance (The Ankh Cross and Freemasonry).

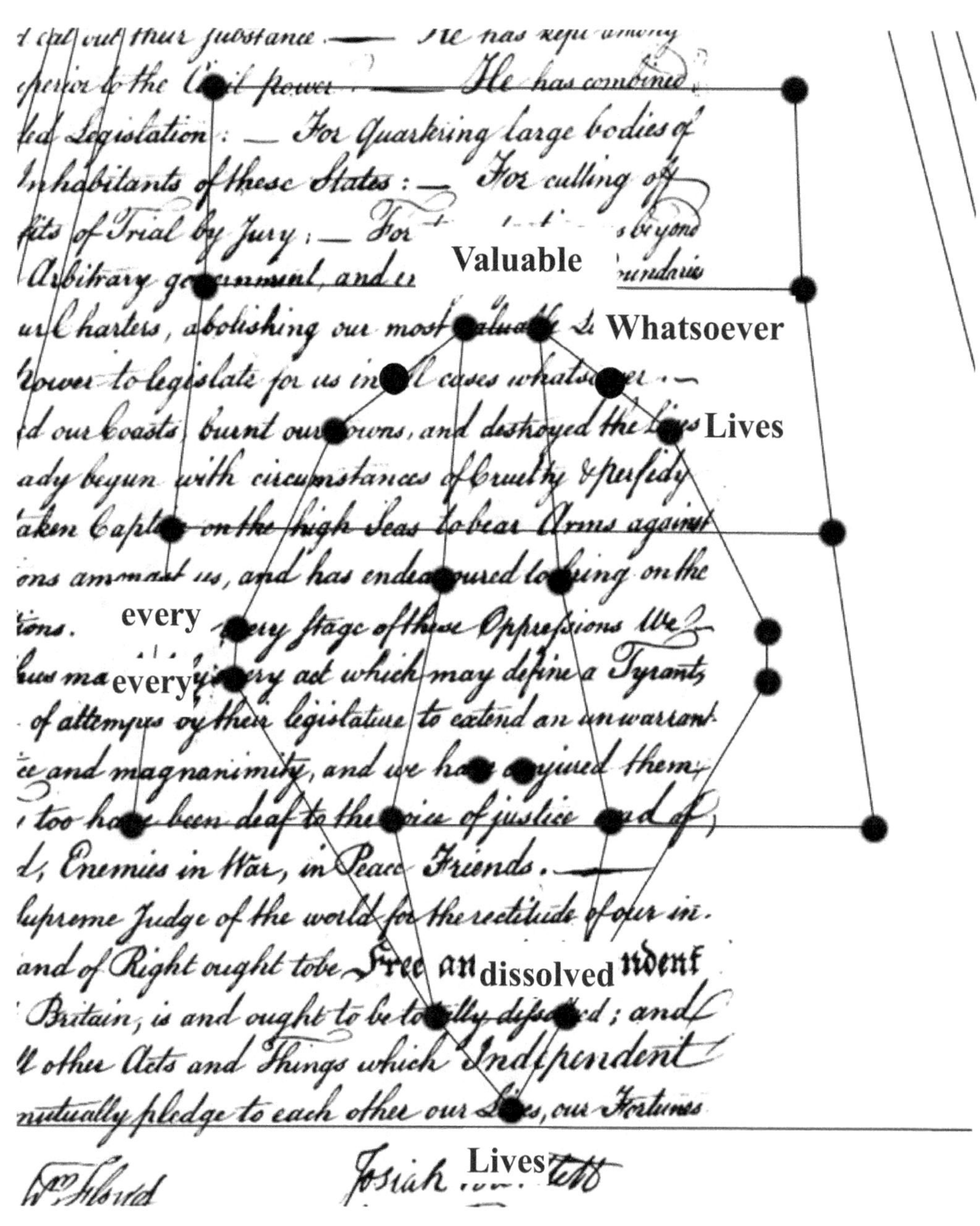

Fig. 31

Unfinished Pyramid

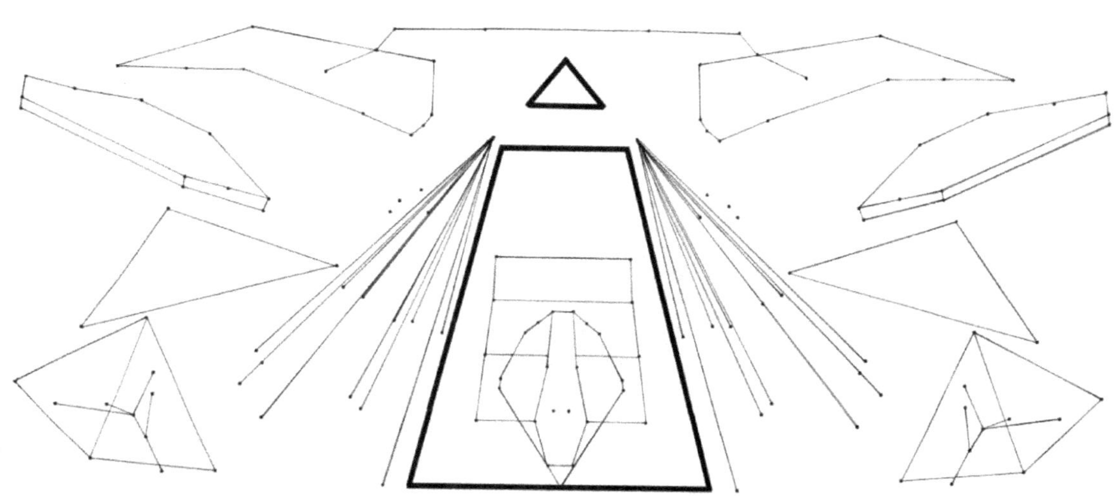

Fig. 32

The coffin, three steps, and Ankh loop align at the center front of an unfinished pyramid (Fig. 32). The pyramid is constructed using the letter V in providence, native, and government. The three points of each letter V are mirrored across the center line. The resulting six points are then connected by lines, to form a trapezoid, or flat-topped pyramid. The floating capstone is created from the letter V, found in the words deriving and invariably. The letter V from deriving serves as the apex and rests directly on the mirroring line. The left base of the capstone is formed by the V from invariably, which, when mirrored, becomes the capstone base, resulting in an isosceles triangle aligned to the center of the flat top pyramid (Fig. 34). The *Declaration's* flat-topped pyramid resembles the 1782 Great Seal of the United States (Fig. 33).

(Great seal of the U.S." reverse side)

Fig. 33

Why do ancient Egyptian themes recur throughout the images of the *Declaration*? The pictures in the *Declaration's* letters feature a Masonic design; thus, the influence of Egyptian mysticism is evident in Freemasonry. Dr. Albert Mackey, a Master Mason and noted Masonic author, wrote, "Egypt was the first country of antiquity to receive the germs of civilization, and there the first Mysteries are supposed to have been invented. We shall, therefore, select the

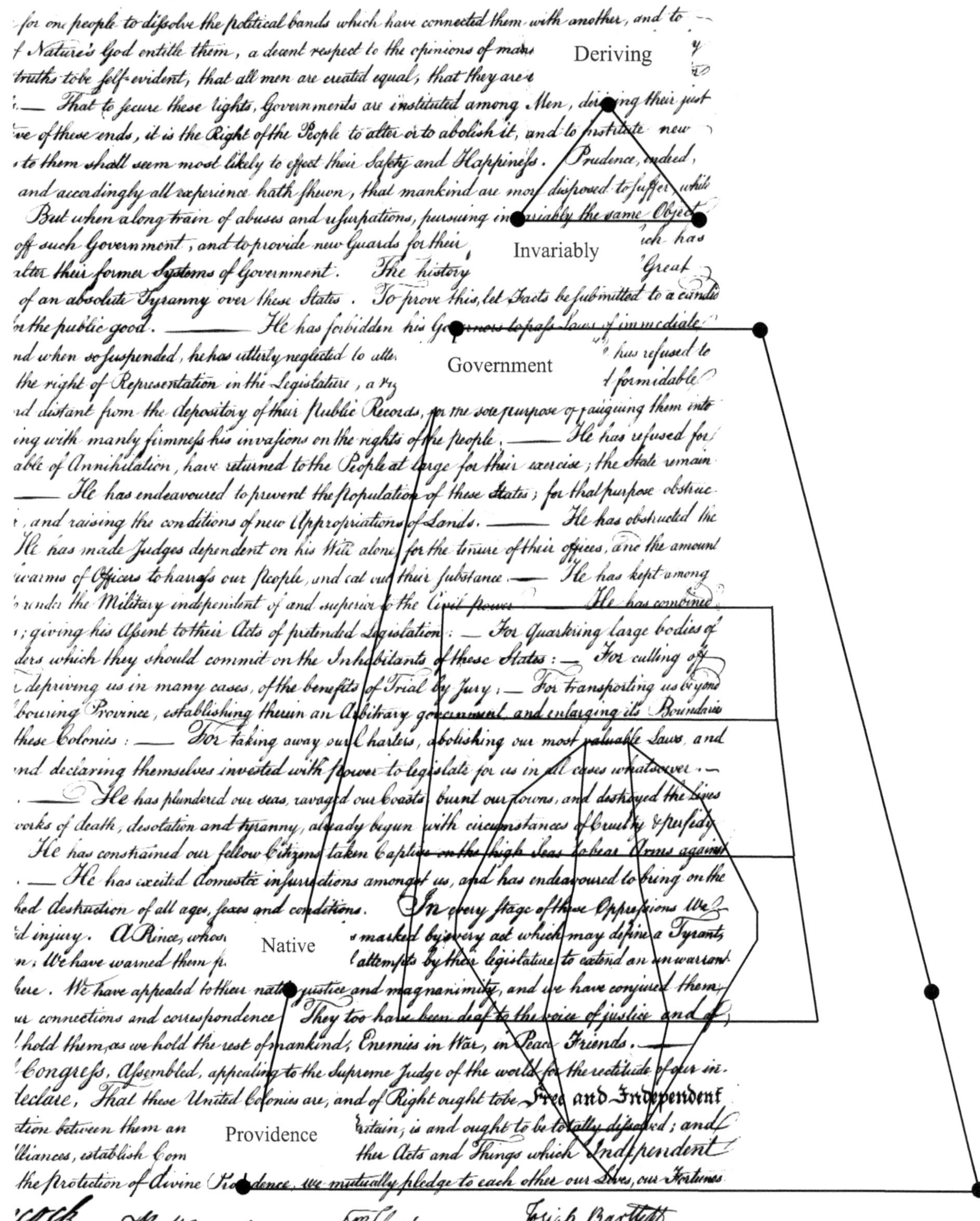

Fig. 34

Osiriac, the most important of the Egyptian Mysteries, as the exemplar from which an idea may be obtained of the character of all the other mysteries of Paganism" (Clegg).

This philosophical lineage provides historical context for the symbolic continuity observed within the *Declaration*'s imagery. It does not establish that such symbolism was deliberately embedded in the *Declaration*, only that the symbolic vocabulary was culturally available

Egyptian symbolism in Freemasonry traces back to the Hermetic rediscovery of antiquity during the Renaissance, spanning the 14th to 17th centuries. This revival was later understood by Masons as Operative Freemasonry, the original guild of craftsmen, which included stonemasons and other artisans who thrived in the medieval era. They built cathedrals and castles, employing specific rituals, symbols, and a hierarchical framework in their practices. As the demand for large stone structures declined, the craftsmen's guilds gradually faded. In search of new funding, the Operative Lodge began accepting non-craftsmen.

Eventually, the Operative Lodge system evolved into a Speculative Masonic system during the 17th and 18th centuries. The Speculative Freemason differs from the Operative Mason in that he is no longer an artisan but instead a philosophical initiate who upholds the customs and rituals of the earlier Operative Masons.

Timothy W. Hogan summarizes this broader syncretic process, noting that Masonic symbolism overlaps with Gnosticism, alchemy, Qabbalah, and Rosicrucian thought. These traditions shared symbolic progressions and initiatory frameworks, though no single lineage can be conclusively established (T. W. Hogan).

Author David Stevenson similarly cautions against treating the formal establishment of the Grand Lodge of England in 1717 as a definitive origin point, emphasizing instead a long and gradual evolution of ideas and practices (Stevenson).

Within this historical context, the pyramid reconstructed from the letter V functions as a geometric structure that coincides with symbolic forms later recognized in Masonic iconography. The reconstruction itself establishes only spatial coherence. Any symbolic resonance arises from historically documented symbolic systems external to the *Declaration.*

The Great Seal of the United States is introduced here solely for contextual comparison. It is not presented as evidence that similar imagery was intentionally embedded in the *Declaration* of Independence.

Worthy Brother Brownell examined the significance of the Great Seal of the United States and the American flag through a Masonic interpretive framework. Brownell's remarks were delivered during an oration commemorating the laying of the cornerstone of the Masonic Hall in Washington, D.C. His address reflects how late nineteenth-century Freemasons understood American national symbols, rather than serving as evidence of eighteenth-century authorial intent. The following excerpt illustrates this interpretive tradition:

"For this Federal Government is represented by a flag which bears the three masonic colors, the red, white, and blue, with a five-pointed star of the ground floor for every member of the Union, and the great seal of our Federal State shows the masonic unfinished pyramid and the Omniscient eye above" (Brownell).

Brownell's statement demonstrates that, by the late nineteenth century, Freemasons openly regarded the Great Seal as resonant with Masonic symbolism. His interpretation reflects internal symbolic continuity rather than documentary proof of original design intent.

John Hodson, who served as Grand Master of Masons in Oregon from 1899 to 1900, offered a more detailed symbolic interpretation of the Great Seal. Hodson's analysis likewise represents a retrospective Masonic reading of national imagery. He notes that Benjamin Franklin, Thomas Jefferson, and John Adams were appointed to an early committee tasked with proposing designs for the Great Seal, and that a range of symbolic motifs, biblical, classical, and allegorical, were considered during its lengthy development. Hodson interprets many of the Seal's final elements as Masonic in character, though such interpretations are not corroborated by contemporaneous design records.

Hodson describes the front of the Seal, the American eagle with shield, arrows, olive branch, thirteen stars, and the motto E Pluribus Unum, as symbolically consonant with Masonic teachings. He associates the eagle with St. John the Evangelist, a figure traditionally honored within certain Masonic rites, and interprets the arrows, olive branch,

(Lossing)
Fig. 35

clouds, and stars through biblical and moral allegory. These associations reflect Masonic symbolic literacy rather than documented design rationale.

Hodson further characterizes the reverse of the Great Seal as explicitly Masonic, focusing on the unfinished pyramid, the Eye of Providence, and the Latin mottos Annuit Coeptis and Novus Ordo Seclorum. He interprets the pyramid's stepped structure, numerical features, and Egyptian form as emblematic of moral progress, liberation, and divine favor. Hodson's reading also links the number of visible stones to the signers of the *Declaration* of Independence. While numerically suggestive, such correspondences are interpretive and remain unverified by primary sources.

Hodson's overall interpretation frames the Great Seal as both a national emblem and a symbolic document that later Freemasons understood through the lens of Masonic philosophy and ritual symbolism (Fig. 35). His account illustrates how American national imagery was subsequently integrated into Masonic cosmology and moral instruction.

Importantly, the Great Seal was adopted in 1782, six years after the *Declaration* of Independence, and was the result of multiple committees, revisions, and compromises. Its symbolism cannot, therefore, be used as evidence that similar imagery was intentionally embedded in the *Declaration* itself. Rather, the Seal demonstrates that symbolic motifs such as the unfinished pyramid, the all-seeing eye, and the number thirteen were culturally available, intelligible, and meaningful to educated elites of the late eighteenth century and to later Masonic interpreters.

Accordingly, the Great Seal is included here for context, not as final proof. It doesn't prove exactly what the authors meant by the *Declaration* of Independence, nor does it confirm the existence of hidden images in the document. Instead, it shows a clear pattern: the same visual and philosophical style found in the *Declaration*'s geometry later appeared openly and clearly in our official national symbols. These same symbols were later recognized by Freemasons as being consistent with their own traditions.

This connection makes it more believable that the geometric patterns found in this study align with symbolic systems that Freemasons knew, valued, and later used. However, on its own, this connection does not prove that these patterns were deliberately put there.

Horned Altar

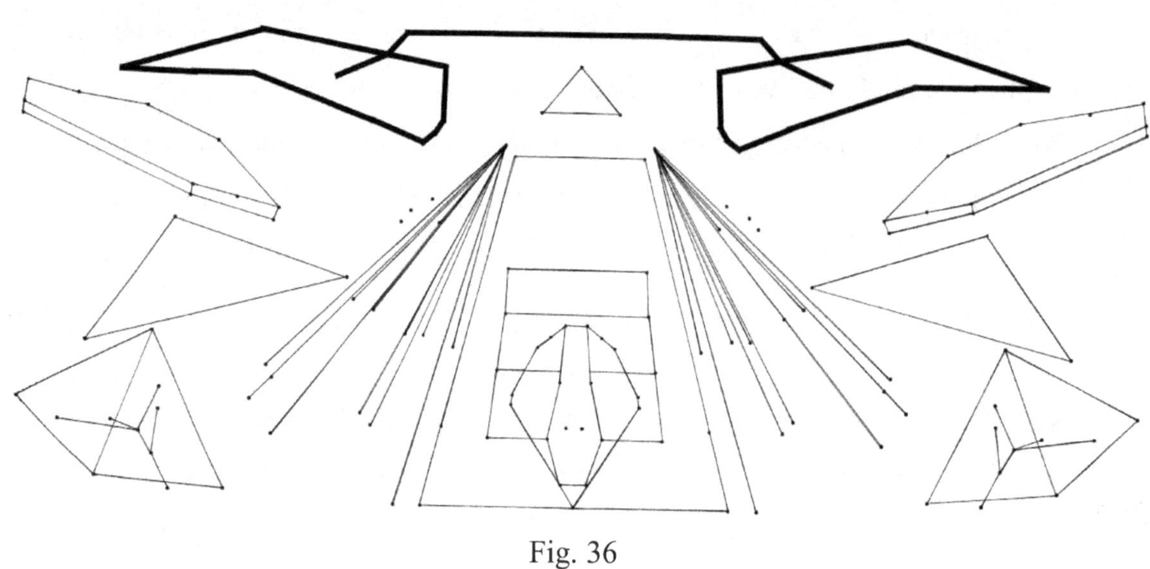

Fig. 36

The *Declaration* of Independence altar is designed using the letter V, fixed in place by the wording of the *Declaration.* The form derived from the words: governed whenever, government, government, over, government, provide, government, self-evident, events, dissolve, and have (Fig. 38). Traditionally, Catholic altars do not have horns, but ancient Hebrew altars did (Fig. 37). They seem to have been associated with the sacrifice of bulls and other animals (Hunt).

The altar at the top of the letter V diagram (Fig. 36) is depicted as a horizontal line with horns extending from either side, positioned above the pyramid's floating capstone. The coffin enters the pyramid across the steps, with both symbols positioned below the altar and its horns. Albert Mackey describes the orientation of the altar, coffin, and steps, and their significance.

(Danckert')
Fig. 37

Mackey explains the ritual relationship between the altar, coffin, and steps as follows: "In Masonic tradition, particularly in higher degrees, a coffin or bier was historically placed before the altar. The specific foot movements made to pass over it and reach the altar symbolized respect for the artisan and the sanctity of the altar. This ritual represents the journey through "three grand steps" from earthly existence toward enlightenment and divine knowledge. As interpreted by Mackey, it's clear that these steps symbolize a transition from ignorance to illumination, either literally or figuratively crossing over a symbolic representation of death, to teach that proper knowledge and eternal life are found beyond the "darkness and ignorance" of this world" (Mackey, *An Encyclopedia of Freemasonry and its Kindred Sciences*).

The Israelites acknowledged the divine power and protection associated with worship by placing horns on sacred altars."In the Jewish Temple, the altars of burnt-offering and of incense had each at the four corners four horns of shittim wood, shittim being a species of acacia having yellowish wood. Among the Jews, as well as all other ancient peoples, the altar was considered peculiarly holy and privileged; and hence, when a criminal, fleeing could hold of these horns, he found an asylum and safety. As the Masonic altar is a representation of the altar of the Solomonic member, it should be constructed with these horns" (Mackey, *An Encyclopedia of Freemasonry and its Kindred Sciences*). The passage draws a parallel between the altar in the Jewish Temple and the Masonic altar in King Solomon's Temple, which should be constructed with horns. This connection highlights the influence of ancient Jewish traditions on Freemasonry.

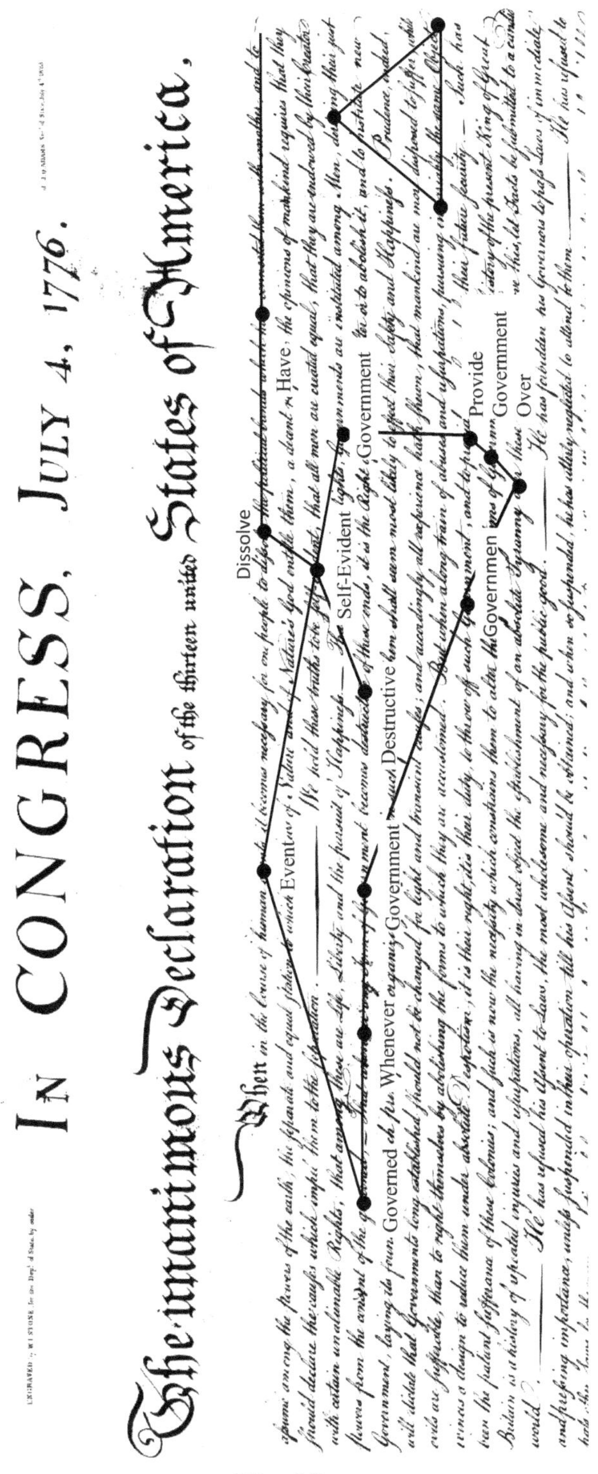

Fig. 38

Image (Fig. 38) shows an edge view of a half altar. This altar has a flat top with a sloping line marking the table's edge and outward-extending horns that taper to a point. The altar is completed by mirroring the table and horns, producing a two-dimensional side view.

Accordingly, the coffin/steps/pyramid/Ankh/altar configuration is presented as a geometric result with symbolic resonance, not as a hidden emblem. Its significance lies in its structural coherence within the reconstruction and its alignment with historically documented symbolic vocabularies available to later interpreters. As with the unfinished pyramid and Great Seal, this correspondence supports plausibility rather than proof and must be evaluated as part of a broader pattern rather than as a standalone claim.

Thirteen Rays of Glory

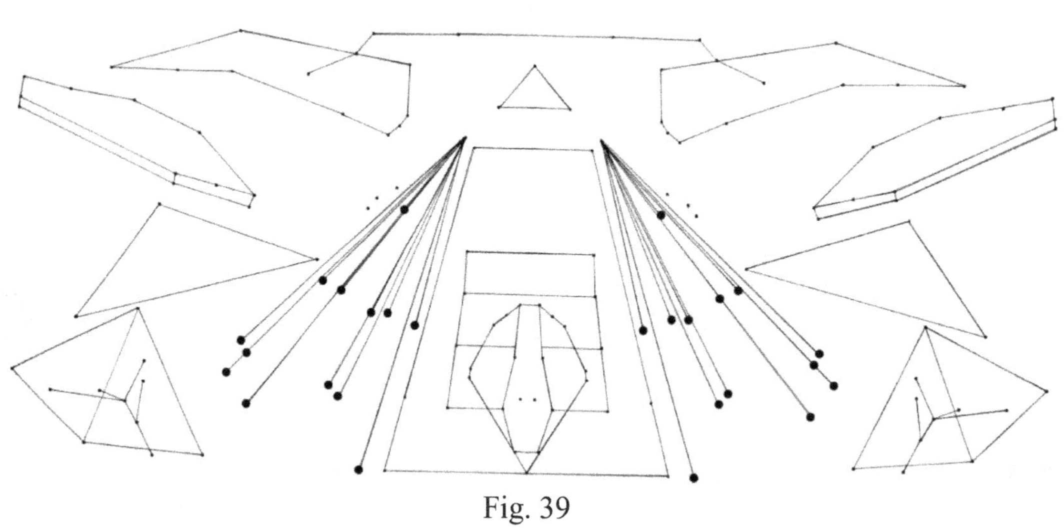

Fig. 39

Located on both sides of the unfinished pyramid near the capstone is the point of origin word "Prove," with thirteen additional points descending, forming thirteen rays created by the letter V.

Thirteen descending points, known as the rays of divine light, are formed from the letter V of the words prevent, depriving, province, invested, themselves, ravaged, civilized, have, themselves, have, have, inevitably, and divine (Fig 42). The word prove serves as the point of origin, from which connecting lines cascade downward to form thirteen light rays. When these letterforms are aligned according to the established reconstruction rules, mirroring across the central axis and connecting corresponding vertices, they produce thirteen linear extensions descending from the apex region. These extensions form a fan-like pattern that is geometrically consistent and repeatable. This configuration is described here as "rays" solely as a visual shorthand. The term refers to straight, descending line segments radiating from a common point, not to an assertion of symbolic intent. The number thirteen arises from the number of qualifying letterforms available within the defined reconstruction space, rather than from a numerological assumption imposed after the fact.

The terms divine light, rays of glory, nimbus, aureole, glory, and gloriole are often used interchangeably in religious and artistic contexts; however, each possesses distinct characteristics and symbolism.

Fig. 40

A nimbus is typically a circular or cloud-like light surrounding the head of a divine or sacred figure (Fig. 40). It symbolizes holiness, sanctity, and divine presence, representing spiritual authority and enlightenment. Nimbuses are commonly depicted in religious art, particularly in Christian symbolism, to indicate the divinity of Jesus Christ, the Virgin Mary, and the saints. These distinctions are introduced here to clarify terminology, not to claim that the reconstructed rays function as religious iconography. The comparison is formal rather than doctrinal: the reconstructed geometry produces straight, radiating lines that visually correspond to a well-established artistic motif.

Rays of Glory are beams of light that emanate from a divine or sacred figure, often depicted as golden or radiant, representing the figure's divine power, majesty, and glory. They can also symbolize enlightenment, inspiration, or a spiritual connection. Divine Light encompasses any luminous or radiant manifestation of the sacred, representing its transcendent nature, illuminating power, and capacity to transform and uplift (Fig. 41).

Dr. Robert Mackey describes rays of glory emanating from a triangle as follows: "It is the symbol of the Supreme Architect of the Universe, the Creator; and when surrounded by rays of glory, it becomes a symbol of the Architect and Bestower of Light" (Mackey, *An Encyclopedia of Freemasonry and its Kindred Sciences*).

(Cross)

Fig. 41

The triangle above the unfinished pyramid, formed by the letter V, features rays of divine light. The capstone, also known as the floating triangle, represents the Eye of Providence, historically associated with the Eye of Horus. The rays emanating from the letter V in the *Declaration* create a line of sight from the all-seeing eye as it watches over us below (Fig. 39).

The all-seeing Eye of Horus, of Egyptian origin, also became known as The Eye of Providence, a Christian adaptation. The Eye of Horus is a symbol from ancient Egypt that represented royal power, protection, and good health. It is also referred to as the Eye of Ra, a symbol associated with another Egyptian deity.

It was not until the Renaissance in Europe that the Eye of Horus began to acquire Christian symbolism. At this time, it became a symbol of divine power and a representation of the Holy Trinity. The Eye was often depicted within a triangle and, in the 17th century, was usually accompanied by clouds and a sunburst.

The prominence of the number thirteen warrants particular caution. Thirteen is undeniably central to the Great Seal of the United States and is commonly explained in historical scholarship as representing the original colonies. Later Masonic writers and commentators have proposed additional biblical and esoteric interpretations, including associations with the tribes of Israel or Masonic organizational structures. These interpretations, while internally coherent within Masonic symbolism, are retrospective and remain debated.

The thirteen rays identified in this reconstruction correspond numerically, but not causally, to the recurring use of thirteen in the Great Seal. This correspondence is noted as a case of striking coincidence rather than as evidence of intentional encoding. The reconstruction demonstrates that a thirteen-ray configuration can be produced consistently from the text using a fixed geometric method, not that the number was selected for symbolic reasons.

The close-up illustration of the origin word "prove" and the descending points (Fig. 42) emphasizes the mechanical nature of the construction. The rays emerge from letter geometry, alignment, and repetition, not from freehand drawing or symbolic embellishment.

As with the unfinished pyramid, altar, and Ankh-like figure, the rays of glory are therefore presented as a geometric outcome with symbolic compatibility, not as a concealed emblem. Their significance lies in their structural coherence within the reconstruction and in their alignment with symbolic systems later recognized and valued by Freemasons and other interpreters. On their own, they do not demonstrate deliberate design; considered alongside the broader pattern, they contribute to a cumulative argument grounded in plausibility rather than proof.

Prove
Prevent
Province
Depriving
Invested
Themselves
Civilized
Ravage
Themselves
Have
Have
Have
Inevitably
Divine

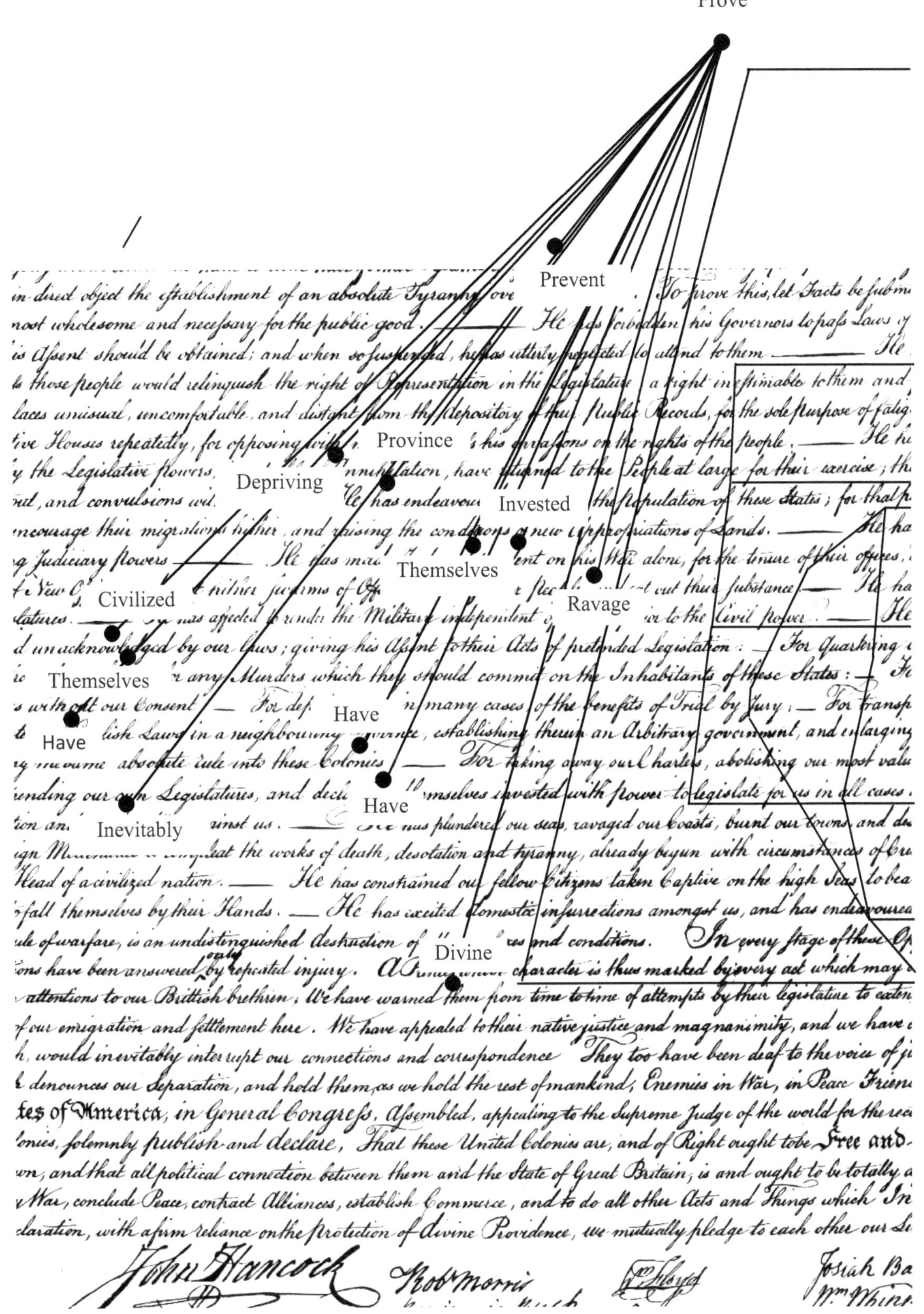

Fig. 42

Orion's Belt

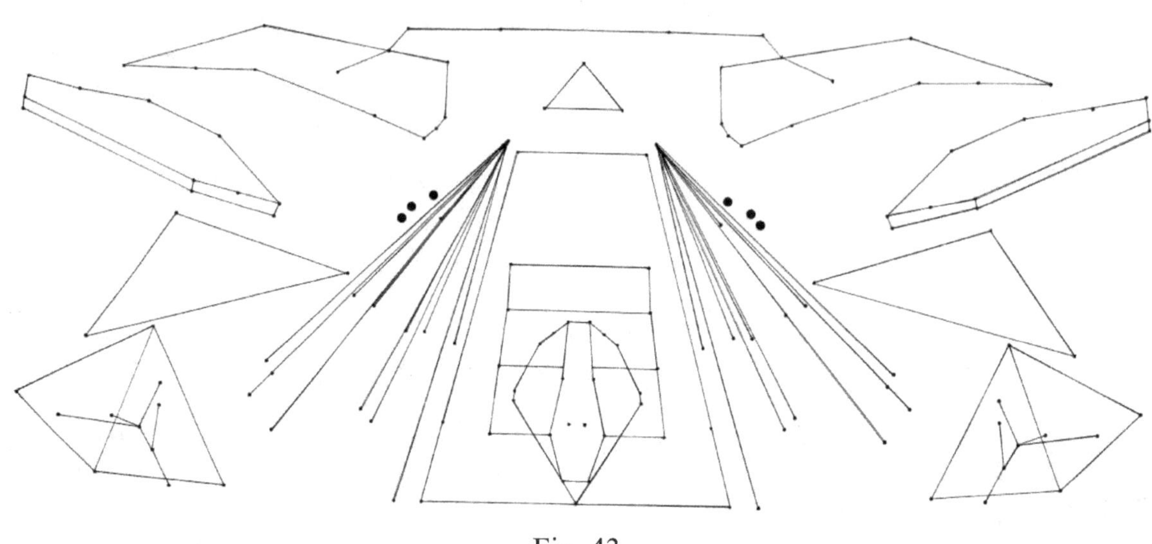

Fig. 43

Next to the rays of glory is a cluster (Fig. 43) of three words that contain the letter V. These letters V are represented as dots in the image above and are taken from invasions, have, and endeavored (Fig. 44). These three letters V align with the same asterism as Orion's Belt, located in the constellation of Orion. Orion's Belt is a well-known pattern of three stars: Alnitak, Alnilam, and Mintaka (Fig. 45).

Orion's Belt is a fascinating aspect of the images formed from the letter V. The Ancient Egyptians believed that the stars in Orion's Belt represented the resting place of Osiris' soul, the god of the afterlife (Orion).

Invasions

Have

Endeavoured

Fig. 44

As noted in *The Asiatic Quarterly Review*, "The Pyramid texts show Osiris Orion, like his Greek namesake, to have been a mighty hunter. The justified dead unite with Osiris, traveling with him daily as Ra also passes to the sky to sojourn with Osiris" (The Asiatic Quarterly Review). "Other constellations won the spiritual regard of the Egyptians. The soul or sahou of Osiris was said to have dwelt in Orion. The Belt of three stars, the middle one being of special interest, could not fail to win attention" (Bonwick).

The connection between Freemasonry, Orion's Belt, and Osiris illustrates the enduring power of ancient symbols and their remarkable ability to transcend time and culture. This connection suggests a shared human fascination with the cosmos, encompassing the mysteries of life and death. These symbols remind Freemasons of their ethical principles and the pursuit of spiritual enlightenment.

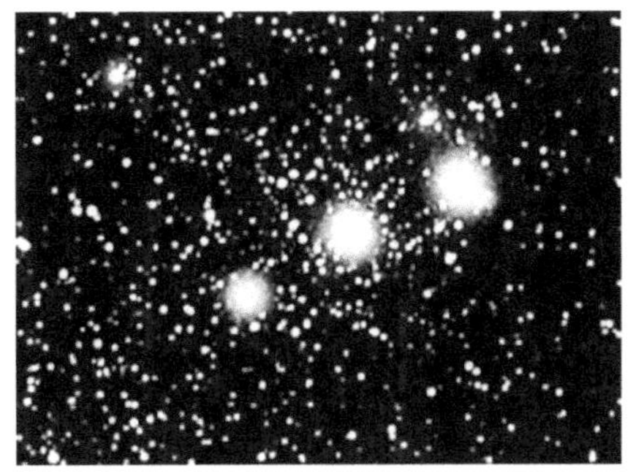

(NASA/JPL)
Fig. 45

"The three stars that form Orion's Belt have significant symbolism in Freemasonry. In Masonic tradition, the Belt of Orion represents the three principal officers of the lodge: the Worshipful Master, Senior Warden, and Junior Warden. ancient Egyptian mythology associated the three stars of the Belt of Orion with Osiris, Isis, and Horus. The three stars were also important to the ancient Babylonians, who referred to them as the 'Three Kings' and associated them with the God Ninurta" (Freemasonry). According to Masonic tradition, the Three Ancient Grand Masters who presided over the construction of King Solomon's Temple were Solomon, Hiram, King of Tyre, and Hiram Abiff, represented by the three stars of Orion.

Modern theories connecting Orion's Belt to the layout of the Giza pyramids, most notably those proposed by Robert Bauval in The Orion Mystery, fall within the field of archeoastronomy and remain debated in academic scholarship. Regardless of their merits, these theories were entirely unknown in colonial America. The astronomical measurements, archaeological data, and theoretical frameworks necessary to propose such alignments did not exist in the eighteenth century.

For this reason, the Orion analogy is not used here to argue for Egyptian transmission, astronomical knowledge, or deliberate stellar encoding in the *Declaration*. Instead, it demonstrates that the reconstructed geometry produces a stable three-point linear pattern that corresponds to one of the most historically significant and symbolically rich triadic forms recognized across cultures.

The relevance of Orion's Belt, therefore, lies not in causation but in symbolic compatibility. The *Declaration*'s reconstructed geometry yields forms, triads, axes, rays, and hierarchies that later interpreters, particularly within Freemasonry, readily associated with established symbolic systems involving death, rebirth, moral order, and cosmic structure.

As with the unfinished pyramid, altar, rays of glory, and Great Seal, the Orion's Belt configuration is presented as a geometric outcome with cross-cultural resonance, not as proof of hidden meaning. Its inclusion strengthens the cumulative argument that the geometry uncovered in this study aligns with symbolic vocabularies historically valued by Freemasons and other esoteric interpreters, while stopping short of asserting intentional design or authorial awareness.

Pyramid, Tetrahedron, *Euclid's Elements*, Book 1, Proposition 5

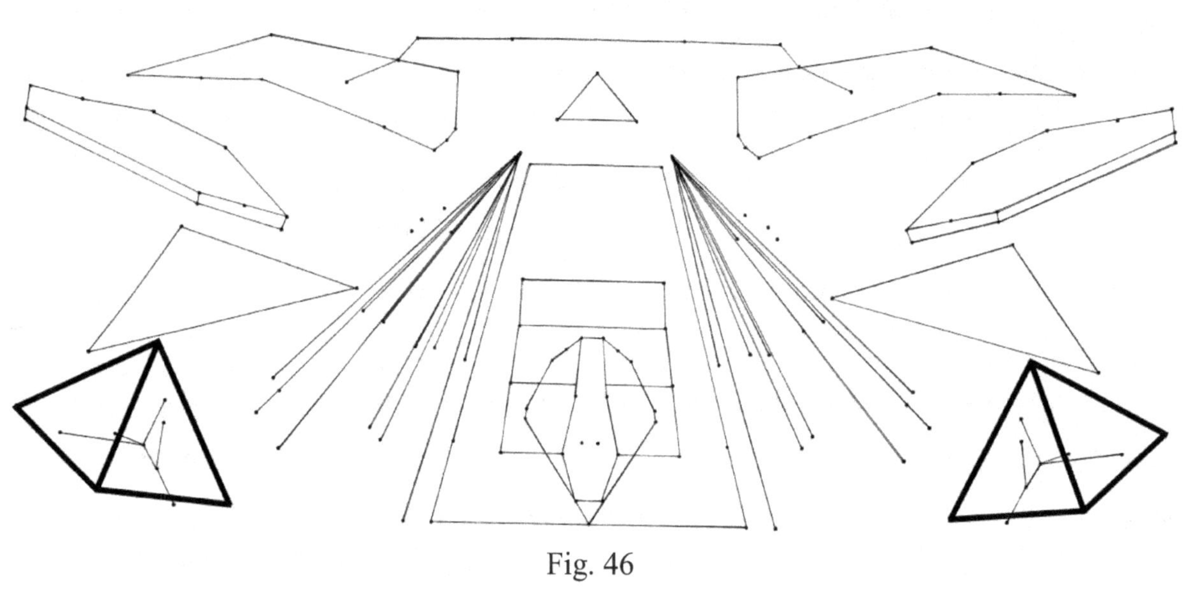

Fig. 46

Similar to the Egyptian Giza Pyramids, the two *Declaration* pyramids flanking the unfinished central monument are built on square bases (Fig. 46). While the structure is grounded on a square base, its visual and geometric form is defined by paired isosceles triangles. This is rooted in Euclid's Elements (Book 1, Proposition 5), where a tetrahedron is illustrated as constructed from two joined isosceles triangles (Fig. 47).

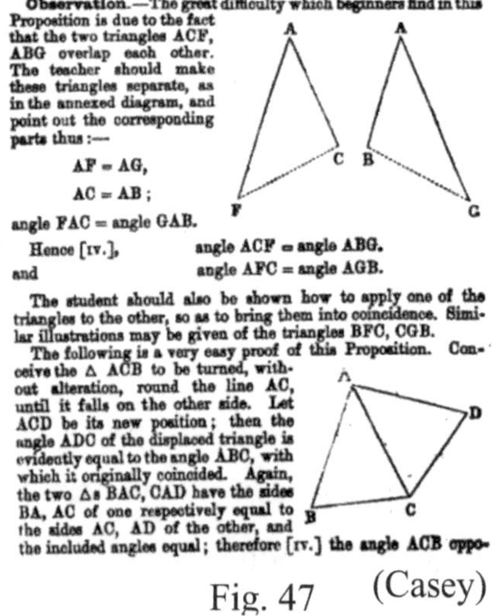

Observation.—The great difficulty which beginners find in this Proposition is due to the fact that the two triangles ACF, ABG overlap each other. The teacher should make these triangles separate, as in the annexed diagram, and point out the corresponding parts thus:—

AF = AG,

AC = AB;

angle FAC = angle GAB.

Hence [IV.], angle ACF = angle ABG.

and angle AFC = angle AGB.

The student should also be shown how to apply one of the triangles to the other, so as to bring them into coincidence. Similar illustrations may be given of the triangles BFC, CGB.

The following is a very easy proof of this Proposition. Conceive the △ ACB to be turned, without alteration, round the line AC, until it falls on the other side. Let ACD be its new position; then the angle ADC of the displaced triangle is evidently equal to the angle ABC, with which it originally coincided. Again, the two △s BAC, CAD have the sides BA, AC of one respectively equal to the sides AC, AD of the other, and the included angles equal; therefore [IV.] the angle ACB oppo-

Fig. 47 (Casey)

This imagery serves as a geometric proof: if a triangle has two equal sides, the angles opposite those sides must also be equal. By aligning two such triangles, the diagram demonstrates the fundamental properties of the shape and provides a visual basis for the pyramid imagery found within the *Declaration* and other Euclidean texts. Comparable illustrations are found in the 1752 editions of Euclid's Elements by Robert Simson and E. Stone, which were known to be part of Thomas Jefferson's library.

The geometric figure on the right (Fig. 48) is a proof from the 1752 edition of *Euclid's Elements of Geometry*, Book 6, Proposition 6, which states that if two triangles have one angle equal to one angle, and the sides about the equal angles are proportional, then the triangles are equiangular and therefore similar, by E. Stone. The image on the right is also found in *The Elements of Euclid* (1752), written by Robert Simson. Book 1, Proposition 5, focuses on the equality of base angles within a single isosceles triangle, a core concept of congruence. In contrast, Book 6, Proposition 6 establishes a condition for the similarity of two different triangles, relying on the proportionality of their sides. The *Declaration's* geometry borrows visual logic from multiple propositions simultaneously; the graphical representation of both Propositions 5 and 6 in the context of Euclid's Elements, as illustrated in the *Declaration's* graphical pyramid, is striking. Both editions of *Euclid's Elements*, edited by Stone and Simson, are known to have been in Thomas Jefferson's Library.

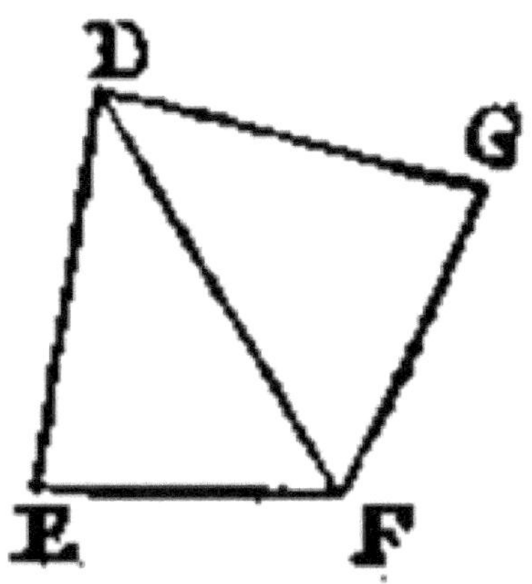

Fig. 48 (E. Stone) (Simson)

The visualization of this Euclidean pyramid within the *Declaration* is based solely on the placement of the letter V in the words' governments, have, absolved, and levy (Fig. 49). The geometric imagery of the outer triptych, including the pyramid, is created without employing any center-mirroring techniques found in the imagery of the center triptych. I believe the reason for placing the pyramid and other more complex images in the outer triptych is the precision and exactness necessary to develop the increasingly complex geometric drawings that follow.

Accordingly, the pyramidal forms identified here are best understood as Euclidean-compatible visual outcomes rather than symbolic declarations. They demonstrate that the *Declaration*'s reconstructed geometry operates within the same proportional and symmetrical logic that governed Enlightenment mathematical thought. Any resonance with Egyptian pyramids, tetrahedral solids, or later symbolic systems emerges at the level of analogy, not proof.

As with the Great Seal, Orion alignment, rays of glory, and altar imagery, the Euclidean pyramid contributes to a cumulative pattern: a geometric field whose forms align with established mathematical and symbolic languages known to later interpreters, particularly within Freemasonry, without requiring that such meanings were consciously embedded by the document's authors.

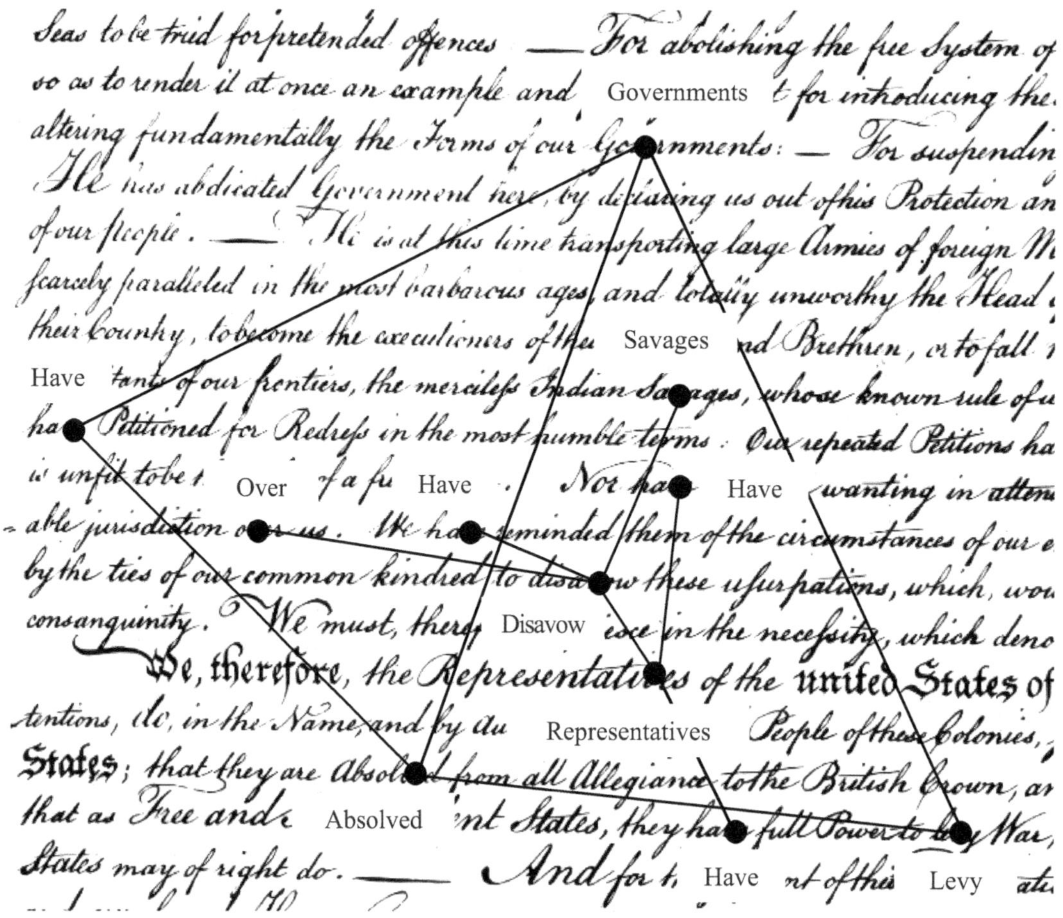

Fig. 49

Sprig of Acacia

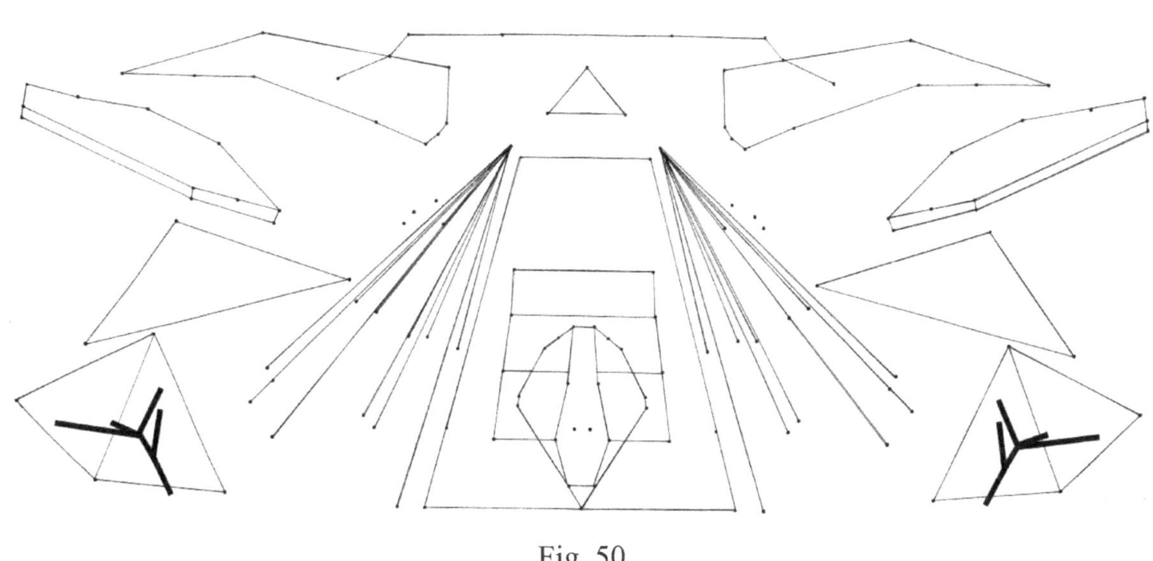

Fig. 50

Within the triangular field defined by the Euclidean Proposition 5, based pyramid, a branching geometric form emerges from the connected points of the letter V (Fig. 50). When the relevant points are joined by straight line segments, the resulting configuration resembles a small offshoot or branch, commonly referred to as a sprig (Fig. 51). This resemblance arises solely from the spatial distribution of the letters as they occur in the text and from the same linear connection method applied consistently throughout this study.

3rd Degree
England 1780
(A Member of the Craft)
Fig. 51

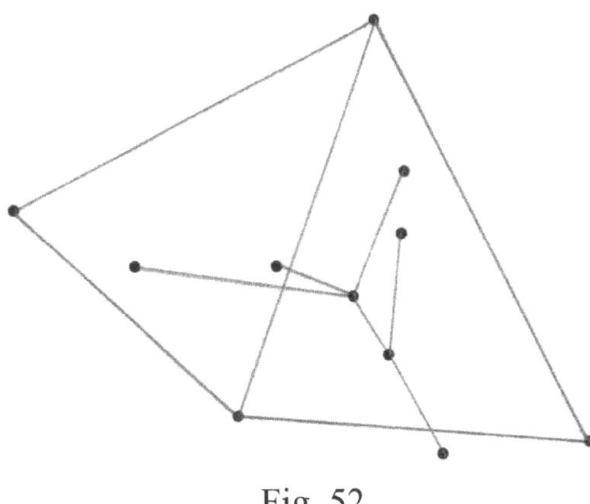

Fig. 52

The visual similarity of this branching form to a botanical sprig is not, in itself, evidentiary. However, within later symbolic traditions, particularly those of Freemasonry, the sprig of acacia occupies a prominent allegorical role. This symbolic association is introduced here not as proof of intent, but as contextual framing for how such a form would be read by trained symbolic interpreters.

In Masonic literature, the acacia tree, often identified with the biblical shittah or shittim wood, is associated with endurance, incorruptibility, and continuity. Albert G. Mackey describes the acacia as "preeminently the symbol of the soul's immortality" within the mythic system of Freemasonry" (Mackey, *An Encyclopedia of Freemasonry and its Kindred Sciences*).

Separately, in Egyptian mythology, the acacia appears in the Osiris narrative. According to later mythological retellings, Osiris was sealed within a chest by his brother Seth and cast into the Nile. The chest eventually lodged against an acacia tree, which grew around it, enclosing the body. The tree was later cut down and fashioned into a pillar, from which Isis recovered Osiris (Short Talk Bulletin - Vol. X November, 1932 No.11). This story associates the acacia with death, concealment, preservation, and eventual restoration.

Importantly, none of these symbolic associations establishes that the branching form reconstructed within the *Declaration* was intentionally designed to represent acacia, Osiris, or Masonic doctrine. The geometric figure itself is generated mechanically from fixed letter positions using the same constrained methodology applied elsewhere in this study. The symbolic reading emerges only after the form is resolved.

Accordingly, the acacia sprig should be understood as a recognizable symbolic analogue rather than a coded emblem. Its relevance lies in demonstrating that the reconstructed geometry produces forms that later symbolic systems, particularly Freemasonry, were already equipped to interpret meaningfully. This supports the broader claim of this study: that non-random structure, once mechanically resolved, can align with established symbolic grammars without requiring claims of deliberate concealment or authorial encoding.

As with the pyramid, altar, rays of glory, and Orion motifs, the acacia sprig contributes to a cumulative pattern of geometric outcomes that are symbolically legible within historical traditions familiar to later interpreters, while remaining methodologically neutral with respect to eighteenth-century authorial intent.

Euclid's Elements, Book I, Proposition 1

The seven points that formed the acacia sprig are from the letter V: savages, have, have, over, disavow, representatives, absolved, and have (Fig. 49). The arrangement of these points suggests an underlying Euclidean structure. When interpreted through Euclid's Elements, Book I, Proposition 1, these points define equilateral triangles, while Proposition 2 establishes proportional relationships among line segments. I removed the lines that formed the sprig and, using a draftsman's compass, began to process the dots as outlined in *Euclid's* Book 1, Proposition 1. The essence of Euclid's Proposition 1 lies in creating an equilateral triangle using the two endpoints of a given line. The Vs that composes the sprig of acacia appear to serve a dual purpose, creating patterns that suggest the formation of Euclidean Propositions 1-3. Some points from Euclidean Proposition 1 seem to have been erased to form the acacia sprig, thereby concealing the underlying Euclidean geometry. One example is the missing point corresponding to the letter (A) (Fig. 53).

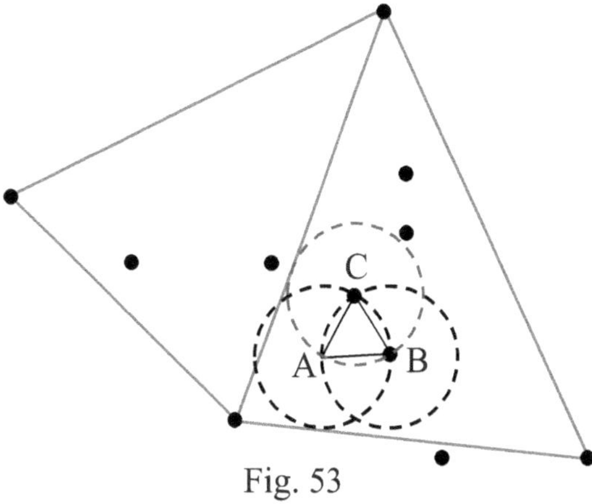

Fig. 53

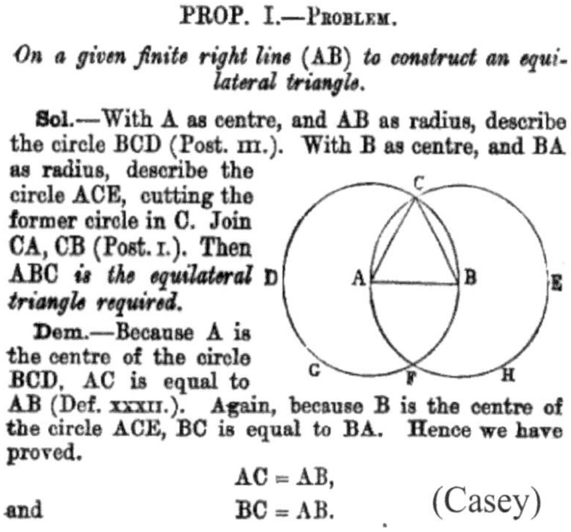

PROP. I.—PROBLEM.

On a given finite right line (AB) to construct an equilateral triangle.

Sol.—With A as centre, and AB as radius, describe the circle BCD (Post. III.). With B as centre, and BA as radius, describe the circle ACE, cutting the former circle in C. Join CA, CB (Post. I.). Then ABC *is the equilateral triangle required.*

Dem.—Because A is the centre of the circle BCD, AC is equal to AB (Def. XXXII.). Again, because B is the centre of the circle ACE, BC is equal to BA. Hence we have proved,

AC = AB,

and BC = AB. (Casey)

Fig. 54

Using a draftsman's compass and following the procedure of Proposition 1. I drew two identical circles using points B and C, with the line segment between them serving as the compass radius. The point of intersection of the two circles, point A, is the third point of the equilateral triangle. I then redrew the centering circle around point A, making Proposition 2 easier to visualize (Fig. 53). The illustration (Fig. 54) is a Euclidean textbook example demonstrating Proposition 1. P. Castells presented a lecture in 1913 on the use of Book I, Proposition 1, within the Masonic Lodge. He illustrated the methods of medieval Freemasons by presenting both the geometrical operation and the mystical interpretation of Book I, Proposition 1 (Castells).

Euclid's Elements, Book 1, Proposition 2

(Fig. 55) illustrates the construction process described in Euclid's Elements, Book I, Proposition 2. Building on Proposition 1, point B is designated as the center of a circle, and point A defines the length of the radius; circle BA. Point A is formed from the letter V from the word "have." Next, a line is extended from point B to the circumference of circle BA, creating point E. Point E is created from the letter V in the word (absolved.) Using point D as the center, then extending a line from point D to point F, which is created from the word (have) makes circle DF. Proposition 2 demonstrates that the line segments BA, CF, and BE are equal in length.

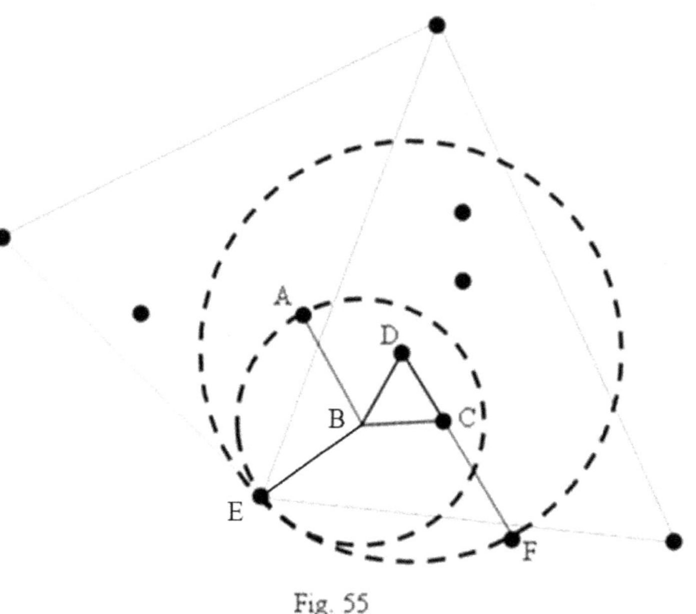

Fig. 55

The dots in *Euclid's Elements* Proposition 2 diagram are generated from the letter V in the words: have letter (A), disavow letter (D), representative letter (C), absolved letter (E), and have letter (F).

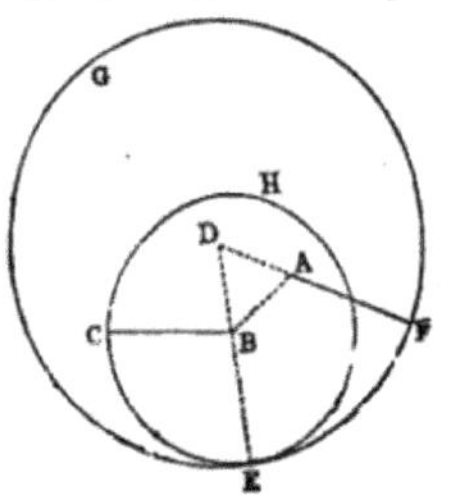
PROP. II.—Problem.

From a given point (A) *to draw a right line equal to a given finite right line* (BC).

Sol.—Join AB (Post. I.); on AB describe the equilateral triangle ABD [I.]. With B as centre, and BC as radius, describe the circle ECH (Post. III.). Produce DB to meet the circle ECH in E (Post. II.). With D as centre, and DE as radius, describe the circle EFG (Post. III.). Produce DA to meet this circle in F. AF *is equal to* BC.

Dem.—Because D is the centre of the circle EFG, DF is equal to DE (Def.

(Casey)

Fig. 56

Textual examples of Euclidean Proposition 2 (Fig. 56) have been illustrated in various forms, with the extended leg [BA] extending in many directions. I located several illustrated examples of Proposition 2 with the extended leg [BA] extending in the same direction as the illustration in the *Declaration*. In the *Declaration*, the tolerances of Propositions 1 and 2 fall within one to two millimeters of the precise compass movements required to establish both diagrams.

Euclid's Elements, Book I, Proposition 3

Euclid's Elements, Book I, Proposition 3, (Fig. 57) builds upon the existing constructions of Propositions 1 and 2.

Proposition 3 (cutting off a lesser line segment from a greater) is demonstrated using line segments CF and CH, where CH is longer than CF.

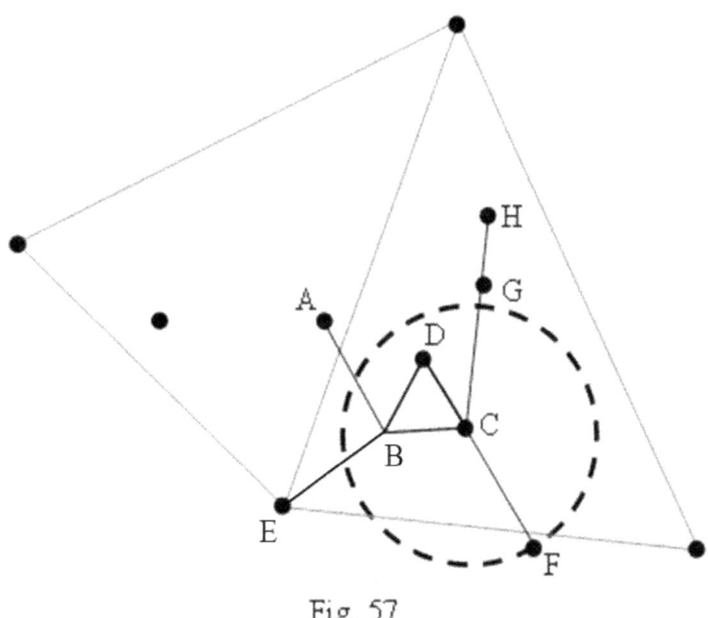

Fig. 57

Circle centered at point C: Place the compass point at C and set its radius to the length of CF. A circle is then drawn. The point at which the circle intersects line CH is the critical point. This point is designated as G. The radius defined by line segment CF intersects CH within a few millimeters at point G, establishing line segment CG, which has been "cut off" from the larger segment CH. The segments CG and CF are meant to be of equal length at true scale (1:1). Figure 58 demonstrates the deliberate discrepancy between CF and CG, which results from a specific length required for a dynamic symmetry spiral construction. This spiral aesthetically positions the three outer shapes: the pyramid, the triangle, and the three-dimensional coffin. Additionally, point G marks the end of the length of an acacia branch, which is referred to as "I to Z line segment 7" in the dynamic symmetry spiral plot described on page 61. Line BA is equal to line CF, and the length of line CF is within a few millimeters of line CG. Point G originates from the word "have," and Point H originates from the word "savages" in the *Declaration*. The three Euclidean propositions in the *Declaration* form a layered collective construct that contrasts with individual textbook illustrations of Propositions 1, 2, and 3.

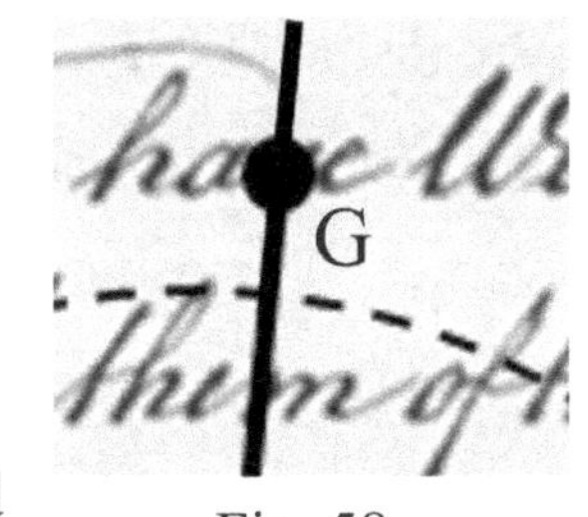

Fig. 58

I believe the arrangement of points using the letter V was designed both to present the propositions and to anticipate the mechanical drawing of a surface development for a four-sided pyramid. The seemingly random placement of points conveys a meticulously measured fit within the pyramid. Combining the three Euclidean propositions in this manner also addresses the limited space available to showcase the artistry of geometry, creating a small but pleasing, esoteric visual package resembling a sprig of acacia.

Euclid I.1–3 as a Closed Geometric System

Euclid's Elements, Book I, Propositions 1 through 3, together establish the minimum operations required for classical plane geometry using only a straightedge and compass: the construction of an equilateral triangle (I.1), the transfer of a line segment to a specified point (I.2), and the subtraction of a lesser segment from a greater (I.3). When these three propositions can be executed within a single, fixed-point field, without introducing new arbitrary points, the field may be described as a closed geometric system.

In the analytical reconstruction presented here, all points required to execute Propositions I.1–3 are derived exclusively from the fixed spatial positions of the letter V within the engrossed *Declaration of Independence.* These points are treated strictly as geometric positions. No supplemental points, measurements, or proportional adjustments are introduced beyond those generated by standard Euclidean compass-and-straightedge procedures.

Proposition I.1 is satisfied through the construction of equilateral triangles using point pairs derived from the letter V placements, with circle intersections producing the required third vertices. Proposition I.2 is satisfied by transferring a given segment length across the field using circular intersections, establishing equal line segments from specified origins. Proposition I.3 is satisfied by cutting off a segment equal to a given lesser segment from a greater one, again using a single compass radius and fixed centers.

Crucially, these three propositions are not executed in isolation. The same finite set of points supports all three constructions sequentially. Segment lengths established in Proposition I.2 function as the given lengths for Proposition I.3, and triangle constructions from Proposition I.1 supply structural relationships reused in subsequent operations. This interdependence demonstrates operational closure: the system regenerates its own geometric resources without external input.

The system's closure is mechanical, not symbolic. Its validity does not depend on allegory, numerology, or interpretive symbolism. It depends solely on whether the prescribed Euclidean operations can be carried out accurately within the constraints of the point field. The observed tolerances, generally within one to two millimeters at full scale, are consistent with manual drafting practices and reproduction limits and do not compromise the operational integrity of the constructions.

This configuration differs materially from textbook presentations of Euclid, where each proposition is typically illustrated independently with unconstrained point placement chosen for pedagogical clarity. Here, the propositions are resolved within a spatially constrained environment, where point positions are fixed in advance and cannot be optimized for convenience. That the three foundational propositions remain executable under these constraints is a nontrivial geometric fact.

Importantly, the existence of a closed geometric system does not, by itself, establish intentional design, authorship, or symbolic purpose. A system may be mechanically coherent without being deliberately constructed to convey meaning. What this demonstration establishes is a condition of feasibility: the *Declaration*-derived point field behaves as a functional Euclidean workspace capable of supporting the foundational operations of classical geometry. Only after this mechanical closure is established do symbolic or philosophical interpretations become analytically admissible. Without closure, such interpretations would rest on coincidental alignments. With closure, they rest on a demonstrable geometric substrate, even if the motivations behind that substrate remain historically indeterminate.

Accordingly, Euclid I.1–3 function here as a geometric litmus test. The *Declaration*'s letter-derived point field either sustains the full sequence of foundational constructions or it does not. The analysis demonstrates that it does. This conclusion does not assert why the system exists, only that it exists, and that it operates within the strict rules of Euclidean geometry.

Euclid's Elements of Solid Geometry by Thomas Rudd

In 1570, Dr. John Dee wrote an extensive preface for Henry Billingsley's first English translation of *Euclid's Elements of Geometry* (Fig. 59). Billingsley's translation is notable for its pasted flaps of paper that can be folded to create three-dimensional models of the propositions in Book XI, making it one of the oldest 'pop-up' books (Billingsley).

Fig. 59 (Billingsley)

The first English translation of *Euclid's Elements* by Billingsley also contained *A Brief Treatise of Mixed and Composed Regular Solids* and *Euclid's Elements of Geometry* by Thomas Rudd. Thomas Rudd demonstrated a surface development diagram of a dodecahedron and an icosahedron, which, when cut out and folded, formed three-dimensional geometric models. These diagrams are located at the end of the volume.

After completing Euclid's Proposition 3, I noticed a single unused point derived from the word (over) within the Euclidean pyramid (Fig. 60). I again observed a visual connection between this singular point and four nearby points in adjacent geometries.

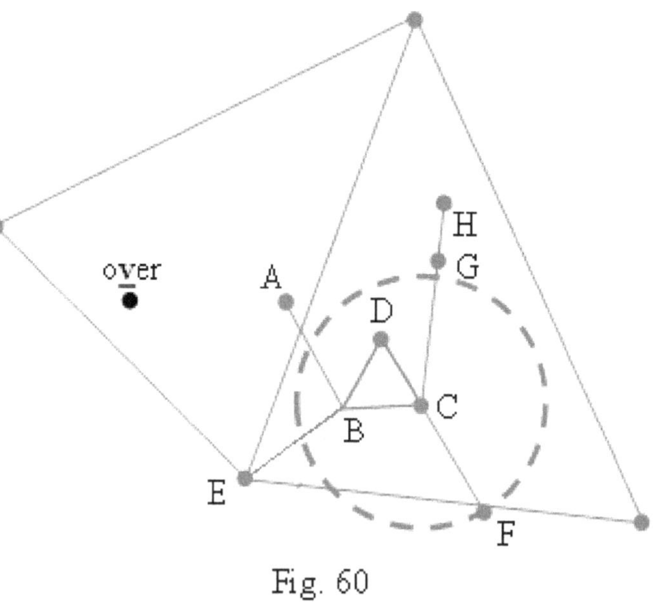

Fig. 60

The five points that appeared to be spaced fairly symmetrically apart, created from the words have, over, have, savages, and governments, establish the appearance of curvature (Fig. 61). Believing the five points had been placed with specific intent, I used a draftsman's compass. I applied the principles of Proposition 1 to the five points, forming four conjoined equilateral triangles. The angular relationships among the triangles create a surface-development pyramid model. I cut out four equilateral triangles, folded them, and taped the free ends together to create a three-dimensional, four-sided pyramid model. This three-dimensional square pyramid (Fig. 62) shares the same geometric design as the square pyramid depicted in the *Declaration*, the four-sided pyramid found in the Isis–Nephthys hieroglyphs, and, more importantly, the pyramid image in Euclid's Elements, Book I, Proposition 5, which features two overlapping isosceles triangles.

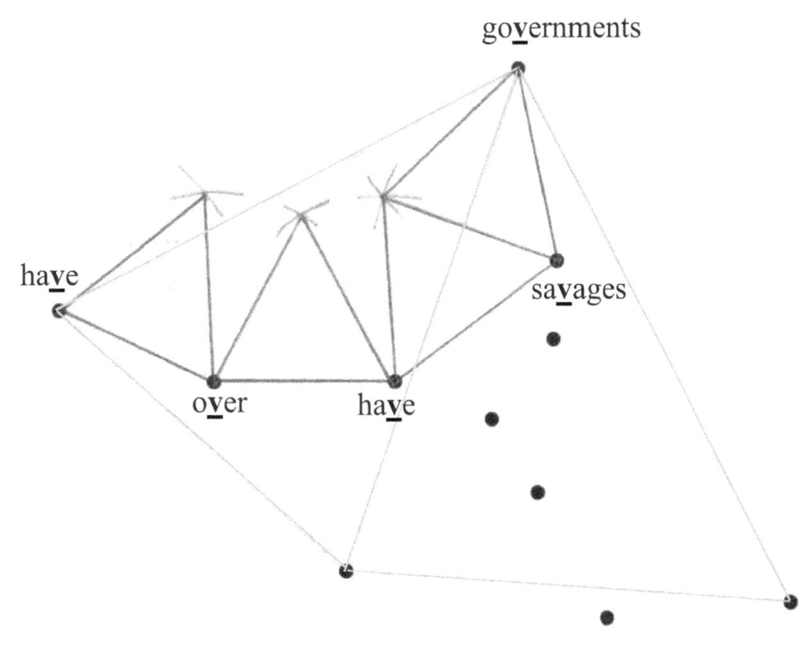

Fig. 61

 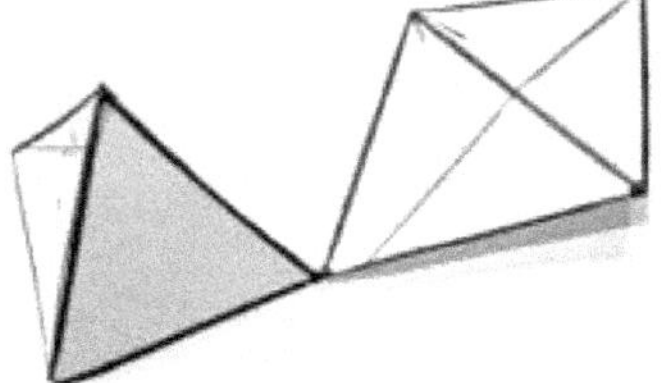 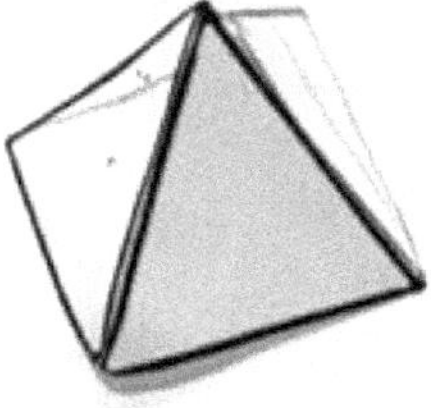

Fig. 62

Phi Triangle

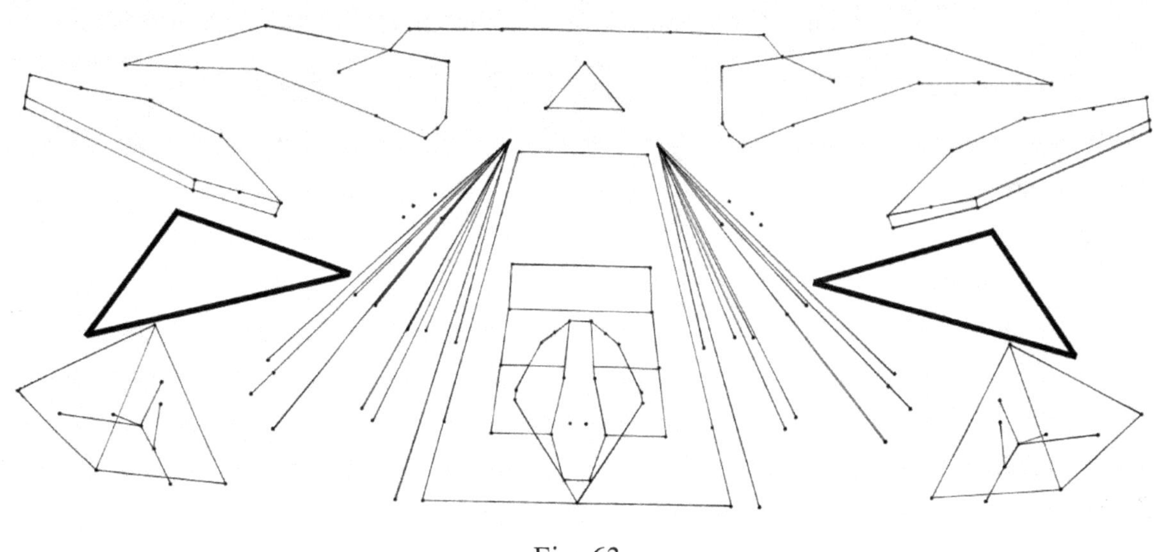

Fig. 63

Initial inspection of the triangular form derived from the letter V suggested a right triangle, a configuration commonly associated with Euclid's Elements, Book I, Proposition 47 (the Pythagorean Theorem). This proposition is frequently referenced in mathematical and architectural traditions and later became prominent in Masonic instructional literature. However, precise measurement of the triangle's sides and angles demonstrates that the figure is not a right triangle and does not conform to a Pythagorean triple (e.g., 3:4:5) (Fig. 64).

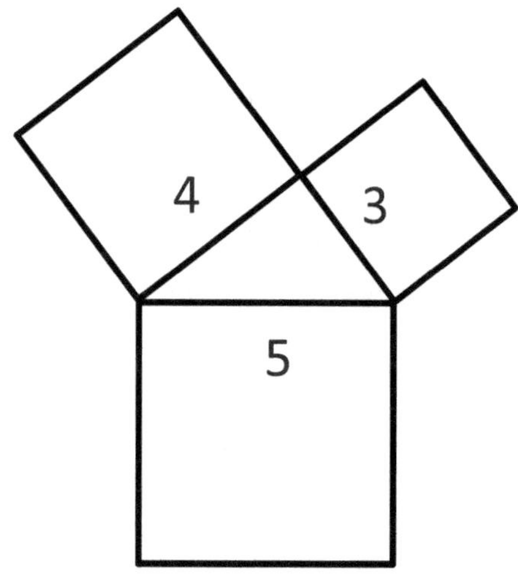

Fig. 64

Instead, the triangle is demonstrably scalene and obtuse. One interior angle exceeds 90 degrees, and all three sides are of unequal length. This classification is based on direct measurement rather than interpretive inference. The observed angles are approximately 40°, 36°, and 108°, confirming that the triangle is neither right nor equilateral.

Given the high degree of geometric coherence observed in previously reconstructed figures, the deviation from a Pythagorean configuration warrants further geometric examination rather than dismissal as error or coincidence. The analysis, therefore, proceeds by testing whether the scalene triangle participates in a larger geometric system already present within the reconstructed field.

The scalene triangle shares spatial proximity with an equilateral triangle previously identified as part of the surface-development pyramid geometry (Fig. 65). Extending the baseline of the scalene triangle toward the equilateral triangle establishes a potential geometric relationship between the two figures. Using the equilateral triangle's endpoint as the compass center and setting the radius equal to its base, a short arc is drawn that intersects the extended baseline. This intersection defines a new point from which a connecting line can be drawn to the apex of the original scalene triangle. Measurement of the resulting configuration shows that the two slanted sides are now equal in length. Through this single compass operation, derived from an already-established radius within the system, the scalene obtuse triangle is transformed into an obtuse isosceles triangle (Fig. 66).

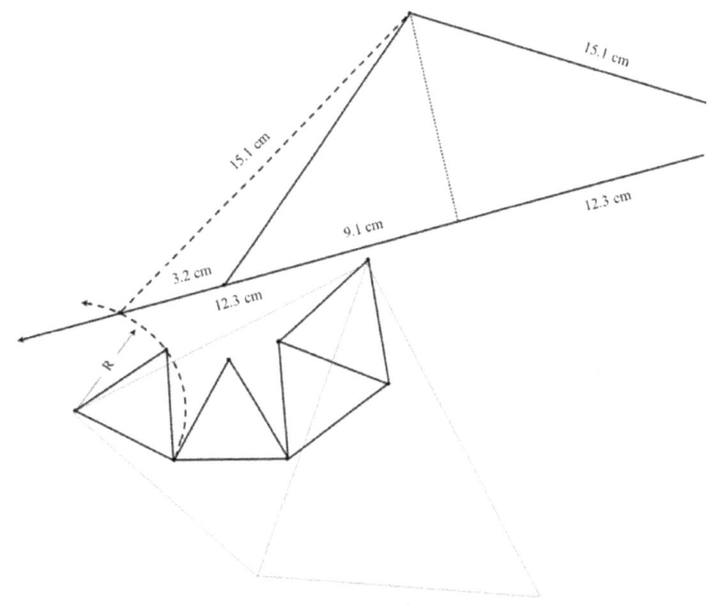

Fig. 65

This transformation does not alter the triangle arbitrarily. It preserves the original apex and base orientation while enforcing bilateral symmetry. The resulting triangle has interior angles of approximately 36°, 36°, and 108°, which correspond to a known geometric form: the obtuse isosceles golden gnomon triangle.

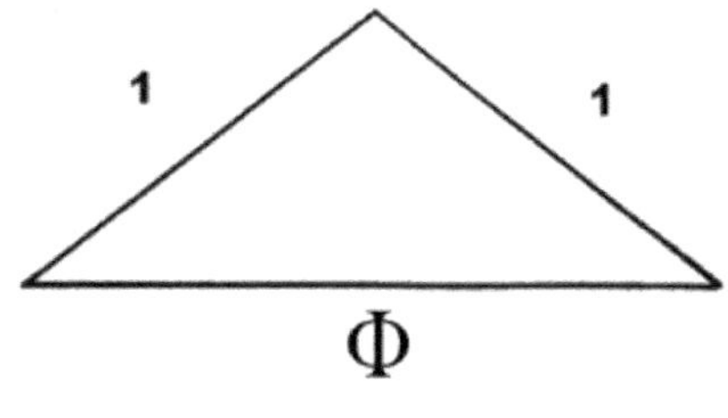

Fig. 66

In a golden gnomon triangle, the ratio of the equal sides (legs) to the base is Φ (the golden ratio, approximately 1.618). Measurement of the *Declaration*-derived triangle yields a leg length of approximately 15.1 cm. Multiplying this length by Φ produces an expected base length of approximately 24.43 cm. The measured base length of the *Declaration* triangle, derived from the letter V placements in go<u>v</u>ernment, in<u>v</u>asion, and gi<u>v</u>ing (Fig. 67), is approximately 24.6 cm. The discrepancy between the calculated and measured base lengths falls within reasonable

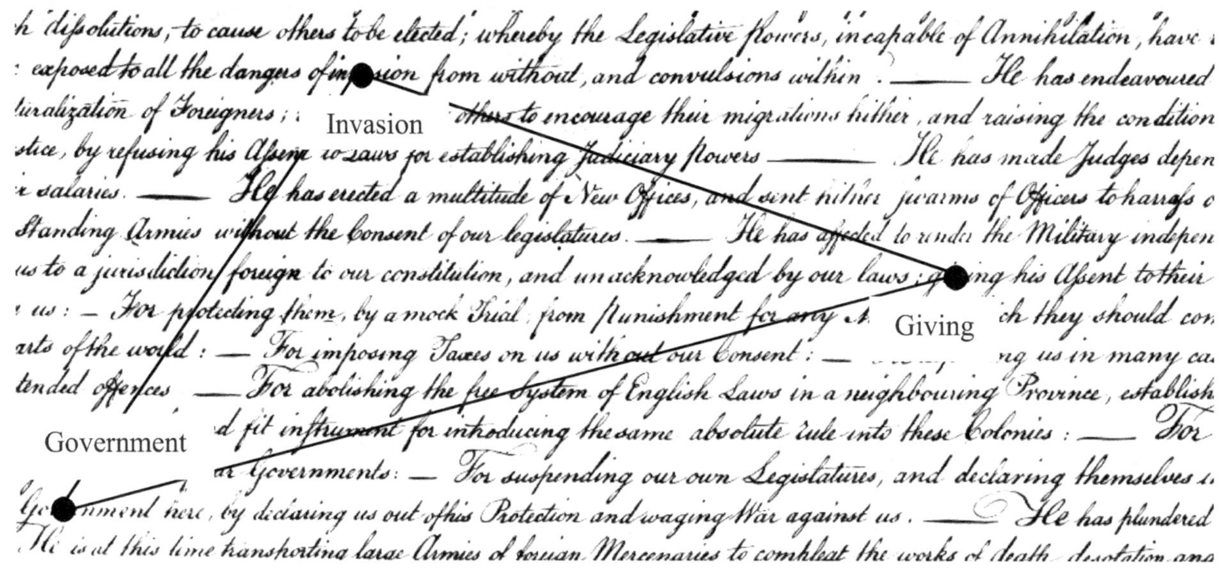

Fig. 67

tolerances given reproduction distortion, photographic scaling, and the fact that the triangle's vertices originate from letterforms rather than constructed points. No rescaling or proportional adjustment was applied to force this outcome.

Notably, the compass radius used to effect this transformation originates from the nearby pyramid surface-development geometry, demonstrating that the triangle's golden proportion is not isolated but dependent on previously established geometric resources within the same system. The transformation, therefore, satisfies the criteria of internal coherence established earlier for a closed geometric field.

Rotating the golden gnomon triangle (Fig. 68) and extending its base produces a larger composite isosceles triangle with angles of approximately 72°, 72°, and 36° (Fig. 69). This configuration is a standard golden triangle in classical geometry, with side lengths in the

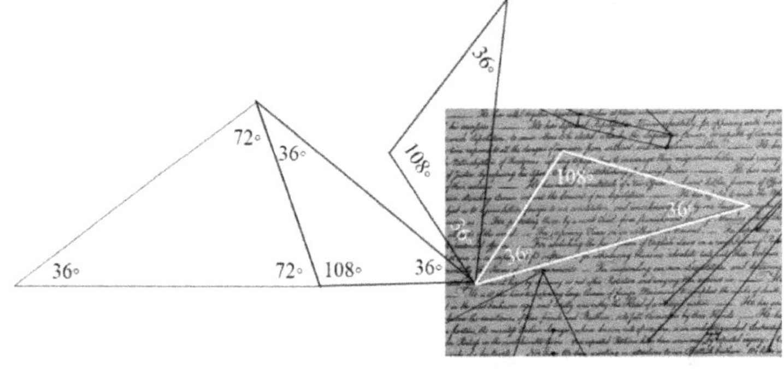

Fig. 68

ratio 1: Φ: Φ−1. The resulting figure exhibits self-similarity and proportional recursion characteristic of golden-ratio constructions. Golden triangles of this type are foundational in the construction of regular pentagons and pentagrams (Fig. 70), where five such triangles interlock through rotational symmetry. The relevance of this observation is geometric rather than symbolic: the transformation demonstrates that the *Declaration*-derived point field supports proportional relationships associated with Φ using only straightedge-and-compass operations and internally generated radii.

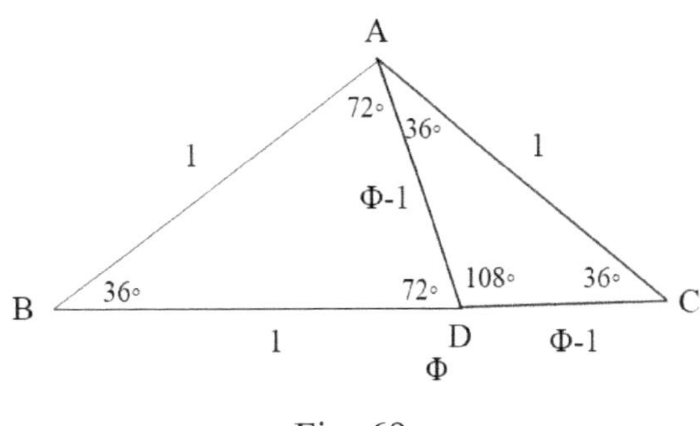

Fig. 69

No historical claim is made that the golden ratio was intentionally encoded in the *Declaration*, nor that its authors sought to embed pentagonal or pentagrammic symbolism. What is demonstrated is that the observed triangle, initially scalene and obtuse, can be mechanically resolved into a golden isosceles form using resources already present in the reconstructed geometry.

Only after this mechanical feasibility is established does the figure acquire interpretive resonance. Geometry has historically been treated, particularly within philosophical and speculative traditions, as a language of proportion, harmony, and order. Freemasonry, among other traditions, later adopted geometric figures, including the square, compasses, and golden forms, as allegorical teaching tools. These later associations do not constitute evidence of intent but provide a contextual vocabulary through which such figures have been understood.

Accordingly, the Phi triangle is presented here not as a symbolic claim, but as a geometric result. Its significance lies in its derivation, proportional accuracy, and dependence on previously established constructions. Like the Euclidean propositions and pyramid surface development preceding it, the golden triangle functions as a mechanically valid outcome within a constrained geometric system whose broader meaning remains open to interpretation rather than assertion.

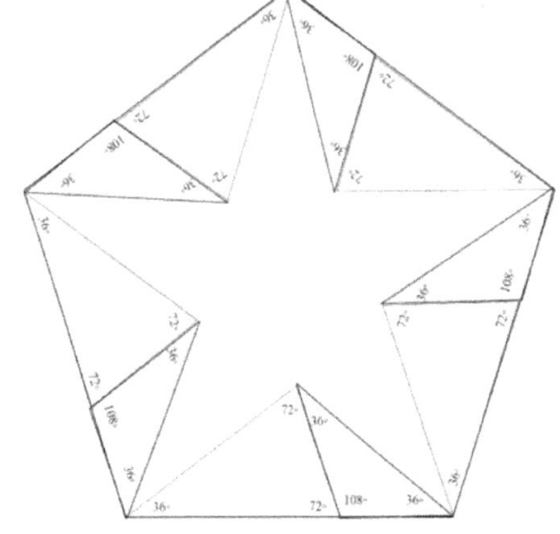

Fig. 70

Dynamic Symmetry Spiral

The connection between geometry and spirituality in Freemasonry is rooted in the belief that geometry serves as a language for comprehending the divine order of the universe and humanity's place within it. By studying geometry and contemplating its symbols, Freemasons aim to develop their moral character, deepen their understanding of the world, and connect with something greater than themselves (Genchi).

12 DYNAMIC SYMMETRY

Greeks covered the point geometrically when they established the fact that in a right triangle, a line drawn perpendicular to the hypotenuse to meet the intersection of the legs, is the side of a square equal in area to the rectangle formed by the two segments of the hypotenuse. (Fig. 3.)

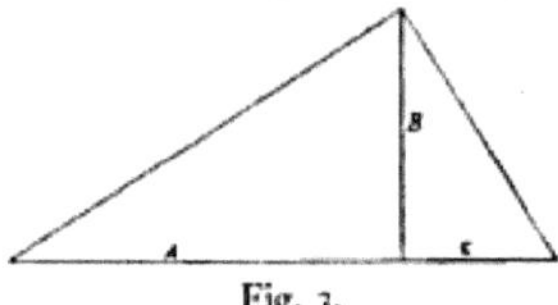

Fig. 3.

These three lines C, B, A, constitute three terms in a continued proportion.

When the three radii vectors are drawn from the center to the circumference of the shell curve, as in Fig. 4,

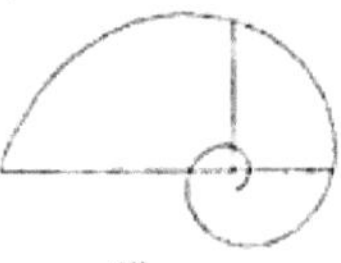

Fig. 4.

and these points of intersection with the spiral are connected by two straight lines, a right angle is created at C and a right triangle formed, ACB. (Fig. 5.)

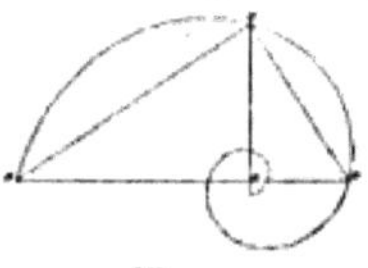

Fig. 5.

If the mean proportional line of this right triangle, ACB, that is, if the line CO be produced through the pole or center of the spiral to the opposite side of the curve, obviously another right angle is created as at B, and by drawing the line BD, the right triangle DBC is formed. (Fig. 6.)

(Hambridge)

Fig. 71

What does a page from *Dynamic Symmetry: The Greek Vase* (Fig. 71) by Jay Hambidge, published by Yale University, have to do with the pyramid, triangle, and 3D coffin images? Discovering geometry within the pyramid and the scalene triangle sparked an examination of the unusual placement of the three images: the pyramid, the triangle, and the three-dimensional coffin. Together, these three images are positioned and angled in relation to one another. The cant of the pyramid, the proximity of the triangle to the pyramid, and the triangle's parallel sides relative to the three-dimensional coffin create an intriguing grouping. The graphical relationship among the three images begins to emerge. In mechanical drafting, specifically in surface development transition images, draftsmen often use line segments from one drawing view to create a surface pattern of the object. In the case of the pyramid, triangle, and 3D coffin, the line segments lie within their respective shapes. These same line segments are represented as *Euclid's Elements* Propositions One, Two, and Three, and a sprig of acacia is also linked to the development of an image that shows how the principles of dynamic symmetry (symmetria) can be used to construct a spiral that approximates the Fibonacci or golden spiral, between the pyramid, triangle, and 3D coffin (Fig. 72) (Hambridge). The ancient Greek term symmetria refers to a system of harmonious proportion, in which the parts of a whole are in a rational, mathematical relationship to each other and to the whole.

Essentially, the image illustrates how the principles of dynamic symmetry can be applied to create a figure that roughly follows the Fibonacci spiral. The two ideas are not identical, but they are connected through related geometric and proportional systems. Dynamic symmetry is a broader system of proportioning, while the Fibonacci spiral is a specific, well-known curve based on a similar mathematical relationship to the golden ratio.

The mathematical order underlying the Fibonacci sequence suggests inherent harmony and balance within nature. Moreover, the spiral visually embodies the interconnectedness of all things, with each part contributing to a greater whole. Many consider the golden ratio, closely linked to the Fibonacci sequence, to be a divine proportion that reflects the universe's beauty and perfection.

Jay Hambidge's dynamic symmetry spiral is based on the ancient Greek methods of symmetria. He argued that the beauty of ancient Greek art and architecture was not a matter of chance or intuition, but was based on a systematic approach to proportioning and design. Hambidge's dynamic spiral is overlaid onto the image's pyramid, triangle, and coffin. The image of the scalene triangle serves as the origin point for developing the dynamic symmetry spiral. This triangle has three vertices labeled X, Y, and Z. The first line segment used in the pyramid is line 1, which was transferred using drafting dividers to form points X and A. Next, line segment 2, measured from vertex X, created the points X to B. The first letter denotes the point of origin, while the second letter signifies the endpoint of the line segment. The remaining points of the dynamic symmetry spiral are generated through this method; however, not all points originate from the vertices X.

Z
I
Y
C
A
D
B
H
X
E
F
G
X to A segment 1
X to B segment 2
A to C segment 5
C to H segment 6
A to D segment 3
A to E segment 4
A to F segment 2
A to G segment 1
I to Z segment 7
4
1
7
6
5
3
2

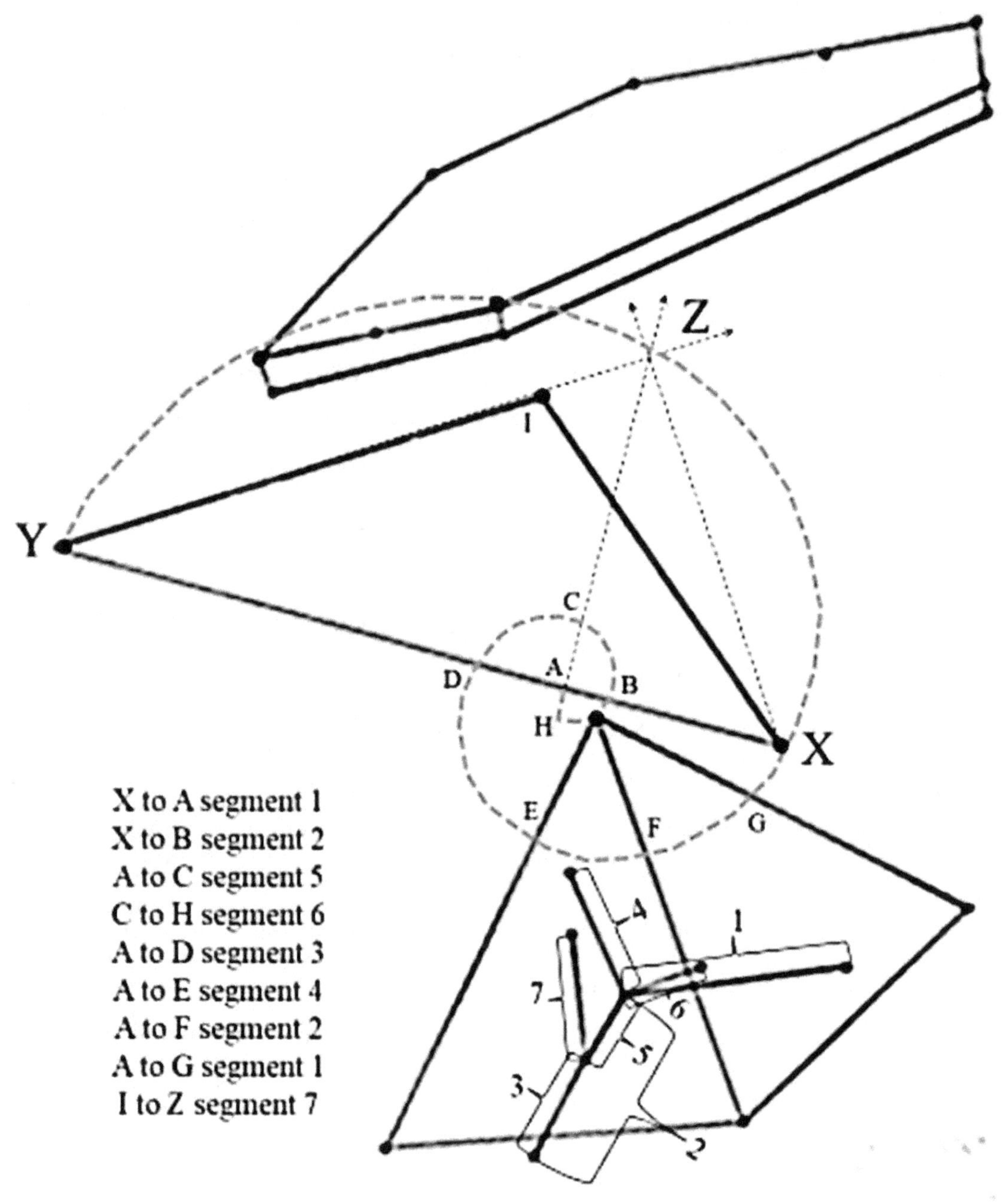

Fig. 72

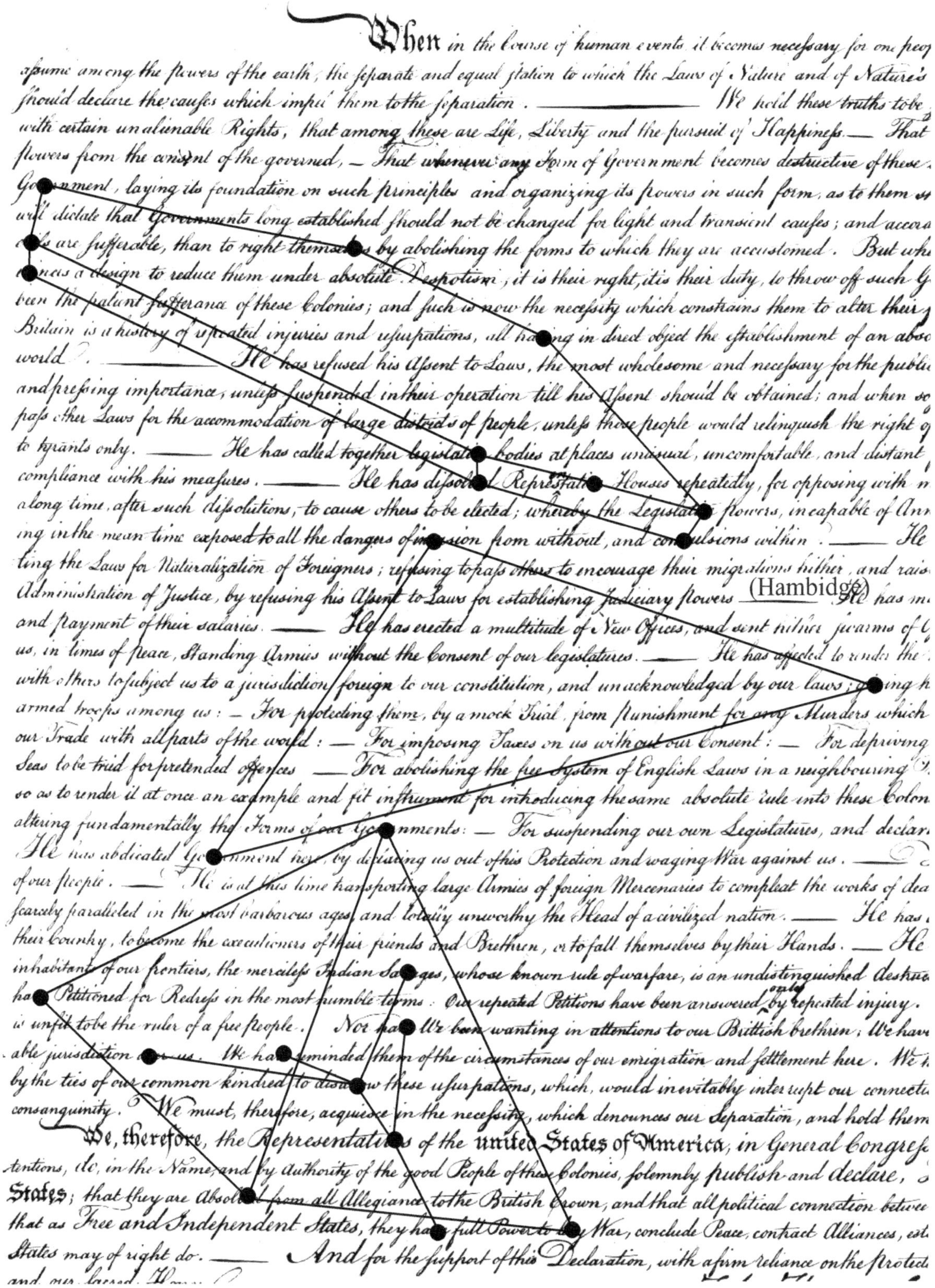

(Hambidge)

Fig. 73

Based on the text from Mackey's *An Encyclopedia of Freemasonry and Its Kindred Sciences*, the three drawings (a pyramid, a triangle, and a coffin) (Fig. 73) tell a powerful story of a Mason's journey through the Blue Lodge, using a symbolic language that is both geometric and deeply spiritual.

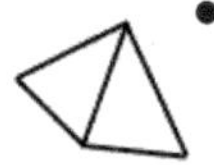

- Entered Apprentice (Square Pyramid): The beginning, the foundation, and the aspiration toward a higher ideal.

- Fellowcraft (Triangle): The journey of learning and the application of intellectual and moral principles used to build a life "on the square."

- Master Mason (Six-Sided Coffin): The culmination of the journey, involving a confrontation with mortality and the hope of immortality through a life well lived and the bonds of brotherhood.

Albert Mackey (1807-1881) was a physician and a prominent figure in Freemasonry, known for his extensive writings on the subject. He held various leadership positions, including Grand Lecturer, Grand Secretary of the Grand Lodge of South Carolina, and Secretary General of the Supreme Council of the Ancient and Accepted Scottish Rite for the Southern Jurisdiction of the United States. Mackey's contributions to Masonic literature include *A Lexicon of Freemasonry, The Mystic Tie, Principles of Masonic Law, Book of the Chapter, Text-Book of Masonic Jurisprudence, History of Freemasonry*, and *Encyclopedia of Freemasonry*. His writings focus on explaining esoteric Masonic history, defining symbolism, and the application of sacred geometry (Drake).

"In the modern rituals, geometry is said to be the basis on the superstructure of Masonry is erected; and in the old Constitutions of the Medieval Freemasons of England, the most prominent place of all the sciences is given to geometry, which is made synonymous with Masonry. Thus in the Halliwell MS. which dates not later than the latter part of the fourteenth century, the Constitutions of Masonry are called the Constitution of the art of geometry according to Euclid, the words geometry and Masonry being used indifferently throughout the document; and in the Harleian MS. it is said, thus the craft Geometry was governed there, and that worthy Master Euclid gave it name of Geometry, and it is called Masonrie in this land long after. In another part of the same MS. it is thus defined: The fifth science is called Geometry, and it teaches a man to mete and measure of earth and other things, which science Masonrie" (Mackey, *An Encyclopedia of Freemasonry and Its Kindred Sciences*).

The Halliwell Manuscript, also known as the *Regius Poem,* serves primarily as a poetic account of the origins of Masonry, associating it with *Euclid* and ancient Egypt. *The Harleian Manuscripts,* a collection of over 7,000 manuscripts housed in the British Library, highlight the connection between geometry and Masonry.

"The Egyptians were undoubtedly one of the first nations who cultivated geometry as a science... From Egypt, which was the parent both of the sciences and mysteries of the Pagan world, it passed over into other countries; and geometry and Operative Masonry have ever been found together, the latter carrying into execution those designs which were traced according to the principles of former. Speculative Masonry is, in like manner, intimately connected with geometry. In deference to our operative ancestors, and, in fact, as a necessary result of our close connection with them, Speculative Freemasonry derives its most important symbols from this parent science. Hence, it is not strange that Euclid, the most famous of geometricians, should be spoken of in all the Old Records as a founder of Masonry in Egypt, and that a special legend should have been invented in honor of his memory" (Mackey, *An Encyclopedia of Freemasonry and Its Kindred Sciences*).

The presence of geometric symbolism throughout the *Declaration* would be viewed as a notable achievement for the Speculative Mason. Mackey's reference to Euclid and his significance to the craft of Masonry, honoring him as the founder of Masonry in Egypt, serves to immortalize him by placing him within the grand design of the Declaration's symbolism. Mackey's commitment to Euclid as the first Freemason of Egypt and the symbolic connection between Euclidean Geometry and Operative and Speculative Masonry. Having established the mechanical feasibility of these constructions, it is appropriate to examine how similar geometric forms have been interpreted within later symbolic traditions, without asserting historical intent. Drawing segmented lines from these points embodies Euclid's first Postulate: "A straight line can be drawn through any two points." Thus, this creates geometric configurations that later Masonic writers would have recognized as symbolically meaningful.

Three-Dimensional Coffin

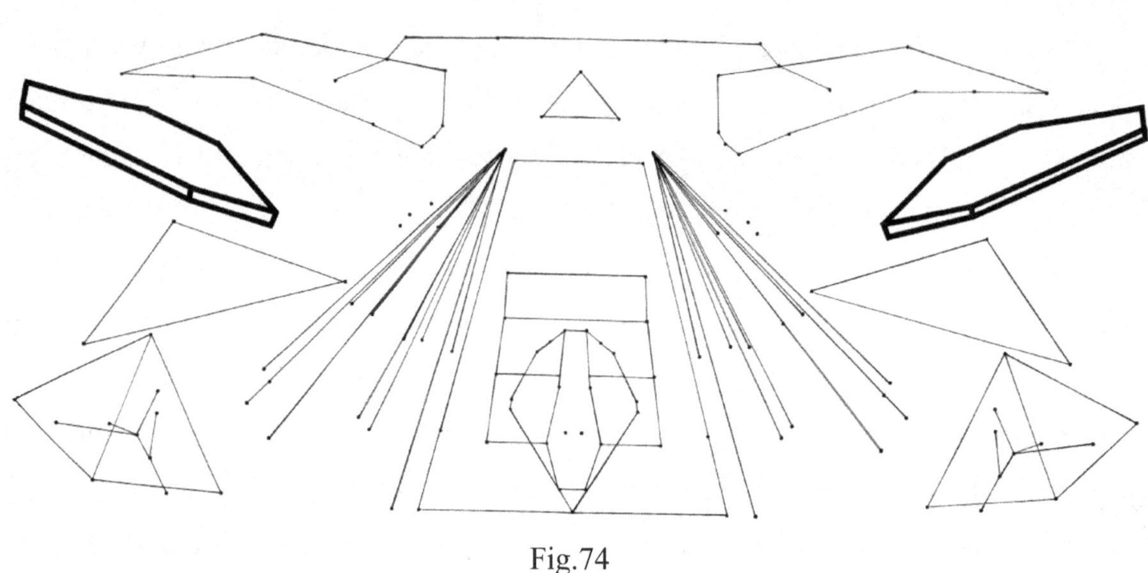

Fig.74

The first image constructed from the letter V is a two-dimensional coffin form. This planar coffin establishes the geometric template for a corresponding three-dimensional coffin, which preserves the same six-sided configuration in spatial projection (Fig. 74). The three-dimensional coffin is derived from letter-V point extractions taken from the following words in the *Declaration*: government (twice), themselves, having legislative, convulsions, representative, dissolved, legislative, evinces, and evils (Fig. 75). These points collectively define the coffin's vertices and spatial orientation.

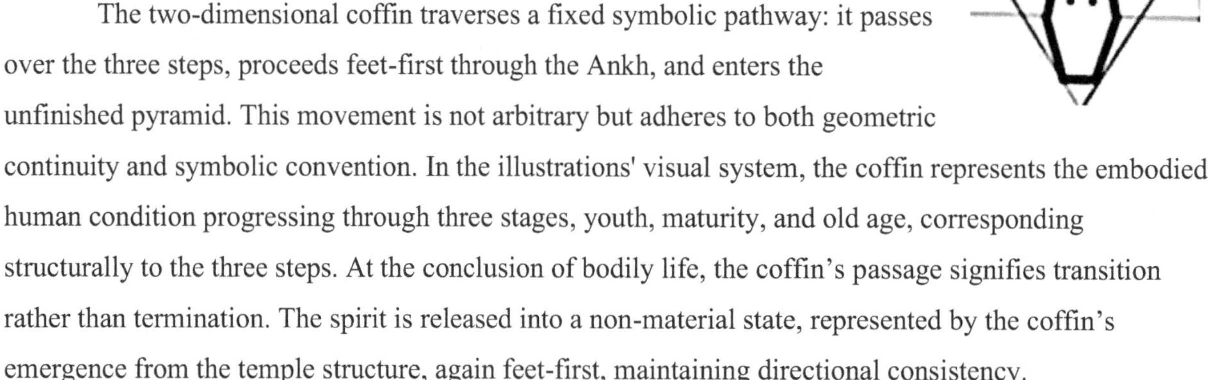

The two-dimensional coffin traverses a fixed symbolic pathway: it passes over the three steps, proceeds feet-first through the Ankh, and enters the unfinished pyramid. This movement is not arbitrary but adheres to both geometric continuity and symbolic convention. In the illustrations' visual system, the coffin represents the embodied human condition progressing through three stages, youth, maturity, and old age, corresponding structurally to the three steps. At the conclusion of bodily life, the coffin's passage signifies transition rather than termination. The spirit is released into a non-material state, represented by the coffin's emergence from the temple structure, again feet-first, maintaining directional consistency.

This sequence aligns with a long-standing symbolic distinction between two-dimensional and three-dimensional perception. Human experience is constrained to planar awareness, life lived "on the surface." Death marks a transition into volumetric existence, analogous to the shift from outline to solid. In this interpretive framework, the coffin functions as both container and threshold.

Metamorphosis and Initiatory Symbolism

The metaphor of metamorphosis has a well-established presence in initiatory traditions. The progression from caterpillar to chrysalis to butterfly provides a structural analogy for transformation rather than a literal claim. Freemasonic author Manly P. Hall articulates this model in *The Secret Teachings of All Ages*, where the butterfly, identified with Psyche, symbolizes the soul's unfoldment through successive stages. Hall describes three phases corresponding to initiation: the unregenerate state, the contemplative state symbolized by the chrysalis or tomb, and the enlightened state represented by the butterfly's emergence (M. P. Hall).

Within this context, the coffin parallels the chrysalis: a temporary enclosure that marks a transition. The imagery does not assert doctrinal belief but reflects a symbolic grammar widely recognized in Western esoteric literature.

Directionality and Ritual Accuracy

The directional movement of the coffin, always feet-first, is a deliberate detail. In Western funerary and ecclesiastical tradition, coffins are carried feet-first as a sign of finality and submission. Head-first movement is reserved exclusively for clergy, symbolizing leadership and guidance of the congregation. The consistent feet-first orientation of both the two- and three-dimensional coffins reinforces ritual accuracy and indicates intentional design discipline rather than incidental illustration.

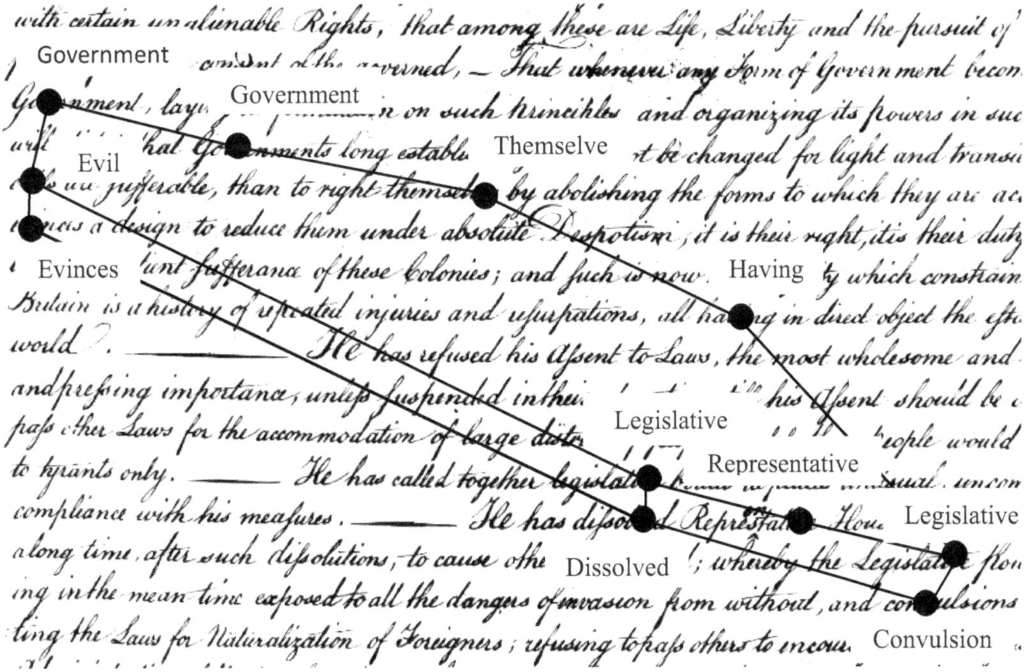

Fig. 75

Proportional Harmony and Visual Constraint

Across the image set, the pyramid, scalene triangle, and three-dimensional coffin are comparable in scale and proportion. Each contains or accommodates Euclidean constructions while maintaining visual equilibrium. The unfinished pyramid, two-dimensional coffin, three steps, Ankh, Orion's Belt stars, rays of glory, and floating capstone exhibit consistent spatial balance. Their relationships suggest deliberate proportional calibration rather than decorative placement.

One element initially resists this balance: the altar with horns. Relative to the surrounding forms, the altar appears oversized. At the time of drafting, its final scale was unresolved. Only later, through analysis of the geometric constraints imposed by the V-based constructions, did the necessity of the altar's size become apparent. Its apparent disproportion is not an error but a consequence of relational geometry that emerges only when the full system is considered. The letter-V diagram was the first of the seven drawings completed, and its internal constraints governed the eventual resolution of all subsequent forms.

Chapter Five

The Letter W

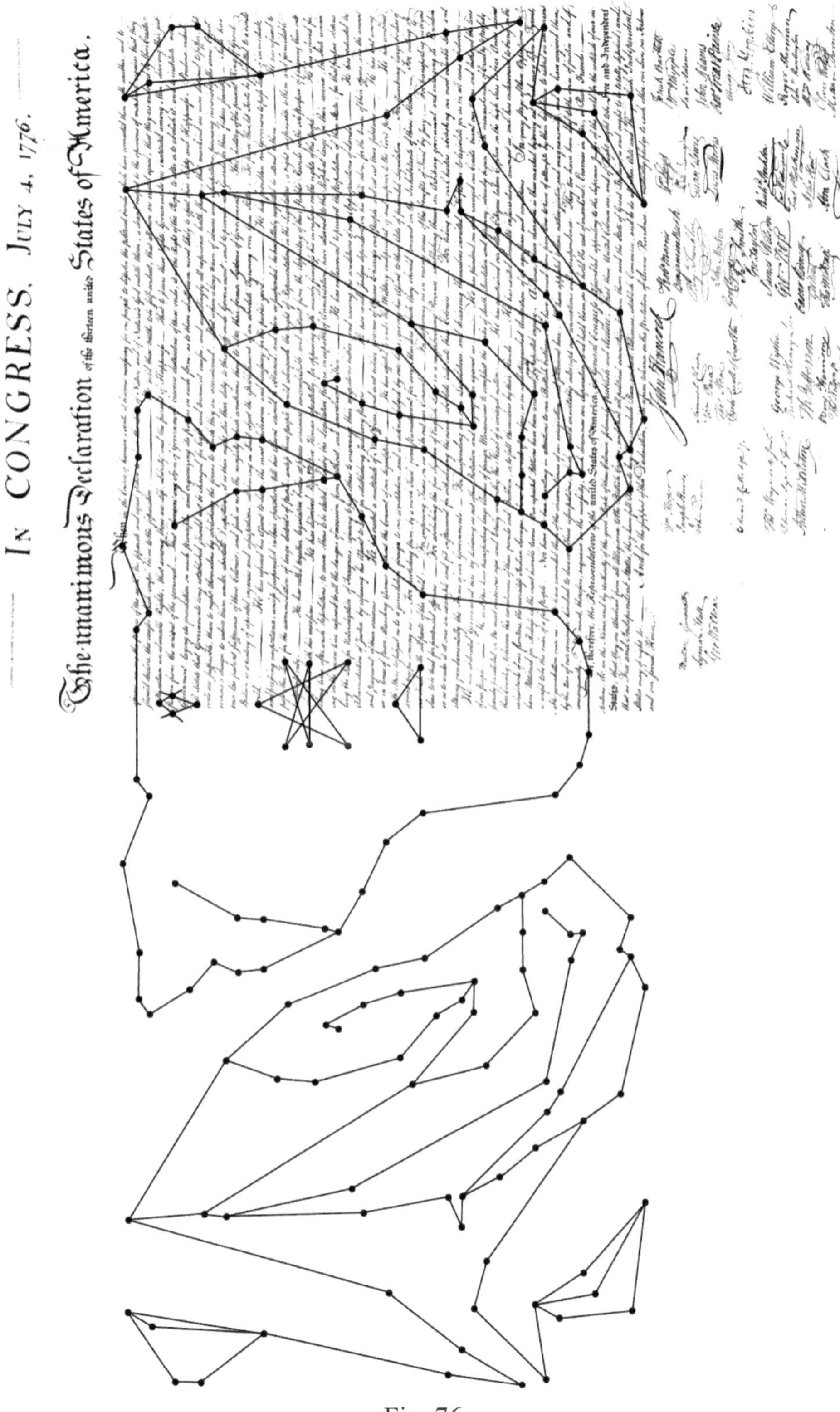

Fig. 76

The unanimous Declaration
Mirror Line
When
Powers/Which/Laws
Which/We
With
Powers/Whenever
Powers
Will
Which
Now/Which
World/Laws/Wholesome
Laws
With
Whereby
Without
Laws
Laws
Without
With
With/World
We
We
We

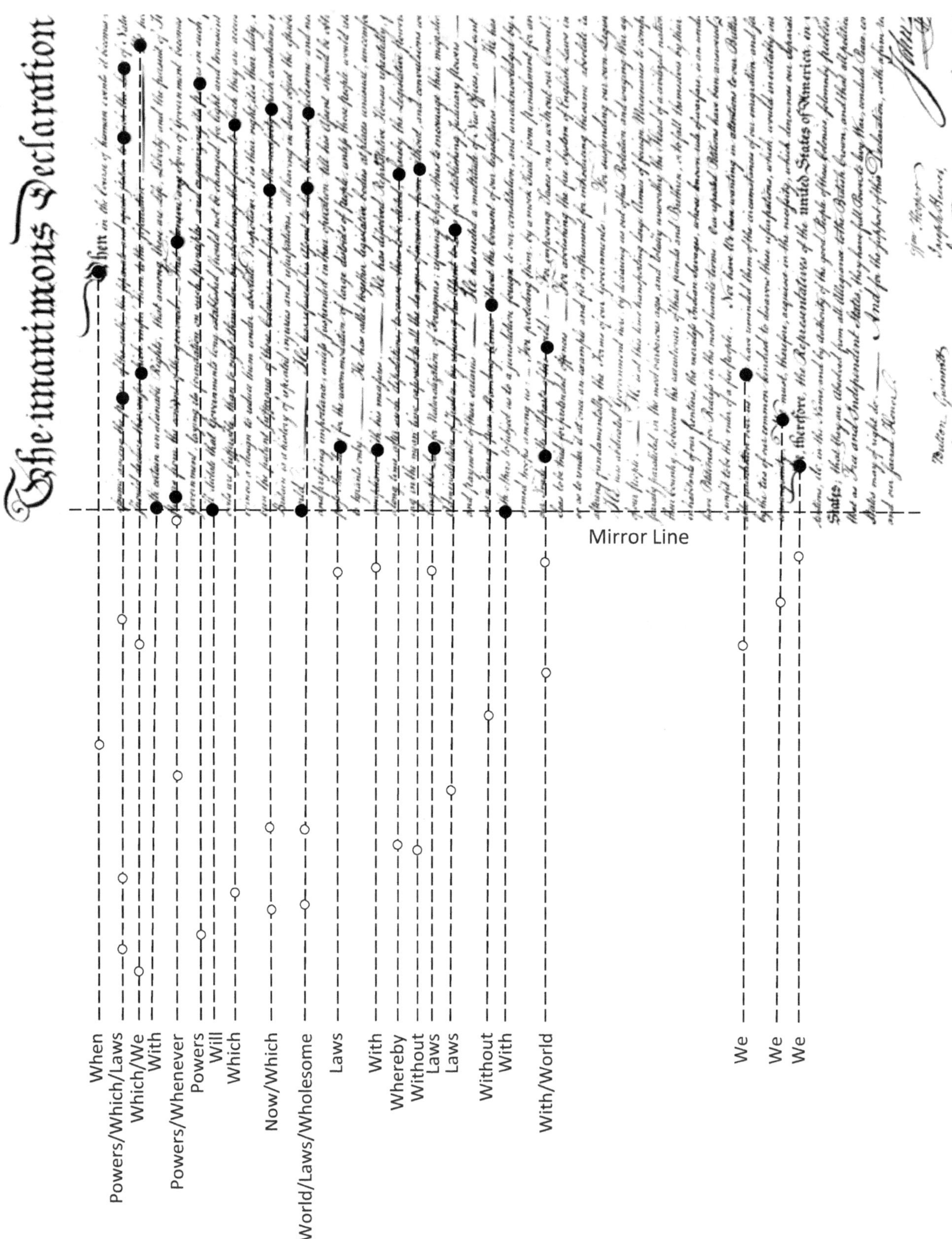

Fig. 77

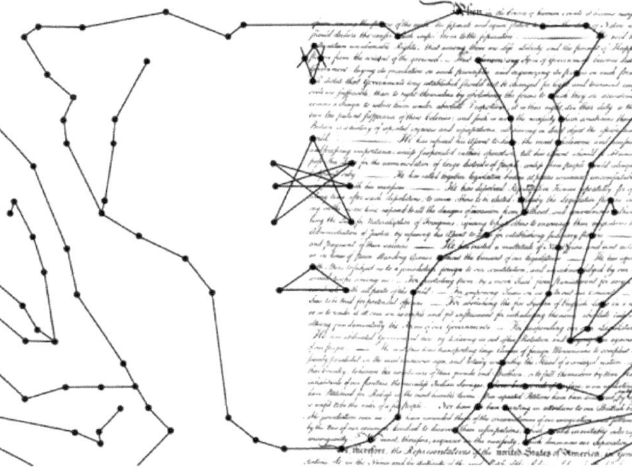

Fig. 78

The letter W-image is the second image identified as having non-random geometry. A lion's head is at the center of the triptych, flanked by a large, mirrored rose blossom on either side (Fig. 76).

Figure 77 illustrates the mirror-line dot process for plotting the lion's head.

The lion head represents the Egyptian God Osiris, the Lion of Judah, and the Father in the Trinity; it is also one of the four living creatures in the *Book of Revelation*. All of these are syncretic representations of God.

On either side of the lion's head, the rose emblem represents the divine; its thorns symbolize suffering, while its bloom signifies eternal life and resurrection. In Rosicrucianism, the rose symbolizes the blood of Christ, and, like Freemasonry, it traces its origins to Hermeticism. The rose symbol embodies the concept of death and rebirth, a theme Martin Luther employed, known as the Luther Seal or Luther Rose. The roses flanking the lion suggest that the lion represents a deity.

Lion of Nectanebo from Heliopolis, Collection of Vatican Museum (Fallaner).
Fig. 79

At the bottom center of the lion image is an upward-pointing triangle. This triangle symbolizes the alchemist's representation of masculinity and the elemental sign of fire. Just above the triangle lies a seven-pointed star shaped like a heptagram. The seven points of the star signify the seven known planets, the seven alchemical metals, and the seven days of the week. Above the seven-pointed star rests an inverted Masonic square and compasses containing symbology whose interpretations vary significantly across Masonic traditions (Fig 78).

Lion, Father, Osiris

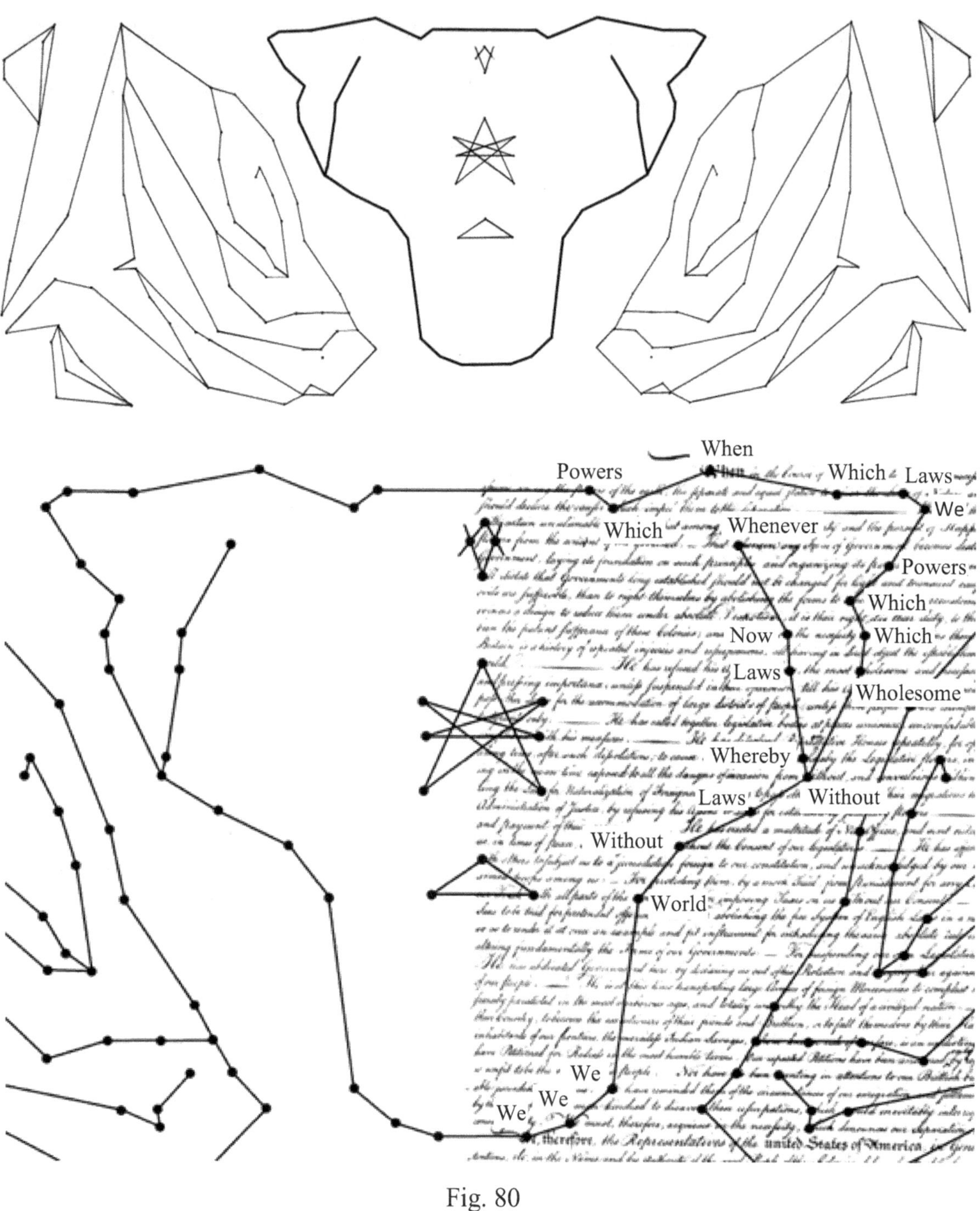

Fig. 80

All points used in this chapter are derived exclusively from occurrences of the letter W in the engrossed *Declaration of Independence*. No letters are added, omitted, substituted, or repositioned. Each W contributes two terminal points, original and mirrored, plotted exactly as they appear within the justified text block, at a fixed scale and orientation. The exception is a single point that lies on the mirror line. Lines are drawn only between corresponding terminal points, using a uniform connection rule applied throughout the chapter. The lion's head is formed by the letter W, plotted from powers, which, when, laws, we, powers, which, which, wholesome, without, laws, without, world, we, we, whenever, now, laws, and whereby (Fig. 80).

Lines connecting each letter W create half of the lion's head, which is mirrored along the line, revealing the completed form. An upward-pointing triangle within the lion's head represents the alchemical symbol for fire and embodies the masculine attribute, indicating that the lion symbolizes masculinity. A seven-pointed star at the center of the lion-head figure is a septagram formed from four' W' letters. The symbol atop an inverted square and compasses is one of the essential symbolic mechanisms of the *Declaration's* graphical constraint (Fig. 78). The inverted square and compasses signify the coming together of the three primary drawings: WVY and BGP.

Throughout Egyptian history, lion-shaped beds and biers have been discovered in tombs and temples (Fig. 79). These symbols of the death and resurrection of Osiris, a key concept in Egyptian mythology, are often depicted on the walls of temples. In Egyptian mythology, Osiris is not represented as a lion, but in Freemasonry, Osiris and the lion are synonymous (Bunsen). “That this change has taken place, we have abundant contemporary testimony. In the Book of the Dead ritual, we find the following: Lord of the earth in a box is thy name….All the Gods to the utmost are humiliated at the words of the Lord of the Chest….The Lion Gods supply his headdress….He is Osiris, the Lion God….I am the Lion God coming forth with a bow" (Finlayson).

In ancient Masonic practices, symbols such as the Lion's Paw and the Lion's Grip are associated with resurrection, a central doctrine of Christianity. The lion, particularly in the Third Degree, symbolizes the resurrection power of Jesus Christ, often referred to as the Lion of the Tribe of Judah (Masonic Encyclopedia).

The phrase "Lion of the Tribe of Judah" is a religious reference to Jesus Christ, who is regarded as a powerful and divine figure. This phrase holds a similar symbolic meaning in Masonic rituals, representing resurrection and a new spiritual life. When candidates reach the third degree of Freemasonry, they undergo a symbolic resurrection reminiscent of the biblical story of Lazarus. This ritual signifies spiritual rebirth and a commitment to a new way of living.

The five points of fellowship, whispered to the candidate, embody the principles and values that should guide their future actions. This symbolism is further reinforced by the tale of Hiram Abiff, a legendary figure in Masonic lore who was murdered but later resurrected. His resurrection is a metaphor for the spiritual transformation that Freemasons aspire to achieve (Kalian).

Mackey describes the importance and symbolism of the lion in Masonic rituals. “The lion was also a medieval symbol of the resurrection. A tradition of a lion has been introduced into higher degrees of Masonry. However, in the symbolism of Ancient Masonry, where the lion is introduced as the third degree in connection with the lion of the tribe of Judah, it is simply a symbol of the resurrection, restoring the symbology of the ages, founded on legend. Therefore, in the Masonic ritual, the phrase ‘lion of the tribe of Judah’ referred in its original interpretation to Christ, who brought life and immortality to light” (Mackey, *An Encyclopedia of Freemasonry and its Kindred Sciences*).

By the grip of the lion's paw, the spirit in man long buried in the sepulcher of substance is raised to life and goes forth as a builder entitled to the wages of a Master Mason (Hall).

Fig. 81

Figure 81 depicts the candidate's resurrection through the lion's paw grip. Notice that the candidate, who is raising, holds the Egyptian Ankh in his left hand. “The master then says, I shall now raise the body of our grand master by the lion's grip, the strong grip of a master Mason, and as the master's word is now lost, the first word spoken after the body is raised shall be a substitute for the master's word until future generations shall find out the right. Some brother now whispers to the candidate to keep himself stiff when he is raised. The master takes him by the master's grip and, bracing his right foot against the candidate with a strong pull, raises him upon the five points of fellowship” (Allyn).

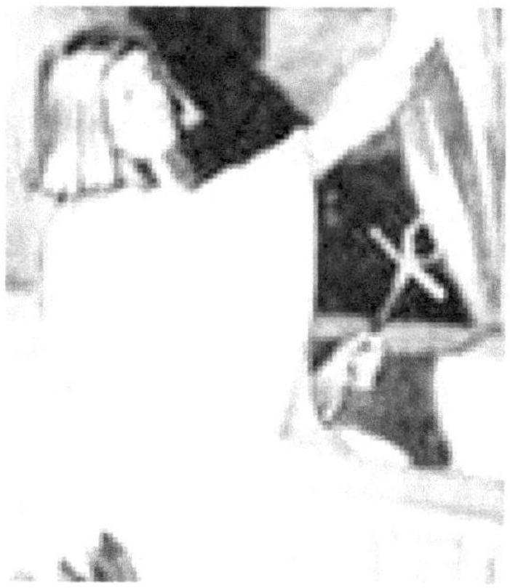

Alchemical Triangle Masculine

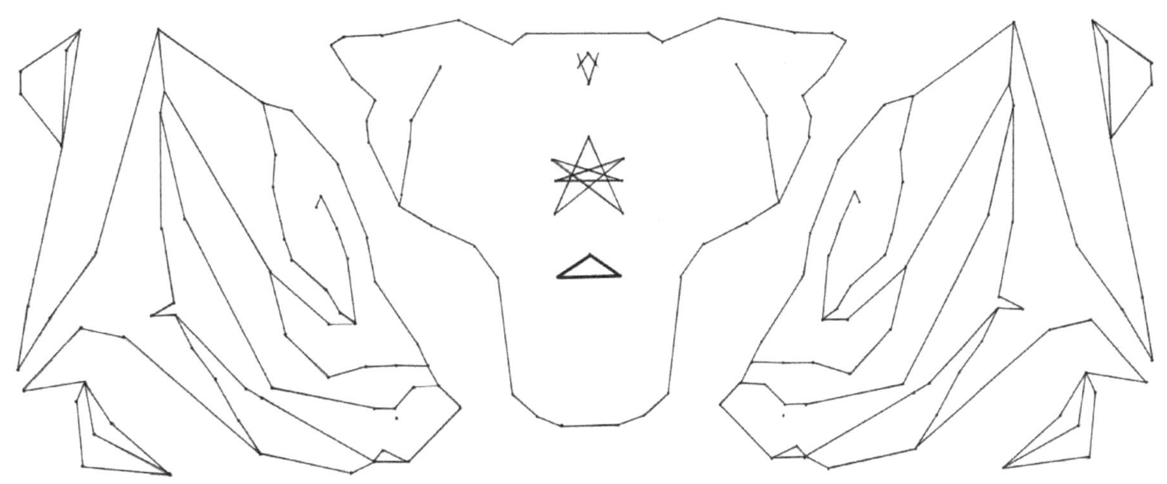

and payment of their s
us. in times of peace, Sta
With
with others to subject us t
armed troops among us
our Trade with all parts
With
Seas to be tried for pretend
so as to render it at once a
altering fundamentally

Fig. 82

The upward-pointing triangle is centered on the mirror line and is formed by the two points of the letter W in the words, **w**ith and **w**ith (Fig. 82). This triangle is the lowest of the three centered symbols on the lion's face. As an alchemical symbol, it signifies the lion's gender as male. The upward-pointing triangle represents the alchemical cipher for fire, one of the four elemental symbols alongside air, earth, and water, each with its own esoteric symbolism. The upward-pointing triangle symbolizes spirit, God, the sun, and the masculine ego. In Christian theology, this triangle represents the Holy Trinity, which comprises God the Father, the Son, and the Holy Spirit.

Albert Mackey described the Rebis illustration in *The Symbolism of Freemasonry* as the best representation of the unification of Freemasonry, Hermeticism, Rosicrucianism, and alchemy (Fig. 83).

"We do not need a better instance of this transmutation of Gnostic talismans into Masonic symbols by a gradual transmission through alchemy, Rosicrucianism, and medieval architecture than a plate to be found in the *Azoth Philosophorum of Basil Valentine*, the Hermetic philosopher who flourished in the seventeenth century. This plate, which is hermetically designed and full of Masonic symbolism, depicts a winged globe inscribed with a triangle within a square, on which a dragon reposes. On the latter stands a human figure of two hands and two heads surrounded by the sun, the moon, and five stars representing the seven planets. One head is male, the other female. The hand attached to the male part of the figure

(Beato)

Fig. 83

holds a compass that, to the female, is a square. The square and compass thus distributed seem to me to indicate that originally, a phallic meaning was attached to these symbols as there was to the point within the circle, which in this plate also appears in the center of the globe The compass held by the male figure would represent the male generative principle and the square held by the female, the female productive principle. The subsequent interpretation given to the combined square and compass was the transmutation from the hermetic talisman to the Masonic symbol" (Mackey, *The Symbolism of Freemasonry: The Sprig of Acacia*).

This image, rich in alchemical and mystical symbolism, resonates deeply with the core tenets of Freemasonry, Hermeticism, and Rosicrucianism. The central figure, the Rebis, represents the perfected being, uniting the male and female principles- a concept fundamental to Hermeticism and central to the transformative goals of Rosicrucianism. While drawing upon these traditions, Freemasonry may interpret the Rebis as a symbol of the Mason's journey toward self-improvement and achieving a higher moral and spiritual consciousness. Other symbols, such as the dual-headed figure, the crown, the globe and triangle, and the sun and moon, all point to the reconciliation of opposites and the attainment of spiritual enlightenment, themes shared by all three traditions. The image's connection to these traditions is further strengthened by alchemical symbols and the word "Rebis," emphasizing the transformative process at the heart of these philosophies.

Seven-Pointed Star

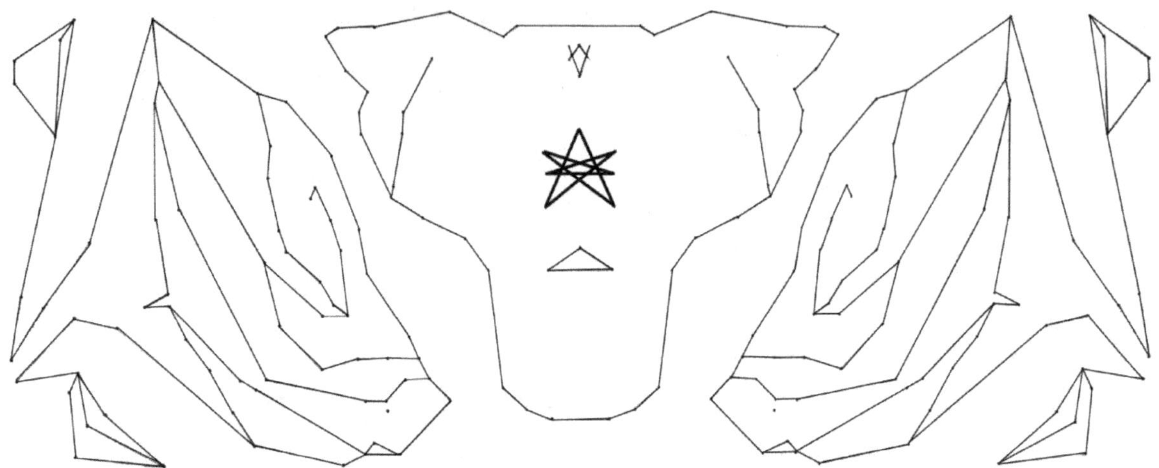

The seven-pointed star is centered on the mirror line and is formed exclusively from the terminal points of the letter W in the word's **w**orld, la**w**s, **w**ith, and la**w**s (Fig. 84). Each point is plotted directly from the justified text block at a fixed scale and orientation, with no added, removed, or repositioned elements. Lines are drawn only between corresponding terminal points using the same uniform connection rule applied throughout this chapter.

The resulting figure is a heptagram, a geometric form defined by seven vertices connected in a continuous sequence. At the mechanical level, the star arises solely from the spatial distribution of the selected letterforms under mirror constraint. No symbolic assumptions are required for its construction.

Fig. 84

Once resolved, however, the heptagram becomes visually legible within a range of symbolic and esoteric traditions that developed long after the eighteenth century. In some branches of Freemasonry, the number seven has been associated with the liberal arts and sciences, stages of moral development, and lodge offices. In alchemical literature, seven is commonly linked to the classical metals and planetary correspondences. Hermetic and Rosicrucian traditions similarly employ sevenfold structures to organize cosmological, philosophical, or initiatory concepts.

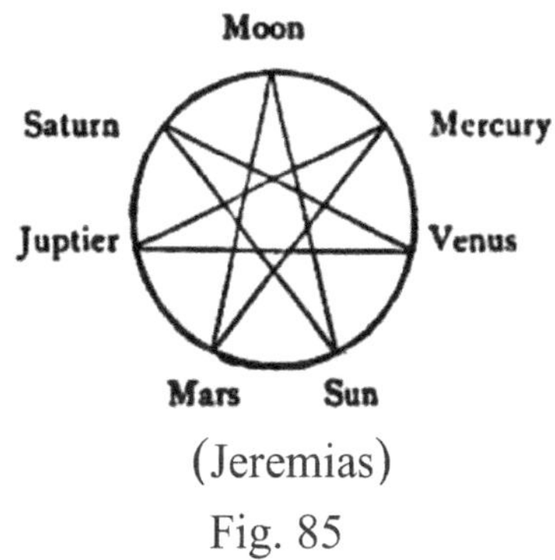

(Jeremias)
Fig. 85

These associations are introduced here not as evidence of intentional encoding, but as examples of how a mechanically derived geometric form can align with established symbolic vocabularies familiar to later interpreters. The presence of a heptagram within the reconstructed field does not demonstrate authorship, doctrinal intent, or esoteric instruction. It demonstrates only that the point field generated from the letter W is capable of producing a stable seven-point configuration recognizable within multiple interpretive frameworks.

(Jeremias)

The historical significance of the heptagram in Babylonian astrology, medieval cosmology, and Renaissance occult diagrams further illustrates the longevity and cross-cultural persistence of seven-pointed geometric structures. Such persistence helps explain why the figure remains symbolically resonant without requiring claims of deliberate placement or concealment.

Accordingly, the seven-pointed star is presented here as a geometric outcome with broad interpretive compatibility. Its relevance lies in the fact that it emerges mechanically from the constrained system under study and that its resolved form coincides with symbolic systems developed and valued in later intellectual and initiatory traditions.

Inverted Square and Compasses

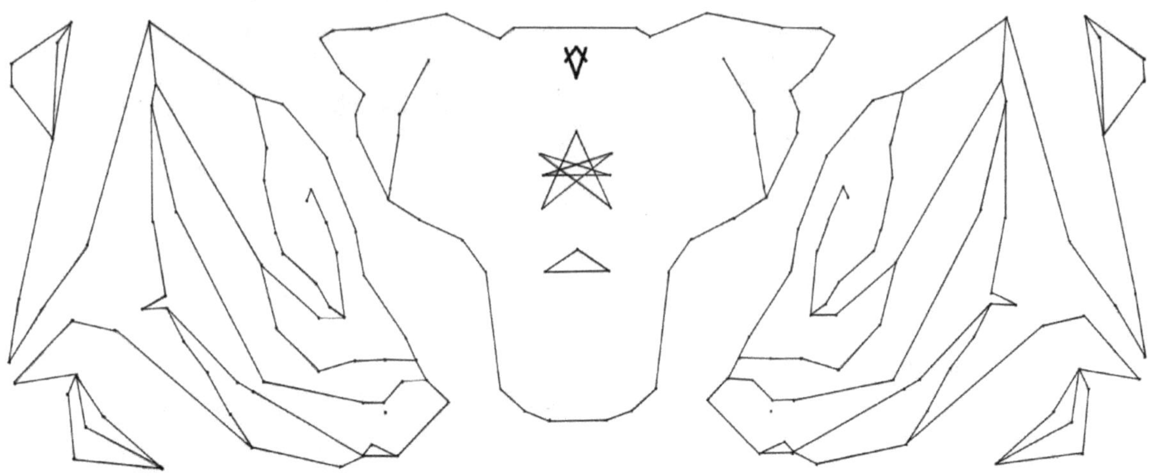

The inverted square and compasses are centered on the mirror line and are formed from the letter W in the words **w**ith, po**w**ers, and **w**ill (Fig. 86). They are among the *Declaration's* most significant images and possess abstract invocations; however, because they are inverted, they embody real-world functionality. The most recognizable Masonic symbolism, the upside-down square and compasses at the top of the lion's head, serves as a functional hinge, acting as the actuator that influences the overall architecture of the seven drawings.

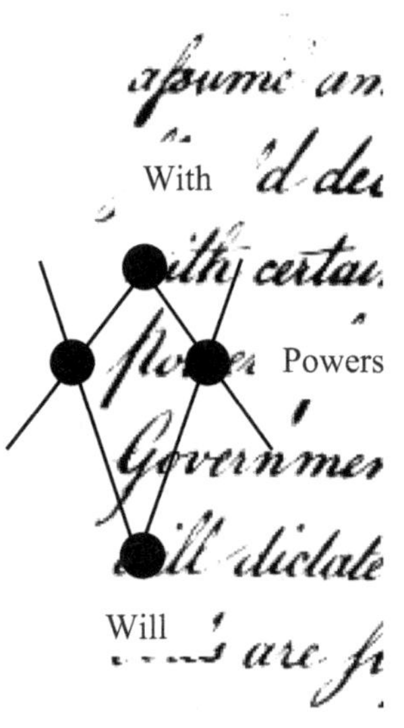

Fig. 86

A description of the four-pointed imagery of the square and compasses by Richard Carlile, the author of the *Manual of Freemasonry*. "Question, Worshipful Master, in what manner did you enter the lodge of Master? Answer. Past Master, upon four points of geometry, formed by the square and compasses united, and the letter G in the center" (Carlile).

You might consider the four points of the Masonic square and compasses as the four cardinal virtues: fortitude, prudence, temperance, and justice. However, Carlile described the geometry

created by the square and the compasses as separate elements that, when layered, create a diamond-like space for the letter G.

The dot pattern outlines the interior space of the square and compasses. The letter G is often placed in this space, symbolizing God, geometry, gnosis, or generative power. Generative power refers to the ability to create or produce something. The shape within the square and compasses is frequently associated with feminine symbolism. The Masonic trowel also features a similar symbolic outline. In the context of the *Declaration*, these four dots could serve the function of the square and compasses, a device for the page rotation (Burkle).

"The square and compasses lie at the heart of Masonic instruction. Recognized as tools of the architect and builder, Freemasons use them to teach moral lessons. The square traditionally admonishes a man to 'act squarely, yet to be honest and upright in his dealings. The compasses remind him to keep his passions within bounds and avoid excess. Together they form a visual reminder to live with balance and integrity in everyday life" (Pennsylvania)

In searching for written references to the inverted square and compasses, I examined the *Collection Made by the Committee on Antiquities of the Grand Lodge Free and Accepted Masons of the State of New York* (1903). The catalogue contains seven entries describing inverted impressions on letters, envelopes, or regalia, each associated with the designation of a Master or Past Master (Andrews). Other references appear on Masonic tombstones and in discussions about whether the points of the compasses should face toward or away from the wearer on a Mason's ring. These examples demonstrate that within Freemasonry, the meaning of a symbol is not fixed but depends on where, how, and by whom it is displayed. Different jurisdictions and periods often use the same emblem in distinct ways.

I then turned to open-access Masonic discussion boards, observing without participating. In one conversation, an Apprentice asked about the significance of the inverted square and compasses. A more experienced Mason explained that, in his jurisdiction, an inverted emblem on a lodge wall indicates an unfinished or imperfect lodge. At the same time, on a paper document, it serves as a cue to turn the document so the emblem faces upright toward the Worshipful Master (*Masonic Social Media Post).

Curious, I rotated the three-foot drawing of the lion head on my kitchen table. When turned 180 degrees, the inverted square and compasses became upright, and the once-lionlike image suddenly resembled the head and bust of a man (Fig. 87). At the time, I did not yet realize the significance of what I was seeing. That act of turning the image would become the interpretive key that unlocked the design embedded within the seven drawings of the *Declaration of Independence*.

(*This quotation is cited as "Masonic Social Media Post" to protect the identity of the Mason who shared information considered proprietary or confidential within the Craft, consistent with ethical research practices in observing online communities.)

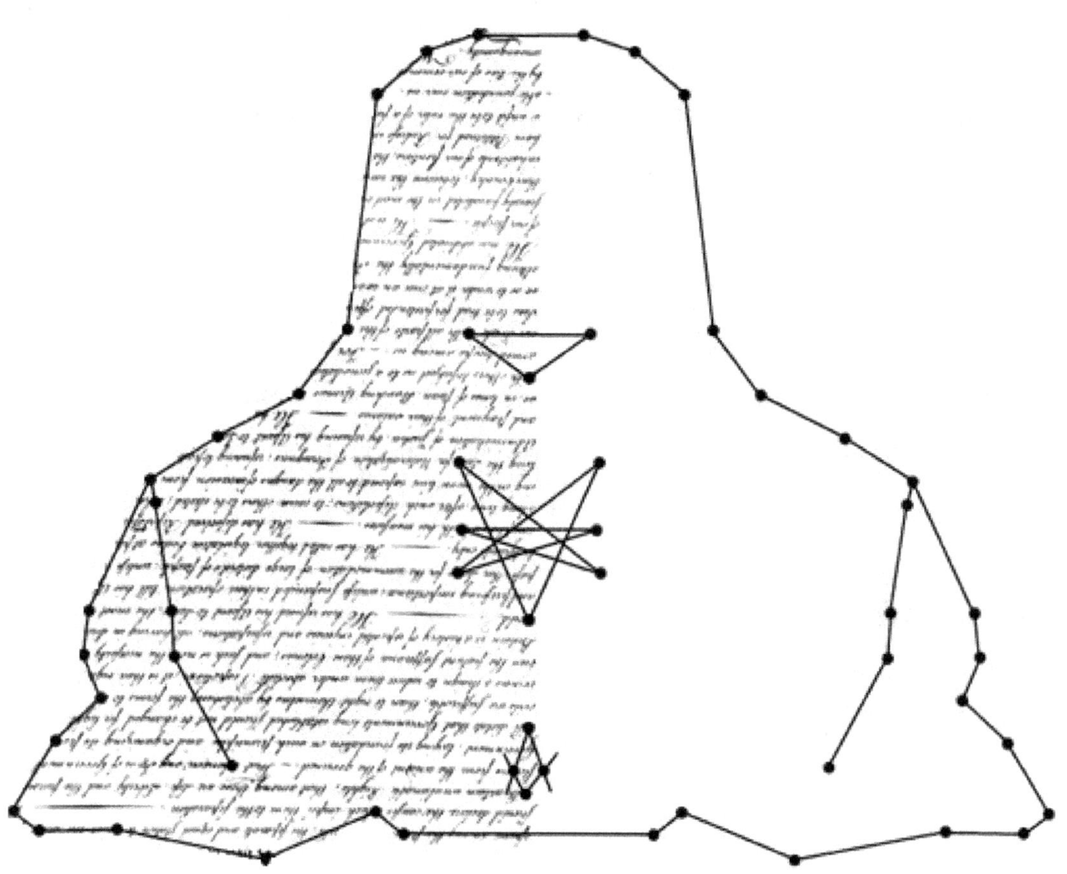

Fig. 87

Rose

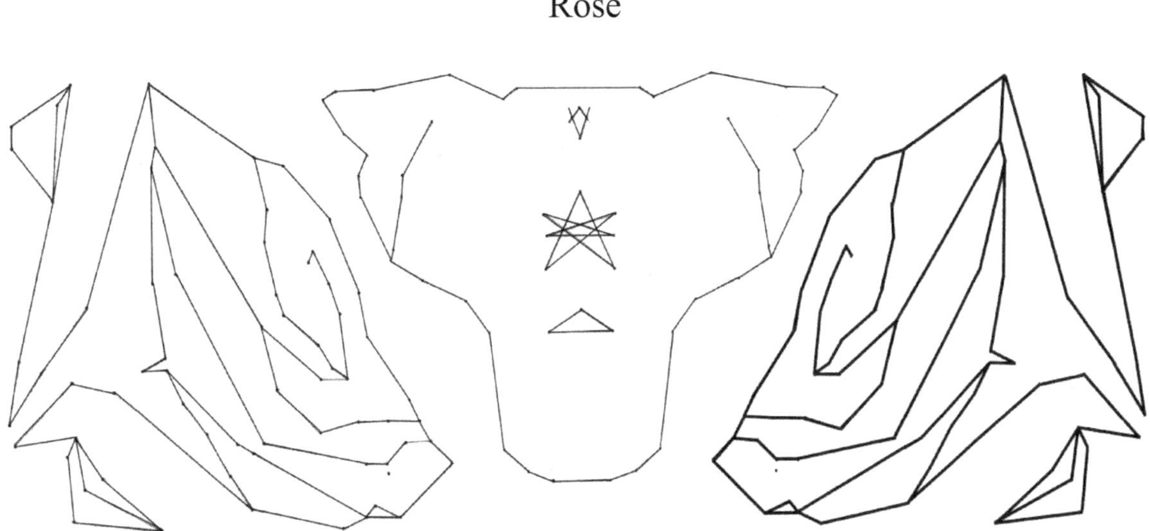

The two mirrored outer panels of the lion head image feature large rose blossoms. The rose design is formed from the letter W in the words: with, endowed, new, while, laws, which, shewn, new, new, will, power, laws, whatsoever, we, unwarrantable, Towns, which, we, war, world, which, we, away, power, with, with, fellow, whose, warned, we, we, between, within, new, power, swarms, unacknowledged, laws, which, with, laws, own, unworthy, waging, war, works, whose, warfare, known, we, wanting, answered, disavow, which, would, which, crown, Power, war, with, throw, would, when, powers, and with (Fig. 88).

Across cultures and traditions, the rose transcends earthly beauty to embody the divine. Its color, fragrance, and transformation from bud to bloom weave a symbolic tapestry pointing toward a higher power (Baring).

The connection between the rose and spiritual rebirth is particularly striking. The term "rose" may be linked to "rose dew rain," suggesting a celestial connection. In ancient Egypt, the rose symbolized regeneration, as exemplified by the tale of Apuleius' regaining human form after consuming rose petals offered by a priest of Isis. The rose serves as a key to unlocking one's true potential, shedding the limitations of earthly existence. The rose's color further enriches its symbolic meaning. Red roses, associated with fire and passion, represent divine love in its most ardent form. White roses, linked to purity and wisdom, symbolize divine intellect. When these two colors unite in a single rose, they signify the harmonious union of love and wisdom within the deity (Portal).

This symbolism extends beyond personal transformation. The rose also serves as a vessel for divine knowledge. The Egyptians believed that sacred knowledge resided within temple walls, and the rose, a symbol of regeneration, was a key to unlocking these secrets. Similarly, the "Mayan Kinal" fire rose is associated with the Holy Spirit, the source of all beings. Finally, the rose's connection to dawn and light reinforces its divine significance. Many cultures view the rose as a symbol of resurrection and eternal life, as it blooms anew from a dormant bud, a metaphor for the potential of spiritual renewal (Portal).

Fig. 88

The rose, a powerful emblem in Freemasonry, Rosicrucianism, and Hermeticism, represents spiritual rebirth, transformation, and the harmonious union of divine love and wisdom. In Freemasonry, the white rose signifies purity, innocence, and the virtue of silence, while the red rose symbolizes sacred love and spiritual passion. Rosicrucianism elevates the rose to a central symbolic position, most notably through the rose-on-the-cross motif, which represents the alchemical transmutation of the soul. In this tradition, the red rose expresses spiritual ardor—often associated with the blood of Christ—while the white rose reflects purity and divine wisdom. Hermeticism likewise connects the rose to Isis, where it signifies regeneration and the transcendence of earthly limitation. Across these traditions, the union of red and white roses symbolizes the reconciliation of opposites—love and wisdom, passion and reason—and marks a crucial step toward spiritual wholeness and enlightenment. In this sense, the rose functions as a key for unlocking latent spiritual potential and attaining deeper insight into the divine.

The historical depth of rose symbolism and the esoteric meanings associated with its colors are further revealed in the following passage:

> The beauty of the rose is matchless, and man ever makes the material thing he most esteems the symbol of the deity he most adores. The Hebrew poets sang of the rose as Solomon in the Song of Songs: I am the rose of Sharon and the lily of the valley. But there was among the rabbins a distinctly religious veneration for the rose they even made it the symbol of the Shekinah the flame of God's presence. The Kabbala reveals this clearly In the Zohar.... Thus, the sacred rose, the supreme flower of light, was made the sign of God's presence, its gentle glories the exponent of the tremendous splendors of the Infinite. The like symbolism continued in the new dispensation Christ was typified by the rose. According to the explanation of St. Jerome, the word Nazareth

means a flower, and Nazareth was situated in Carmel, the garden of God. There was then a peculiar appropriateness in the loving designation of Jesus as the Flower of the Garden, the Rose of the World. An extension of the imagery made the red rose represent the white blossom sprinkled with the Redeemer's blood. In the cultus of the Virgin Mary, the rose soon found a distinguished place, and it was characteristic of her as the lily was of St Joseph. Both the white and the red rose were devoted to her worship, and their religious worth was formally set forth by St Dominic when he instituted the rosary. Indeed, Christian fancy has not hesitated to make the rose a theme for much explication of divine truths. Perhaps the most charming effort in this direction was that of St Basil, though he borrowed the thought from the East. He tells us that in the sinless age, roses bloomed from thornless stems. Then sin entered into the world, men waxed corrupt, and the rose stem put forth thorns as if to guard itself from the vile hands that would gather it. Dante, too, has made use of the rose in his Divine Comedy, employing it after the fashion of the Kabbala as the habitation of God in paradise (Dana).

Fig. 89 (Fludd)

The rose further embodies both masculine and feminine qualities, making it a symbol of balance, polarity, and integration. It is most explicitly associated with the Rosicrucian Rosy Cross, or Rose Croix (Fig. 89). In this emblem, the rose often appears accompanied by a bee, while its twin leaf stems extend outward to form a cross. Together, these elements symbolize spiritual labor, sacrifice, regeneration, and the perfected union of earthly and divine principles.

Chapter Six

The Letter Y

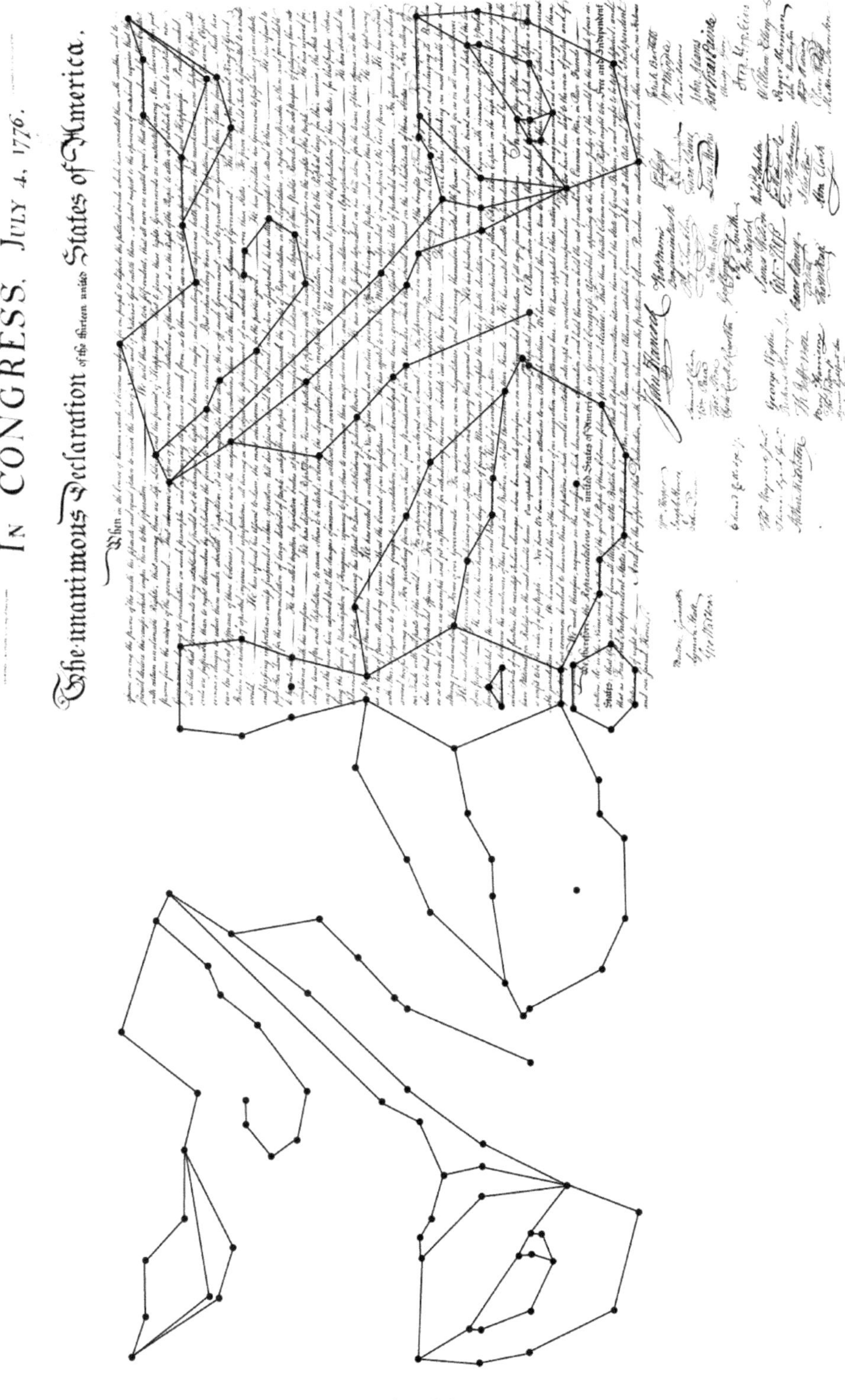

Fig. 90

Mirror Line
Laying
History
Tyrants/Only
By
Payment
By
System
Fundamentally
By
Scarcely/Totally/Unworthy
Country/By
Only
By
By/inevitably
Consanguinity/Necessity
By/Authority/Solemnly
They
They/By
May

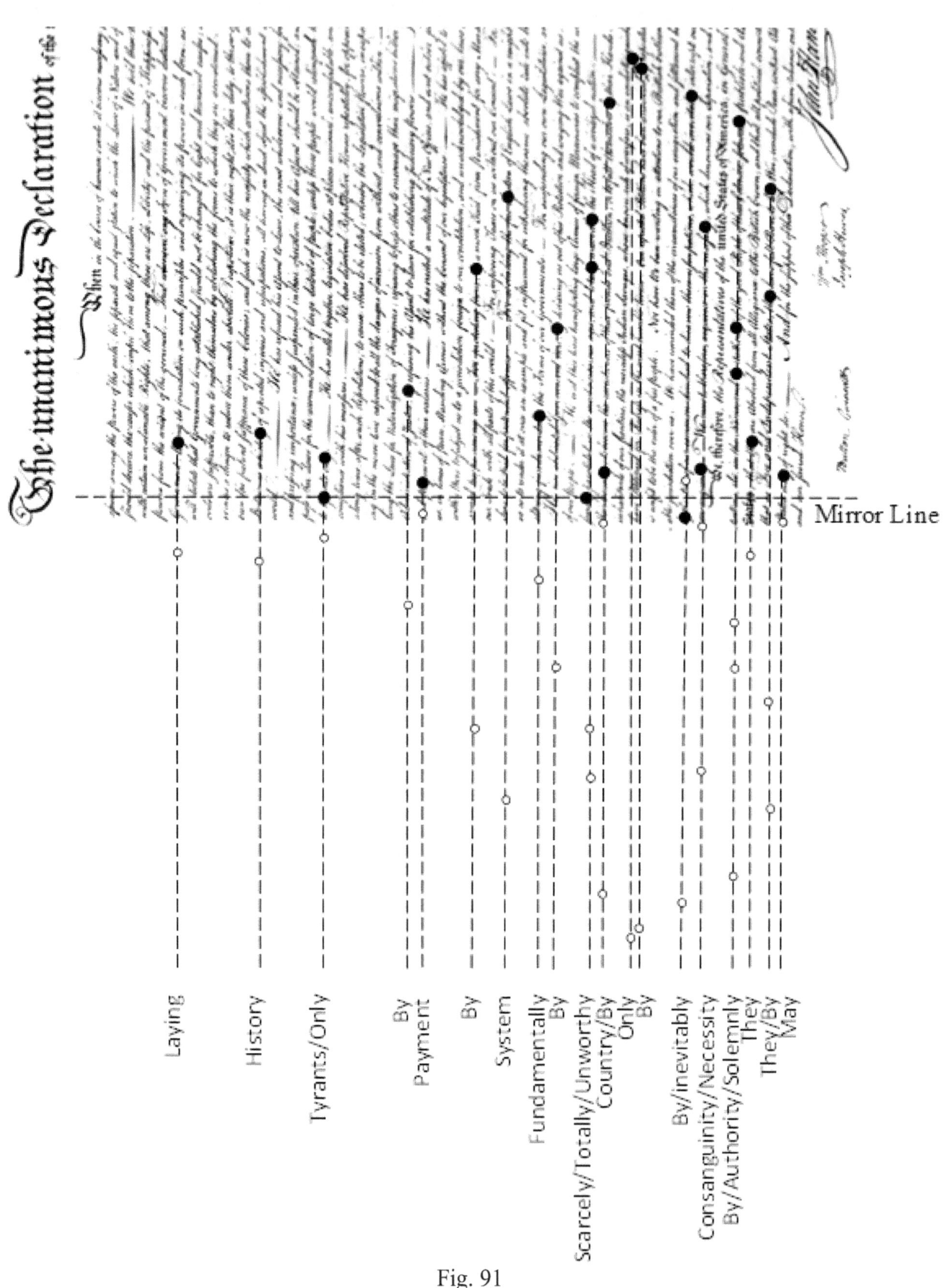

Fig. 91

The letter Y–image is the third image identified as exhibiting non-random geometric behavior. When plotted and mirrored, the resulting form resolves into a winged figure displayed in an inverted orientation relative to the *Declaration of Independence* (Fig. 92). In its descending posture, the figure closely resembles the conventional iconography of a dove, a form long associated in Christian tradition with the Holy Spirit. When the image is rotated 180 degrees, however, the same geometry reads differently, taking on the posture and attributes of the Egyptian goddess Isis.

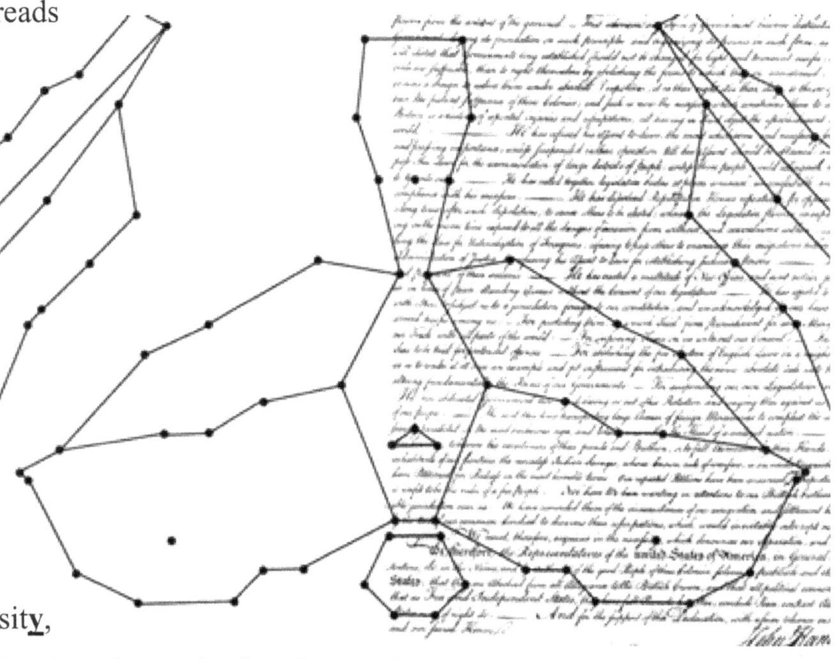

This image is constructed exclusively from the letter Y, drawn from the words: laying, history, only, tyrants, payment, by, by, system, fundamentally, by, totally, unworthy, by, only, by, necessity, solemnly, by, by, consanguinity, they, by, authority, they, and may (Fig. 92). No letters are altered, repositioned, or selectively emphasized. Each Y contributes two terminal points, plotted at a fixed scale and mirrored across the central axis.

(Cino)

At the head of the inverted winged figure is a six-sided shape that functions visually as a nimbus. In Christian art, the nimbus or halo signifies divine presence, and while circular forms are most common, polygonal nimbuses—often hexagonal—appear in depictions of allegorical or spiritual figures (Ferguson). In this orientation, the hexagonal nimbus reinforces the identification of the figure as the descending Holy Spirit, consistent with the Gospel account of Christ's baptism: "And he saw the Spirit of God descending like a dove, and lighting upon him" (Matthew 3:16).

(Bles)

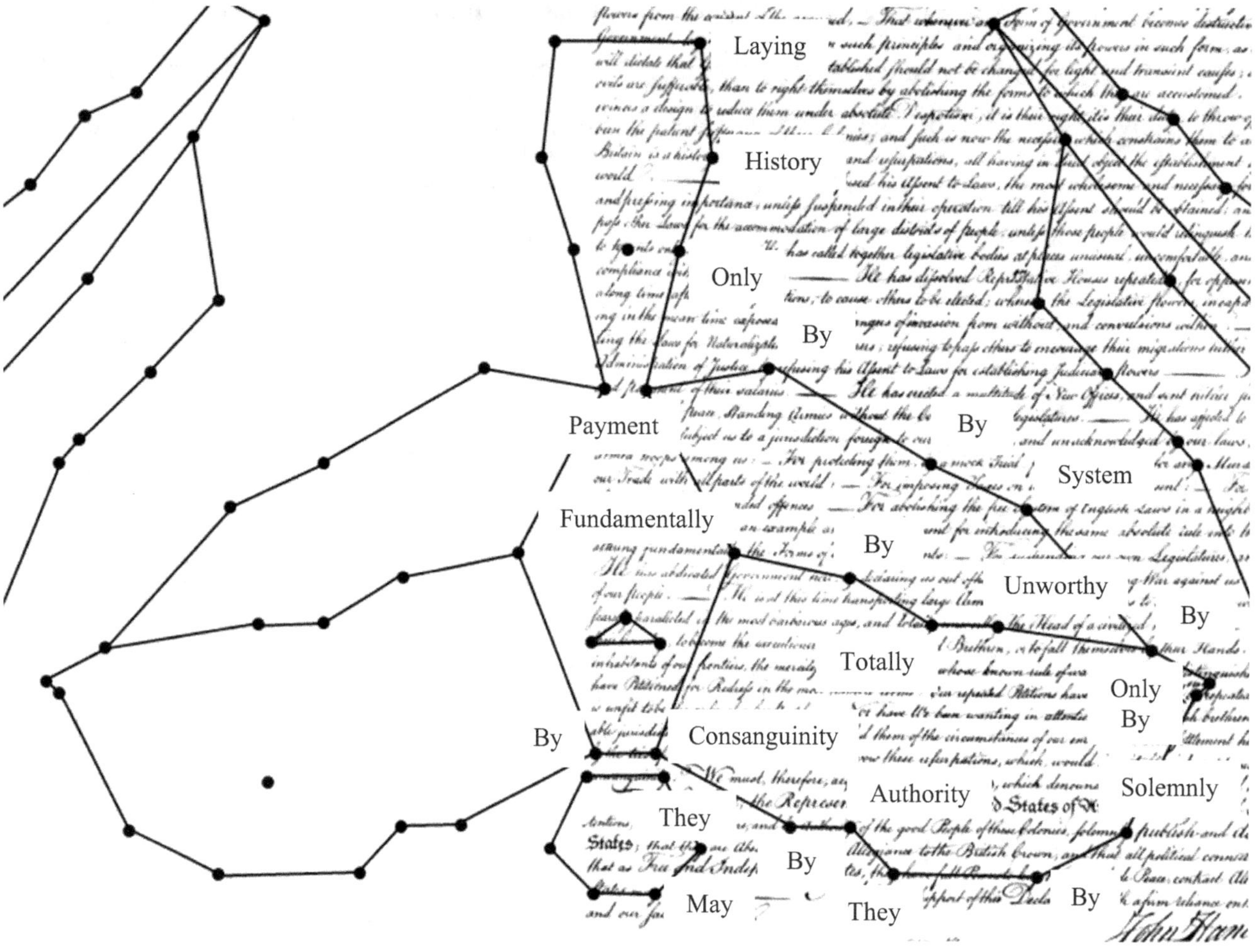

Fig. 92

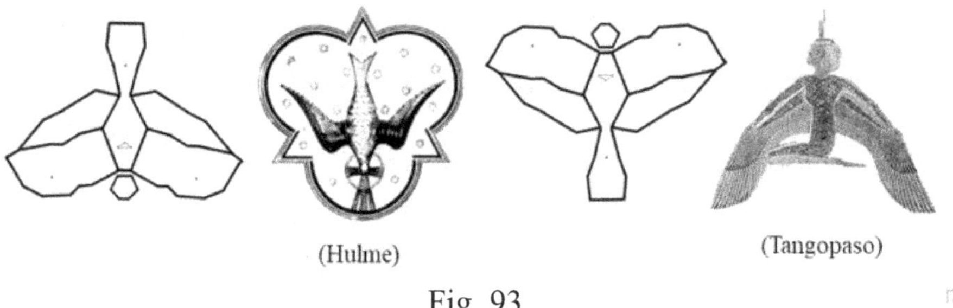

(Hulme) (Tangopaso)

Fig. 93

When the image is rotated 180 degrees Fig.93, the same hexagonal form assumes a different resonance. In Egyptian cosmology, the star Sirius, closely associated with Isis, marked rebirth, renewal, and divine order. The correspondence between the hexagonal nimbus and stellar symbolism invites comparison rather than certainty, but the association is strengthened by the figure's posture, wings, and internal geometry.

Within the body of the rotated image, downward-pointing triangles emerge. One is formed from the letter Y in the words scarcely and country; another is defined by three points drawn from necessity and tyrants. These triangles align closely with the alchemical symbol for water and the feminine principle. Their placement and orientation contrast directly with the upward-pointing triangle previously identified in the letter W image, which aligns with fire and the masculine.

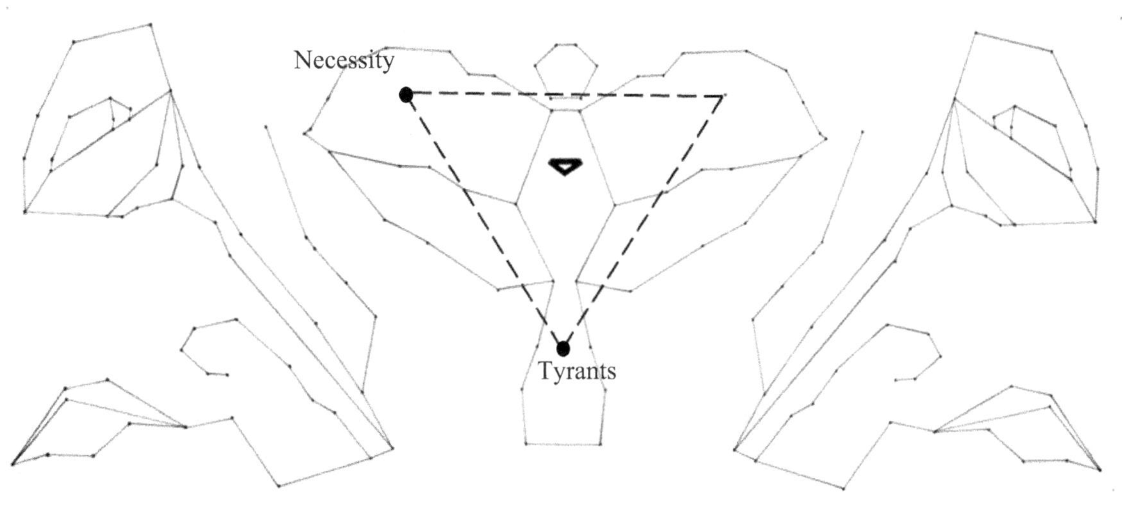

Fig. 95

This opposition is not imposed but emerges naturally from the geometry. The masculine triangle of the lion image and the feminine triangle of the winged image align along the same central axis, inverted relative to one another. Read symbolically, this pairing recalls long-standing symbolic structures: Osiris and Isis in Egyptian myth, Father and Spirit in Christian theology, and complementary principles in alchemical tradition.

Further reinforcing this reading, three additional points, derived by mirroring the letter Y in tyrants and necessity, form a nearly equilateral triangle across the wings and tail of the figure. These three points align along the centerline of the image, a configuration unique within the system. Whether read as a geometric coincidence or a symbolic triad, the configuration echoes trinities found across religious traditions: Osiris, Isis, and Horus; Father, Son, and Holy Spirit.

At this stage, the image does not demand a single interpretation. Rather, it demonstrates a capacity to hold multiple symbolic identities simultaneously, depending on orientation and relational context. What emerges is not a claim of encoded doctrine, but a demonstrable geometric structure capable of supporting layered symbolic readings consistent with traditions known to the period.

Rose, Lily, Lotus

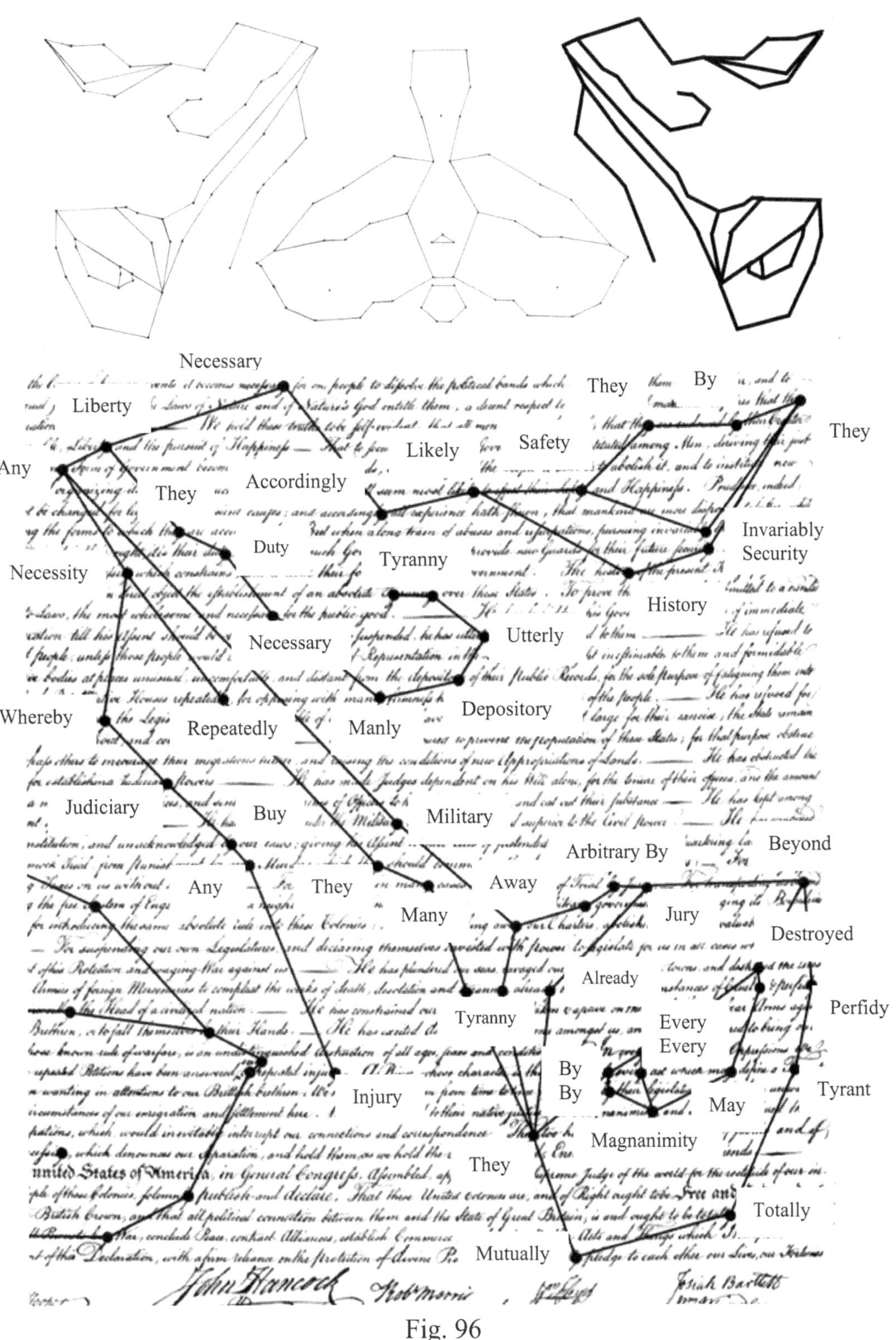

Fig. 96

As in the letter W image, the presence of large mirrored floral forms flanking the winged figure suggests divinity rather than ornament. These flowers—read variously as roses, lilies, or lotuses—are derived entirely from the letter Y in the words: necessar**y**, accordingl**y**, likel**y**, safet**y**, the**y**, b**y**, the**y**, invariabl**y**, histor**y**, securit**y**, libert**y**, the**y**, dut**y**, necessar**y**, depositor**y**, utterl**y**, tyrann**y**, an**y**, necessit**y**, repeatedl**y**, whereb**y**, judiciar**y**, b**y**, manl**y**, an**y**, militar**y**, the**y**, man**y**, awa**y**, arbitrar**y**, b**y**, jur**y**, be**y**ond, t**y**rann**y**, alread**y**, the**y**, injur**y**, destro**y**ed, cruelt**y**, perfid**y**, ever**y**, b**y**, b**y**, ever**y**, ma**y**, t**y**rant, magnanimit**y**, totall**y**, and mutuall**y** (Fig. 96).

signify regeneration and maternal protection. In Christian symbolism, the lily conveys purity and divine favor, while the rose often signifies sacrificial love. The lotus, rising unblemished from murky waters, carries parallel meanings of resurrection and spiritual renewal.

The mirrored placement of these flowers on either side of the winged image reinforces the impression that the central figure occupies a divine or archetypal role. Whether interpreted as Isis, the Holy Spirit, or a syncretic convergence of both, the floral framing situates the image within a symbolic grammar shared across religious systems rather than confined to one.

Taken together, the unfinished pyramid, the lion image, and the winged figure, the system operates much like Masonic symbolism itself: not as a single declaration, but as a layered structure "veiled in allegory and illustrated by symbols" (Grand Lodge of Maine). Meaning emerges not from isolated elements, but from their alignment, inversion, repetition, and proportional restraint.

At this point in the sequence, the veil has not been removed entirely. But it has been cut thin enough that the forms beneath it can no longer be dismissed as arbitrary.

Chapter Seven

WVY-YVW

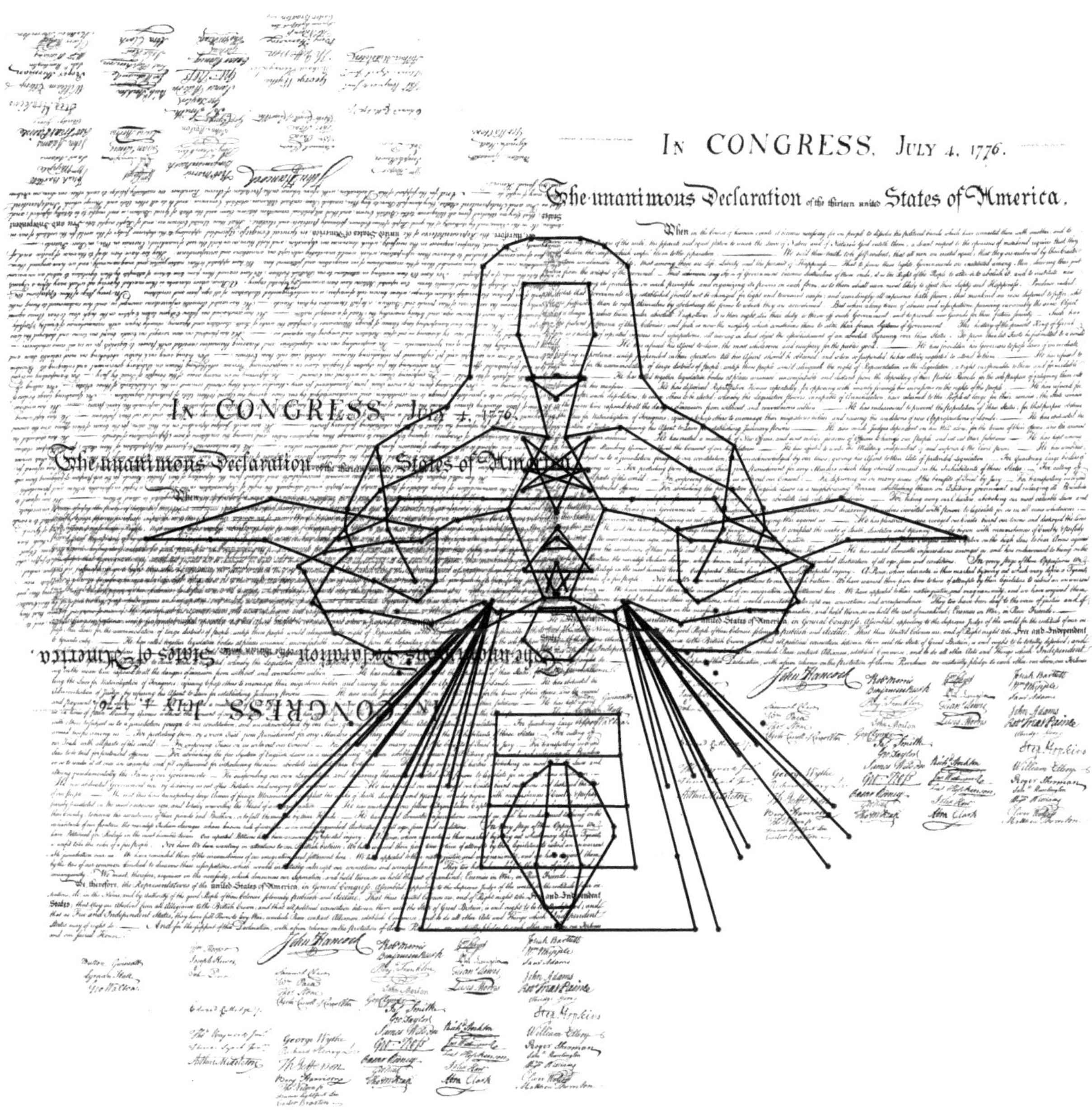

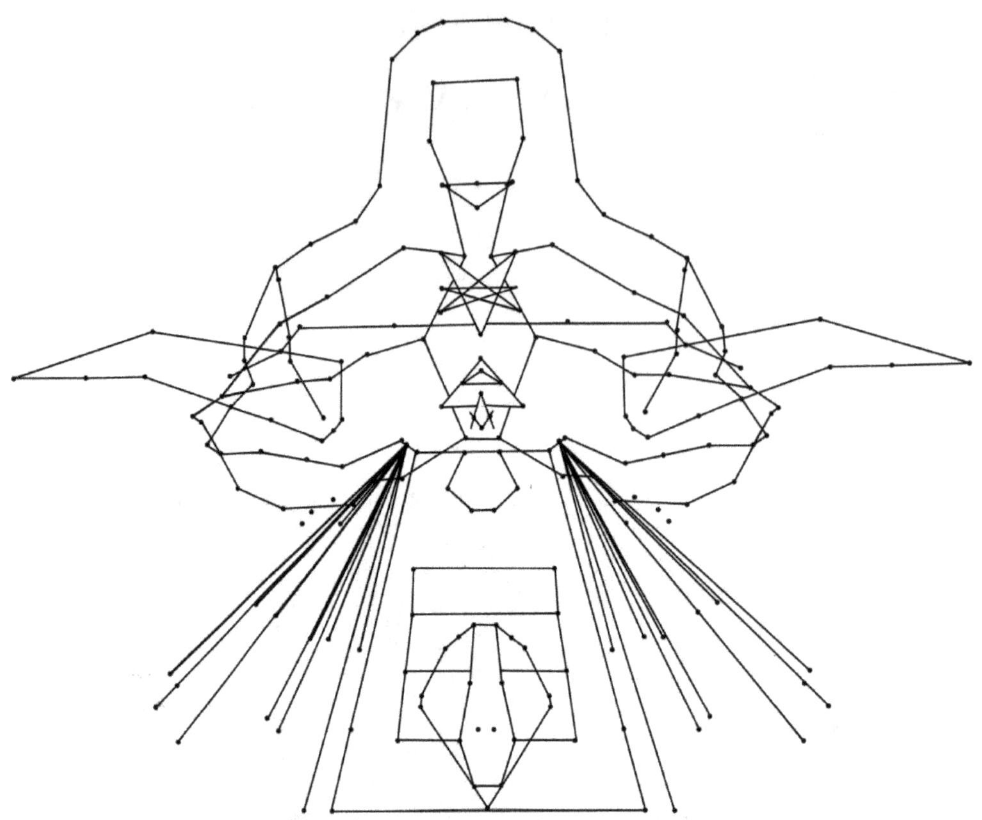

The first three *Declaration* drawings, labeled V, W, and Y, were completed within a week. As I prepared for a short trip out of town, I found myself reflecting on the relationship between these three letters and the images they produced. During long stretches of highway driving, I began asking why these letters, in particular, had emerged as structurally productive, and whether their sequence held any significance beyond their individual constructions.

Out of curiosity, I examined all six possible permutations of the letters W, V, and Y: VWY, VYW, WVY, WYV, YVW, and YWV. English readers naturally interpret the sequence left to right as WVY. Hebrew, however, is read from right to left, prompting consideration of the reversed sequence YVW.

A visual comparison between the mirrored WVY geometry and several Hebrew letterforms suggests an interesting correspondence:

English Letter	Visual Analogy	Hebrew Letter	Sound
Y	Similar form	Yod (י)	Y
V	Closest equivalent	Vav (ו)	V/W
W	Trident-like form resembling a three-pronged structure	Shin (ש)	Sh

Read from right to left, the sequence becomes Y–V–W, which may be compared visually to the Hebrew sequence ש–ו–י. This is not the standard spelling of Yeshua (ישוע), nor does it constitute a linguistic transcription. Rather, it represents a graphic or symbolic correspondence based upon visual form.

The observation becomes more intriguing when considered alongside the broader WVY imagery, which throughout this study has been associated with themes of divine authority, resurrection, and sacred kingship. Whether the apparent resemblance between the WVY geometry and Hebrew letterforms is meaningful, coincidental, or simply another example of the human tendency to recognize familiar patterns remains open to interpretation. Nevertheless, the correspondence offers an additional symbolic layer through which the WVY sequence may be viewed.

The observation did not arise from theological motivation but from orthographic coincidence. In Hebrew, the name Joshua (Yehoshua) is often shortened to Yeshua ([wvy), and in some contexts further abbreviated to Yeshu (wvy). Scholars continue to debate whether this shortening was purely linguistic or carried polemical overtones, but its existence is not disputed (Botkin). The distinction between Yeshua ([wvy) and Yeshu (wvy) lies in the presence or absence of the letter ayin (ע), represented in transliteration by a bracketed symbol. The ayin denotes a guttural consonant unfamiliar to many modern speakers and is frequently softened or omitted in casual or later usage.

Archaeological evidence supports the historical variability of these spellings. An Aramaic inscription on a first-century ossuary, commonly known as the James Ossuary, reads: "James, son of Joseph, brother of Jesus," with the name Jesus rendered as Yeshua ([wvy). Scholarly analysis confirms that multiple spellings of these names coexisted during the period (Lemaire).

The relevance of this correspondence lay not in proving intent, but in recognizing convergence. The same three letters that had independently generated the lion, the winged figure, and the unfinished pyramid now appeared, when read together, as a historically attested contraction of the name Jesus. That realization reframed the drawings not as isolated discoveries, but as candidates for combination.

During the drive home, I began imagining whether the three images might relate spatially, much as the letters themselves relate linguistically. Initially, I tried to visualize the drawings interlocking edge-to-edge, like puzzle pieces. Using the square and compasses as a reference anchor, I noted that the lion image would need to be inverted; the winged image was already inverted on the *Declaration*; and the Eye-of-Providence pyramid was oriented in its conventional reading position. After several mental attempts, it became clear that edge-matching was less promising than layering.

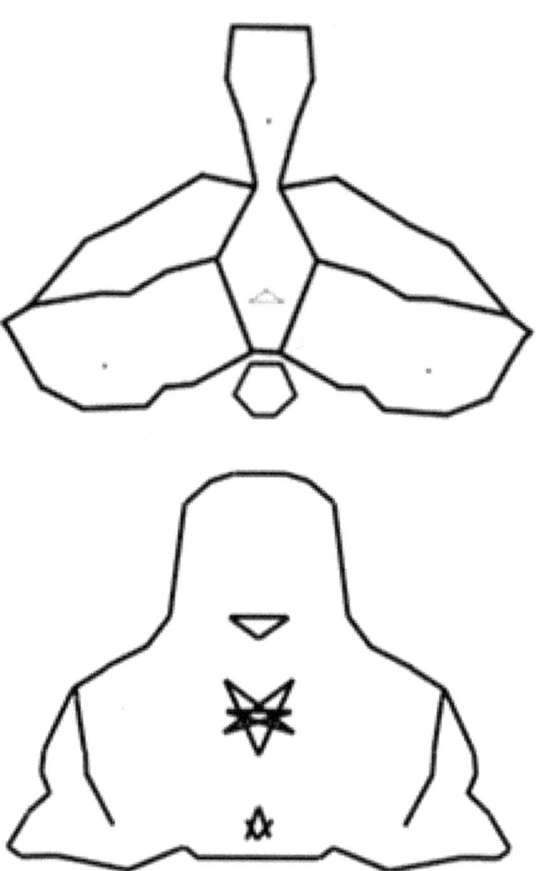

Once home, I laid the three full-sized drawings across the kitchen table and placed the Y drawing, the winged Isis/Holy Spirit image, onto the lightbox. With the lightbox set to full brightness, I placed the W drawing, the lion/Osiris figure, on top. Slowly rotating the lion image 180 degrees, I aligned the inverted square and compasses so that they faced upright, toward the traditional position of the Worshipful Master (Fig. 97).

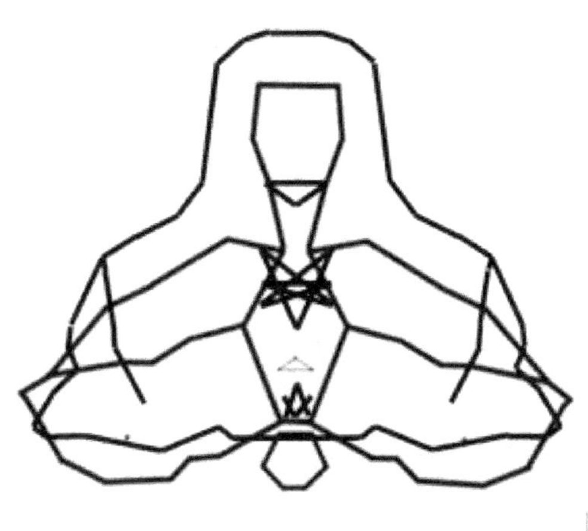

(Roberts)
Fig. 98

At that point, the two drawings resolved into a single, coherent figure. The combined image read unmistakably as a human form. Within Egyptian mythological structure, Horus is the son of Osiris and Isis; within Christian theology, the Son proceeds from the Father and the Spirit. The resemblance to conventional Sacred Heart iconography was sufficiently strong to warrant comparison rather than dismissal. For reference, I placed alongside the composite a nineteenth-century wood engraving of the Sacred Heart of Jesus (Roberts), 1866) (Fig. 98).

In Masonic and esoteric geometry, the right triangle is sometimes described as a triadic structure: the base representing Osiris, the vertical leg Isis, and the hypotenuse their generative product, Horus. Whether or not that symbolism was intended here, the geometric correspondence was exact. The two drawings shared a one-to-one scale and aligned without distortion.

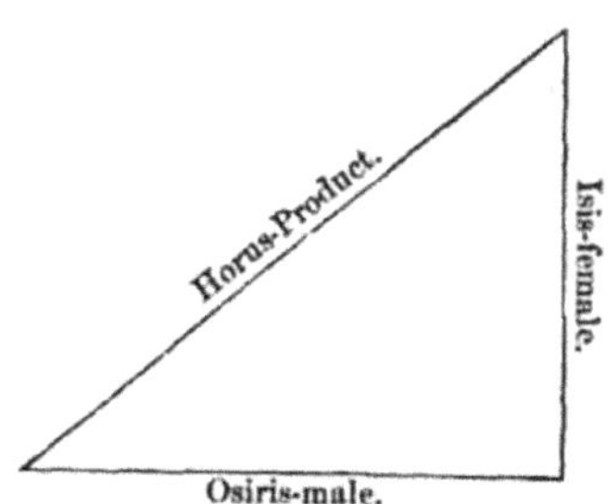

I then placed the V drawing, the unfinished pyramid with the Eye of Providence, over the combined figure (Fig. 99). With all three drawings layered, a new image emerged: a standing human figure with arms extended outward. The previously oversized altar horns now aligned precisely with the span of the outstretched arms. What had appeared disproportionate in isolation resolved naturally once the full system was assembled. For visual comparison, I placed beside it a lithograph of The Ascension of Christ by Friedrich Wilhelm Wehle (1884) (Fig. 100).

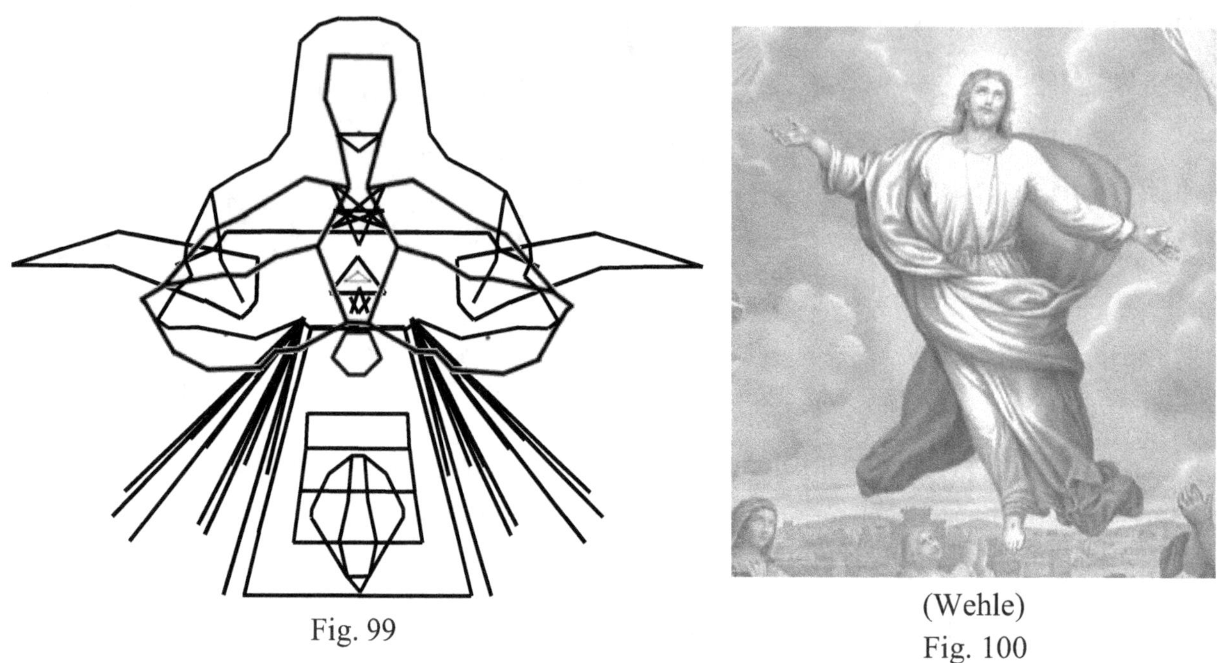

Fig. 99

(Wehle)
Fig. 100

At the center of the composite, the downward-pointing triangle derived from the Isis figure aligned perfectly with the pyramid's floating capstone, forming the Eye of Providence—also recognizable as the Eye of Horus. The geometric center of the figure encompassed all points of the Kabbalistic Tree of Life except the uppermost sephira, Keter, traditionally associated with divine source and unmanifest origin (Fig. 101).

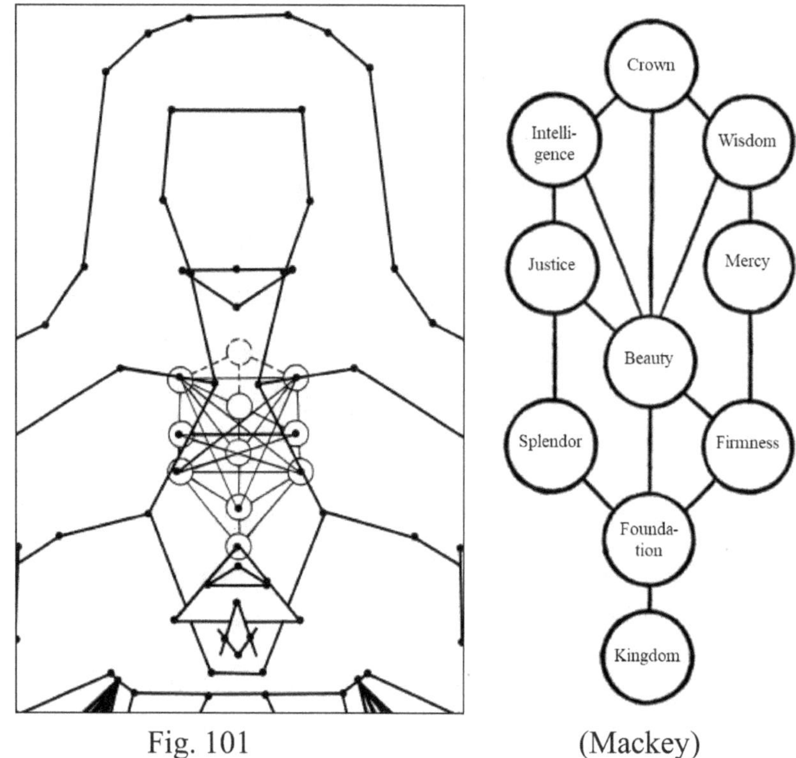

Fig. 101 (Mackey)

Curious whether the alignment would persist under inversion, I secured the layered drawings with painter's tape and rotated the entire assembly 180 degrees on the lightbox. The result was immediate and unexpected. The figure transformed into the image of Apis, the Egyptian bull-god (Fig. 102). The head and shoulders of the human figure became the head of the bull; the outstretched arms became horns. The unfinished pyramid and its thirteen rays formed a crown. At the crown's center, the ankh loop and coffin dots resolved into the uraeus—the rearing cobra associated with royal authority and divine wisdom.

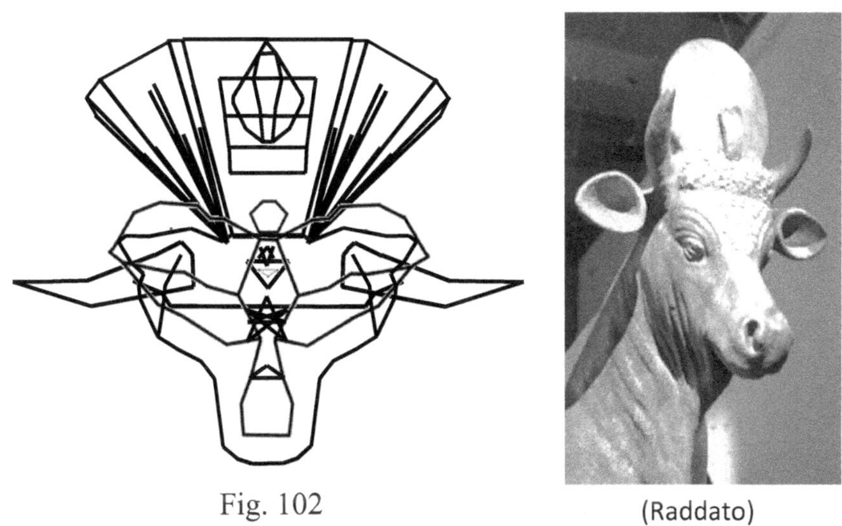

Fig. 102 (Raddato)

Within Masonic symbolism, the uraeus positioned before the three steps suggests guidance along the initiatory path from apprentice to master. Again, the reading was not imposed; it arose from alignment.

Taken together, the transformations yielded four distinct figures: the lion (Osiris), the eagle or winged form (Isis), the man (Horus/Jesus), and the bull (Apis). These correspond

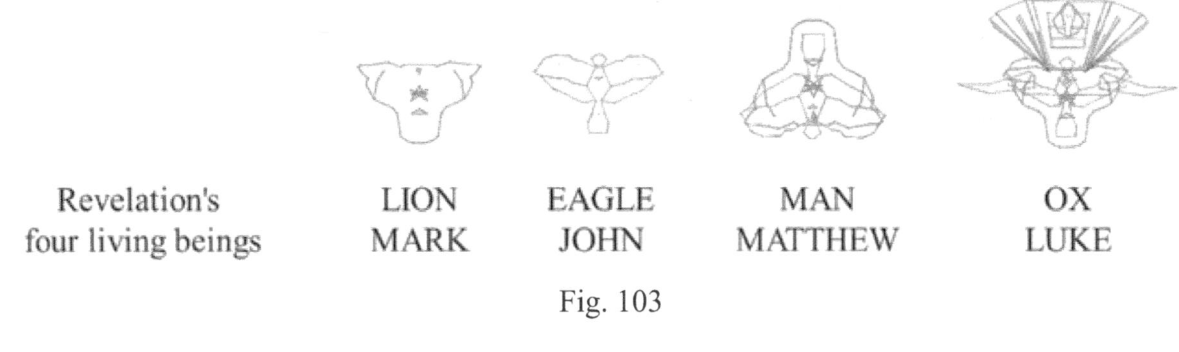

Fig. 103

directly to the four living creatures described in the Book of Revelation: lion, eagle, man, and ox (Fig. 103). The same four figures are traditionally associated with the Evangelists, Mark (Lion), John (Eagle), Matthew (Man), and Luke (Ox), and appear on early Masonic banners, including those of the Ancient Grand Lodge (1764) and the United Grand Lodge of England (Fig. 104) (Dermott).

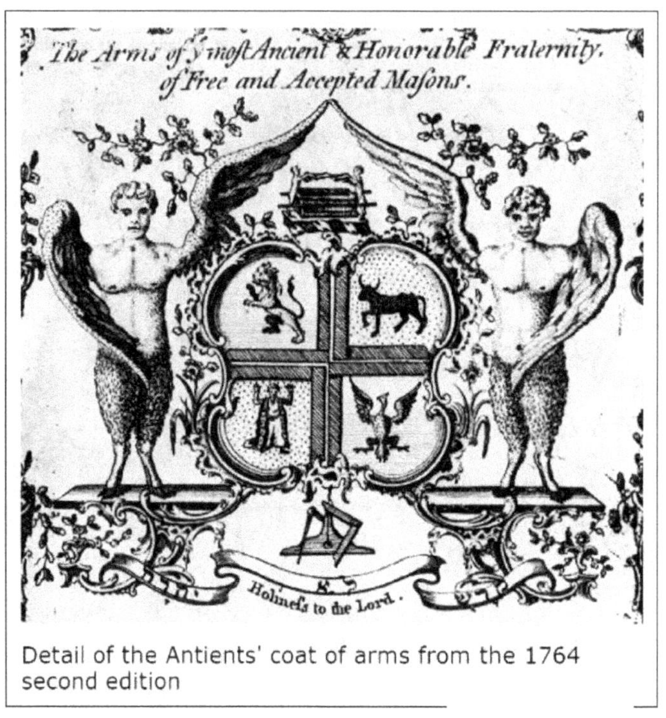

Detail of the Antients' coat of arms from the 1764 second edition

Fig. 104 (Dermott)

The system's precision becomes most evident when the pyramid and lion drawings are examined together. The flat top of the pyramid aligns exactly with the flat top of the lion's head, creating a stable contact plane. When all three drawings are layered, the hexagonal nimbus of the winged figure also locks into this plane (Fig. 105).

At this stage, the question is no longer whether symbolic meaning can be read into the drawings, but whether the drawings consistently resolve into historically coherent symbolic structures under constrained geometric rules. The images do not assert doctrine. They demonstrate alignment.

Letter W
Letter V
IN CONGRESS, JULY 4, 1776.
The unanimous Declaration of the thirteen united States of America.

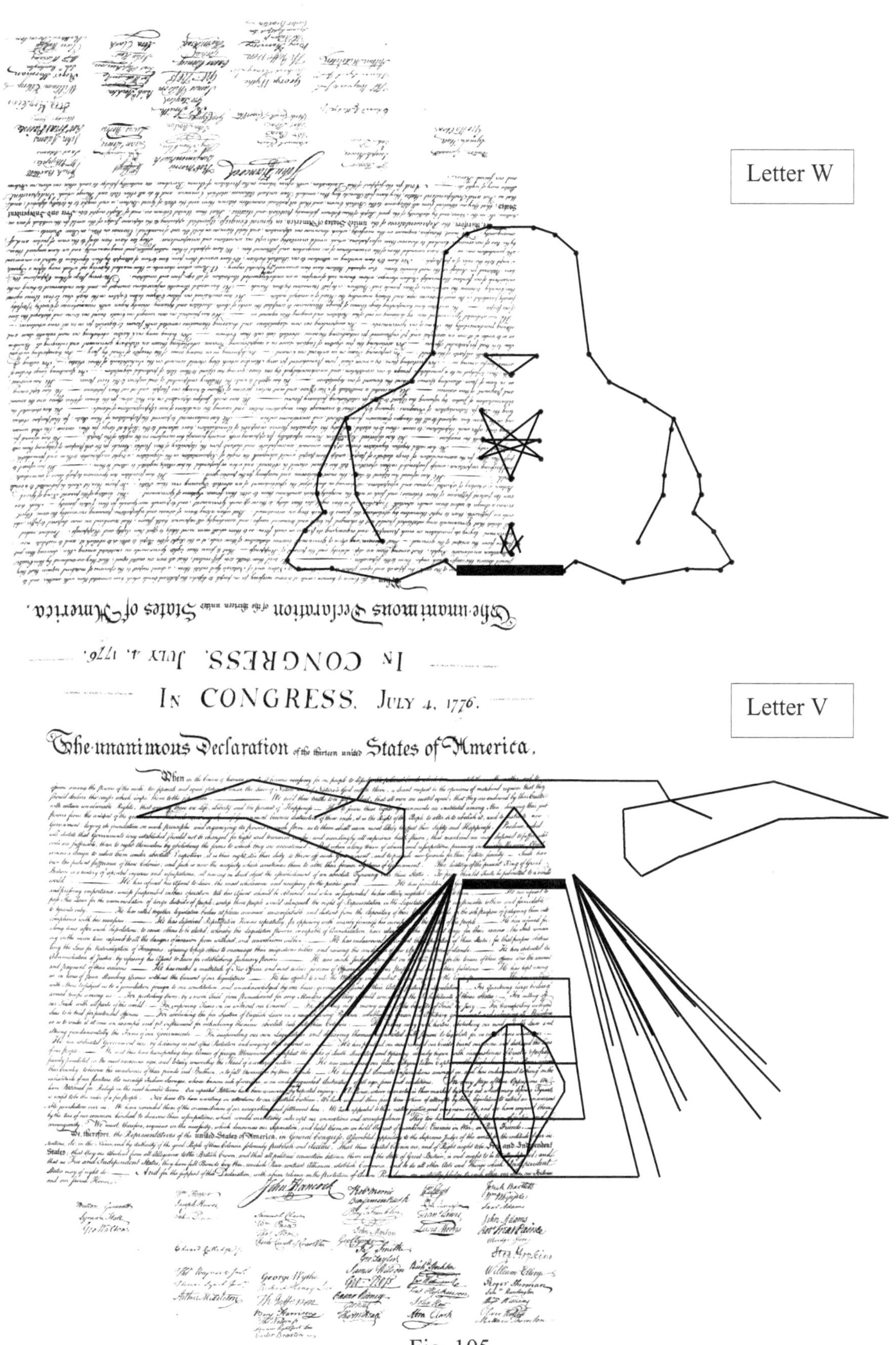

Fig. 105

The Vanishing Point of the Architect

The dashed extension lines within the composition employ a radial projection system, derived from the angular edges of the three steps and the unfinished pyramid. When extended, these lines converge at a single central axis: the apex of the Compasses, while the pyramid's flanks resolve toward the base of the Square. This axial convergence visually frames the Square and Compasses, establishing them as the geometric center of the layered drawing (Fig. 106).

The perspective framework is superimposed over the combined Lion (Osiris/Father) and Eagle (Isis/Holy Spirit) drawings, which together form the underlying facial structure of the Man (Horus/Jesus). Within this arrangement, the Square and Compasses are positioned directly upon the face, occupying the point toward which all architectural lines recede. The effect is not decorative but optical: the eye is guided, by drafting logic alone, to a single locus of attention.

Within traditions that employ architectural metaphor as moral instruction, particularly Freemasonry, the Square and Compasses function as didactic instruments, representing measured conduct and disciplined aspiration. When viewed through that interpretive framework, the alignment of perspective toward these tools suggests a visual analogy: progress through structured stages, oriented toward an organizing principle rather than a literal endpoint.

Importantly, this reading does not depend on asserting encoded intent. The perspective system operates regardless of interpretation. What it demonstrates is that the composition is organized around a vanishing point that coincides with symbols historically associated with order, measure, and construction. Whether understood as moral allegory, spiritual aspiration, or formal design coherence, the convergence itself remains mechanically demonstrable.

In this sense, the "vanishing point" functions less as a declaration of meaning than as a question posed by the drawing: what, within a constructed system, ultimately governs orientation?

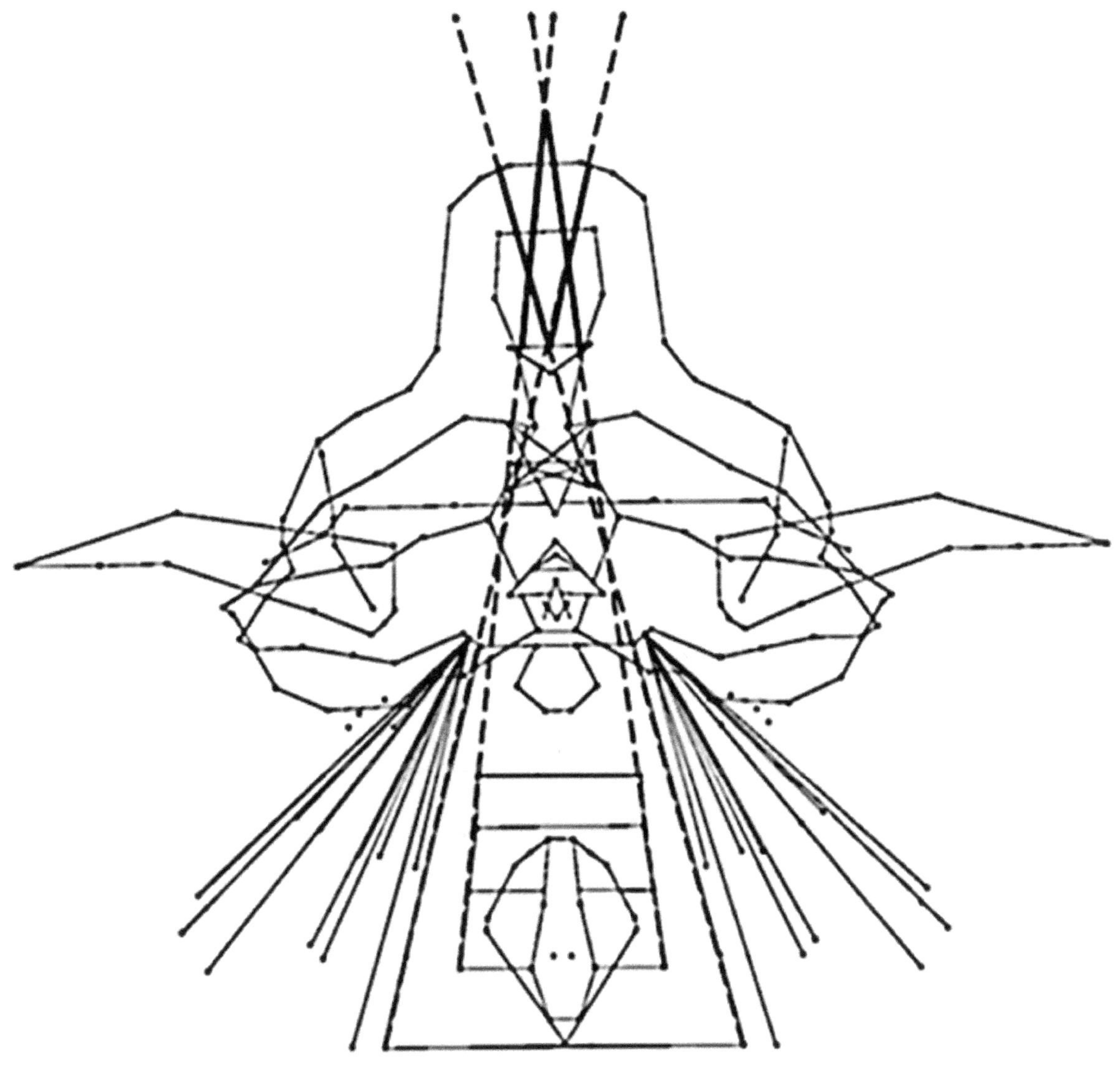

Fig. 106

Chapter Eight

The Five Lines

I did not initially recognize any connection between the five-line flap on the first page of the Rough Draft of the *Declaration* of Independence (Fig. 107) and the rays descending from the letter V, the Eye of Providence, in the engrossed *Declaration*. That relationship only became apparent after I completed the full-scale WVY drawings. Once the geometry was finished, the rays of glory became an intellectual itch I could not scratch. Their angular relationships suggested a form I knew I had encountered elsewhere, but I could not immediately place it.

Driven by that uncertainty, I dug through bins of archival notes until I rediscovered a photocopy of the Rough Draft. On the lower-left edge of the first page, a small paper flap, technically a tab, is affixed. This document represents the Committee of Five's preliminary version. Historian Julian P. Boyd suggested that it may not have been the copy circulated in Congress, though no evidence has ever surfaced to confirm that speculation.

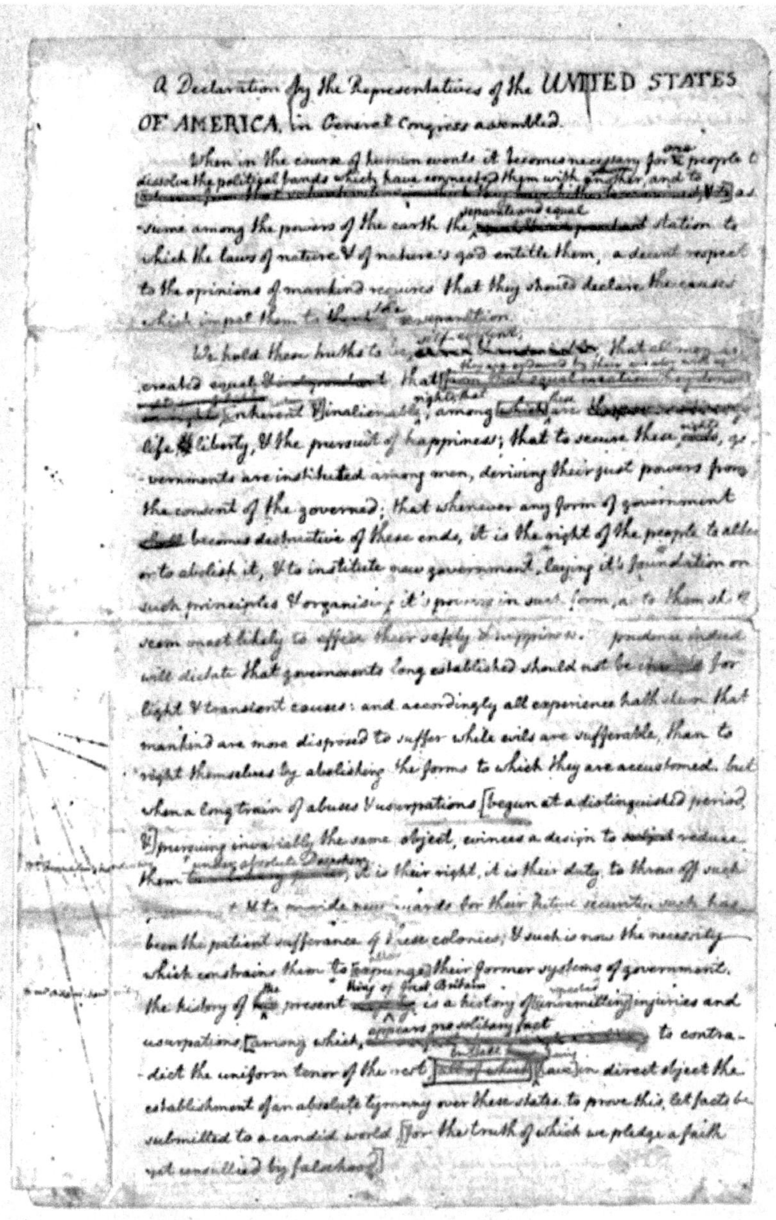

A Declaration by the Representatives of the UNITED STATES OF AMERICA, in General Congress assembled.

Fig. 107

Fig. 108

The flap contains two brief handwritten notes identifying edits as "Franklin's Hand" and "Adams' Hand," each marked with a small symbol. Visually, however, the flap is dominated by five conical lines, three vertical and two horizontal (Fig. 108). Jefferson could easily have written the small notes directly in the margin; the flap's physical presence seems disproportionate to the minimal text it carries. When I contacted the Library of Congress, a government-documents librarian characterized the lines as random markings on a reused scrap of paper. Boyd's extensive study of the *Declaration* likewise makes no reference to them.

Because my work with the Eye of Providence drawing depended entirely on scale, I requested the exact physical dimensions of the Rough Draft from the Library of Congress. Using those measurements, I resized the digital image to its original 1:1 scale. At actual size, a relationship emerged that was not evident in reproduction: the two horizontal lines shared the same angular vertex as the three vertical lines (Fig. 109).

When the two horizontal lines were rotated into vertical alignment and overlaid onto the V drawing on a lightbox, the five Rough Draft lines condensed into three. These three lines aligned cleanly with three of the descending rays inside the letter V of the Eye of Providence drawing (Fig. 110).

The correspondence is not approximate. Angle, spacing, and orientation allow for direct superposition. While coincidence cannot be ruled out, the likelihood of five independently drawn lines aligning so precisely with a specific geometric template, when treated as geometry rather than decoration, is extremely low. One way to conceptualize this relationship is as a key fitting a lock. The thirteen descending rays in the Eye of Providence drawing form the lock; the three condensed Rough Draft lines function as the key. For such a match to occur, correspondence is required not merely in number, but also in angle and position. This alignment favors deliberate human construction over random chance, though intent cannot be established from geometry alone.

The correspondence also raises questions about chronology. If elements present in the Rough Draft align geometrically with features of the later engrossed *Declaration*, one possible explanation is that an earlier hand-scribed or geometrically structured working version of the *Declaration* existed prior to Jefferson's Rough Draft. Other explanations—such as shared drafting conventions, reused compositional guides, or preparatory diagrams now lost—remain possible.

Fig. 109

Regardless of the explanation, the alignment invites reconsideration of how the *Declaration* was visually constructed and planned. The five lines on the Rough Draft flap, long dismissed as incidental, appear instead to participate in a continuity of design that extends from early drafting stages to the final engrossed document. At minimum, they suggest that geometry played a more deliberate role in the formation of the *Declaration* than has generally been acknowledged.

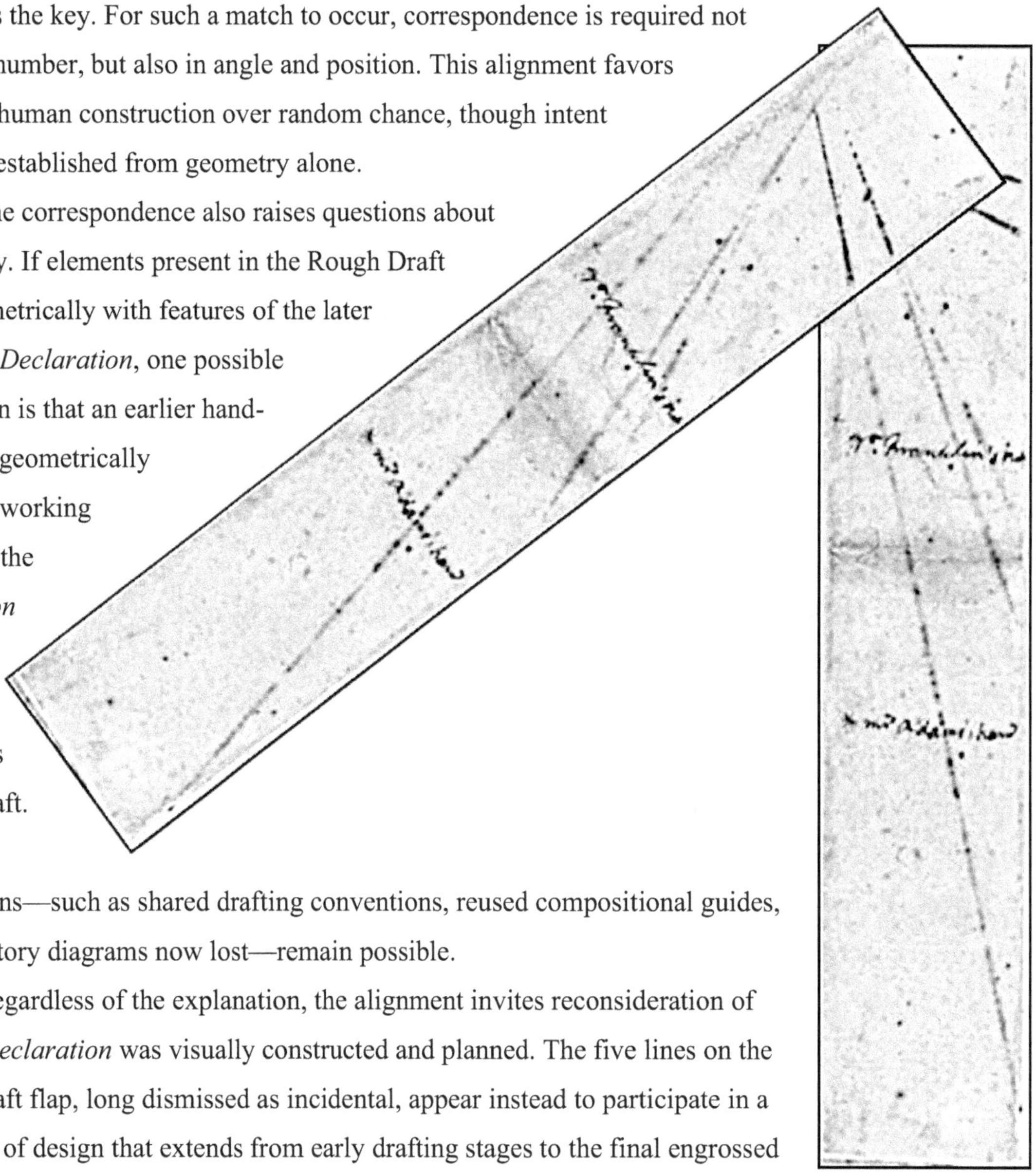

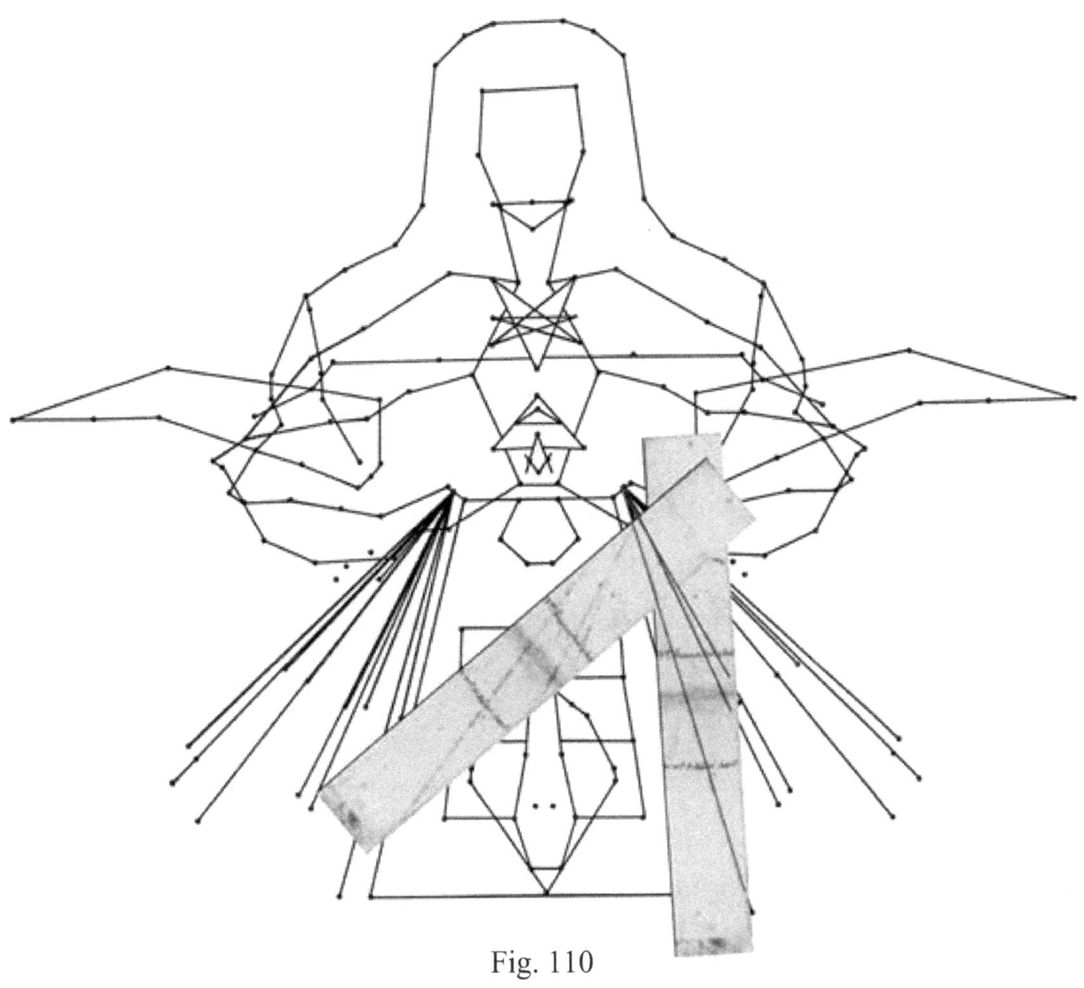

Fig. 110

Chapter Nine
BGP and *The Two Babylons*

The *Declaration of Independence* appears to encode a specific symbolic trinity through three distinct letter-derived images: a queen bee (representing Semiramis) derived from the letter B, a composite deity (Baal-Nimrod) from the letter G, and a butterfly pupa (Tammuz) derived from the letter P. These figures, Nimrod, his consort Semiramis, and their son Tammuz, form the central triadic configuration described in The Two Babylons, the 1853 work by Rev. Alexander Hislop.

It is important to note at the outset that modern scholars overwhelmingly reject The Two Babylons as pseudohistory. Critics argue that Hislop relied on speculative linguistic parallels and selective sourcing to support a pronounced anti-Catholic polemic. However, whatever its scholarly deficiencies, the book circulated widely in the nineteenth century and was absorbed into the broader symbolic discourse. Copies reside in several prominent Masonic libraries, including the Grand Lodge of Iowa and the Supreme Council, 33°, in London.

Hislop was clearly familiar with the symbolic language used by secret societies, noting that "the secret system of Freemasonry was originally founded on the Mysteries of the Egyptian Isis." While Hislop viewed these rituals with hostility, his work reveals an awareness of the same allegorical frameworks that Freemasonry acknowledged. Indeed, the figures of Nimrod, Baal, and Tammuz appear independently in recognized Masonic sources, such as James Anderson's *Constitutions of the Freemasons* (1723) and Albert Mackey's *Encyclopedia of Freemasonry*.

This symbolic pairing predates Hislop's specific narrative. Decades before Hislop published, Lord Byron's dramatic work *Sardanapalus* (1821) featured the same legendary framework of Ninus (Nimrod) and Semiramis. This suggests that the "BGP" triad was part of a pre-existing literary and mythological tradition already in circulation among the era's intelligentsia.

Within Freemasonry, these figures were treated as archetypes rather than literal ancestors. In *Morals and Dogma*, Albert Pike frames Nimrod as a symbol of early human authority and empire-building, while the "Great Mother" (Semiramis) represents the feminine divine principle. Tammuz, the dying-and-rising figure, symbolizes nature's cycles and regeneration. While Hislop sought to expose a pagan conspiracy, Pike treated these figures as a symbolic language conveying moral and metaphysical ideas.

In the context of the *Declaration*, the images formed from the letters B, G, and P combine to create a Mesopotamian leopard associated with Nimrod, while the inverted geometry evokes a "Light Bringer" figure. These constructions do not depend on Hislop's historical accuracy for their validity. Instead, they align with the Masonic principle that the Craft is "a system of morality, veiled in allegory and illustrated by symbols."

Whether or not the historical Nimrod ever existed, the symbolic architecture described by Hislop reflects mythic themes that appear woven into the *Declaration*'s very letters. From the perspective of the "Mystery Schools," where meaning is layered rather than linear, the convergence of these three figures into a single geometric lesson becomes intelligible, a hidden curriculum protected by the tradition of oral transmission.

Chapter Ten

Letter B

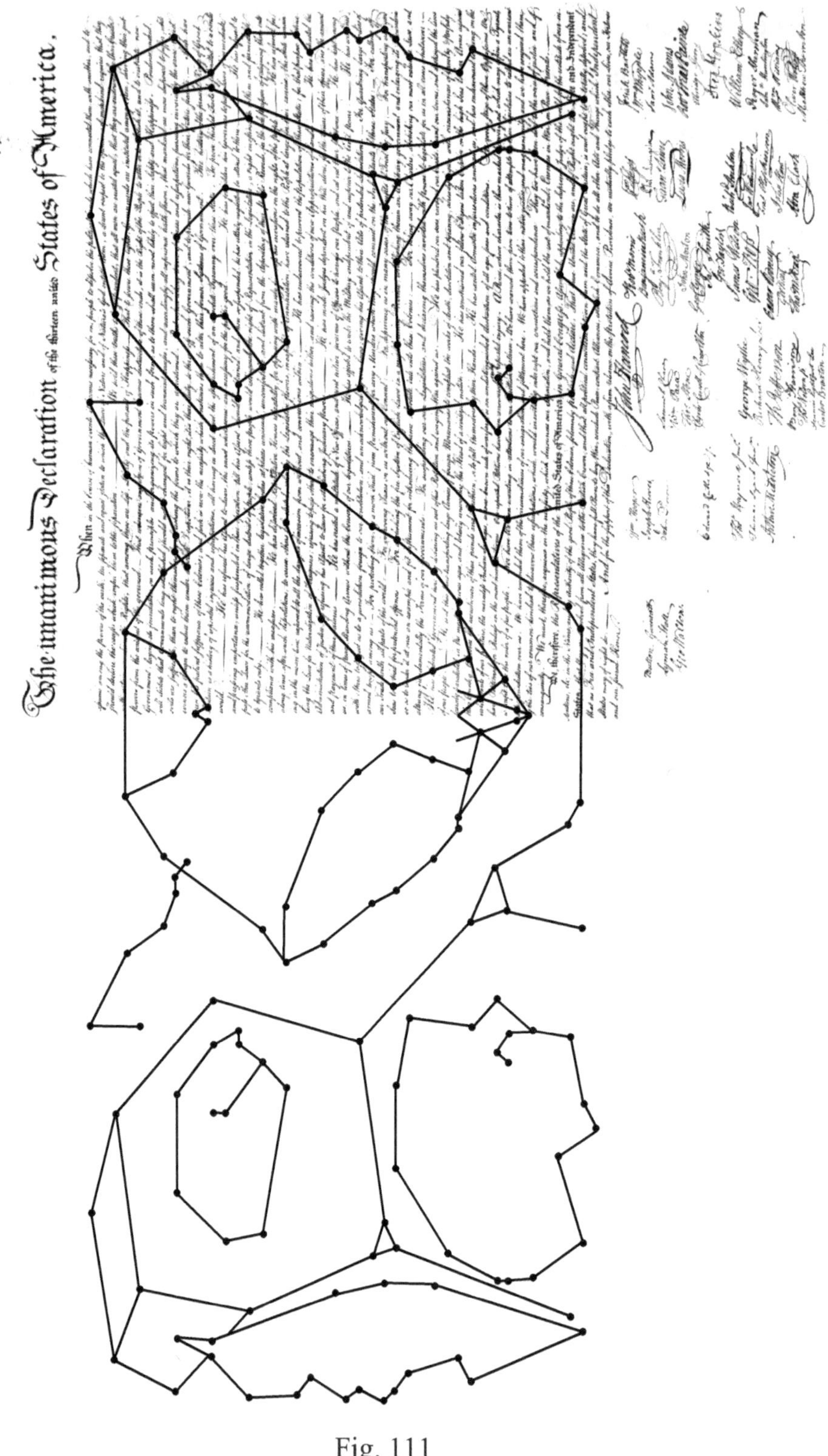

Fig. 111

Becomes
Unalienable/Libert
Becomes
Established/Be
Sufferable/Be/Abolishing
Absolute
Been
Britain
Bodies
Be/Whereby
By/Establishing
Subject
By
Be/Abolishing
Abdicated/By
Barbarous
Becomes
Inhabitant
Be
Able
By
Mirror Line

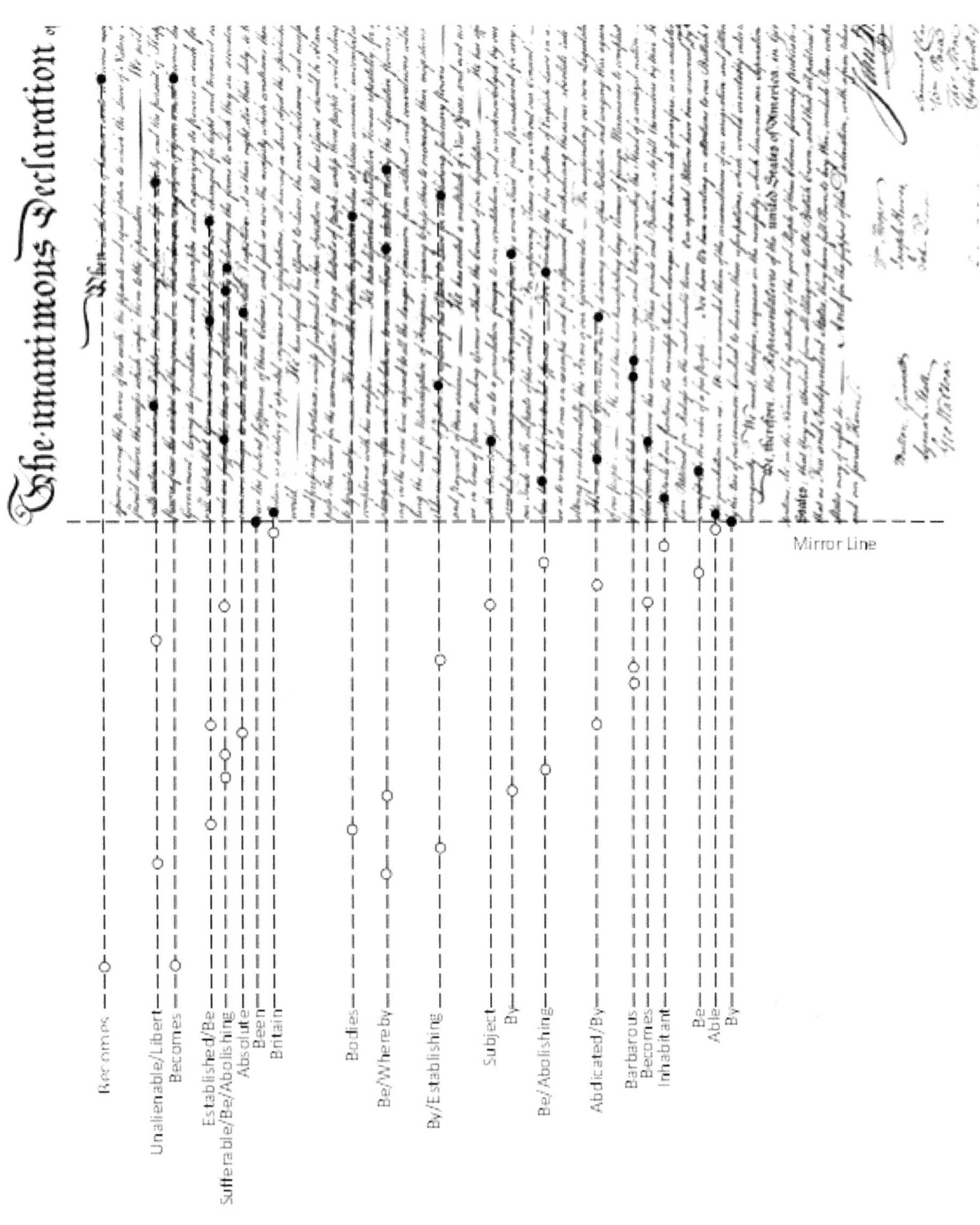

Fig. 112

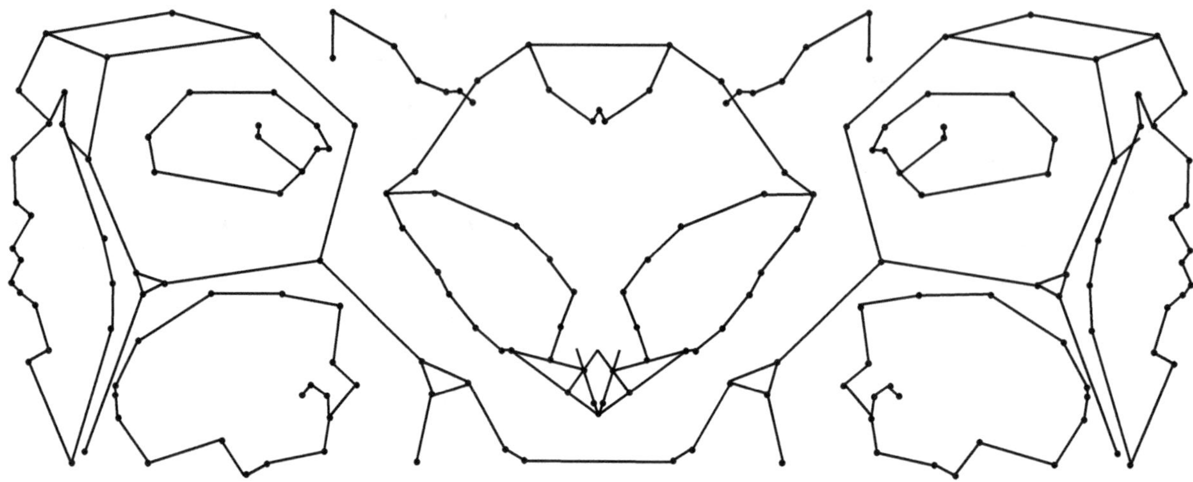

After completing the WVY images, I processed the remaining letters of the alphabet, looking for possible geometric anomalies. I soon recognized that the letters B, G, and P produced geometric patterns similar to those found in the W, V, and Y images. The letter M also generated geometry, but unlike WVY and BGP, its results were naturally multifaceted. The M images did not require layering and then rotation to create additional forms, whereas the WVY and BGP drawings required both techniques to reveal new perspectives.

I processed the B, G, and P geometries first, leaving the more complex M imagery for last. To begin, I ordered four full-size reproductions of the *Declaration* of Independence on faux parchment from the National Archives website, one for each letter in the BGP-M set.
When the reproductions arrived, I unrolled the first copy and placed it on a magnetic whiteboard. I applied sticky dots to every letter **B**, using the same methodology and mechanics established during the WVY drawings. After placing a large sheet of poster paper over the dotted *Declaration* and transferring the dots using a lightbox, I folded the page along the mirror line, mirrored the dots with a Sharpie, and connected them (Fig. 111).

All points used in this chapter are derived exclusively from occurrences of the letter B in the engrossed *Declaration* of Independence. No letters are added, omitted, substituted, or repositioned. Each B contributes two terminal points, original and mirrored, plotted exactly as they appear within the justified text block, at a fixed scale and orientation. The exception is a single point that lies on the mirror line. Lines are drawn only between corresponding terminal points, using a uniform connection rule applied throughout the chapter.

The resulting drawing revealed the image of a queen bee. The central panel of the triptych, formed by the mirrored B-points, depicts a stylized queen bee's head (Fig. 112). Its unusual shape stems from the irregular distribution of the B-point. It anticipates the shapes that later layer with the G and P drawings to form the Mesopotamian leopard and the Light Bringer. The two outer panels form symmetrical honeycomb cells containing larvae, and along the outer edge, an elongated queen cell has been torn open from the side.

The immediate connection between the letter **B** and the bee image was striking. After completing the poster drawing, I began researching the possible significance of the oversized bee head, honeycomb forms, and torn queen cell that emerged from the B-graphical plot.

Queen Bee

The queen bee head image is plotted from the letter Bs in words: unaliena**b**le, suffera**b**le, **b**een, **B**ritain, esta**b**lished, **b**y, a**b**solute, a**b**olishing, **b**e, li**b**erty, **b**ecomes, **b**ecomes, **b**odies, be, where**b**y, **b**y, su**b**ject, esta**b**lishing, **b**y, **b**e, a**b**dicated, a**b**olishing, **b**y, **b**ar**b**arous, inha**b**itants, **b**ecome, a**b**le, **b**e, and **b**y (Fig. 113). At first, the appearance of a queen bee emerging from these letters seemed like a peculiar coincidence. However, after mapping the figure of a monarch butterfly pupa from the letter P and then plotting the horned god Moloch-Baal-Nimrod from the letter G, a consistent first-letter pattern emerged.

Bee Symbolism

My bee research led first to Benjamin Franklin, a patron of beekeeping, and then to the symbolic beehive imagery frequently found on Freemason tracing boards. In Masonic symbolism, the beehive represents the lodge itself, with each brother fulfilling a specific role under the guidance of the Worshipful Master, just as all bees serve the queen (Cross, True Masonic Chart).

(Cross)

I next examined Rosicrucian symbolism, notably the Rosy Cross, which includes a rose with a bee hovering beside it. The Latin inscription *"DAT ROSA MEL APIBUS",* "The Rose Gives the Bees Honey", encodes duality, a theme underscored by the small spider and web often overlooked in the lower-left corner. The rose provides both honey and venom, symbolizing the interplay of light and dark, good and evil (Fludd).

(Fludd)

Queen Bee Goddess

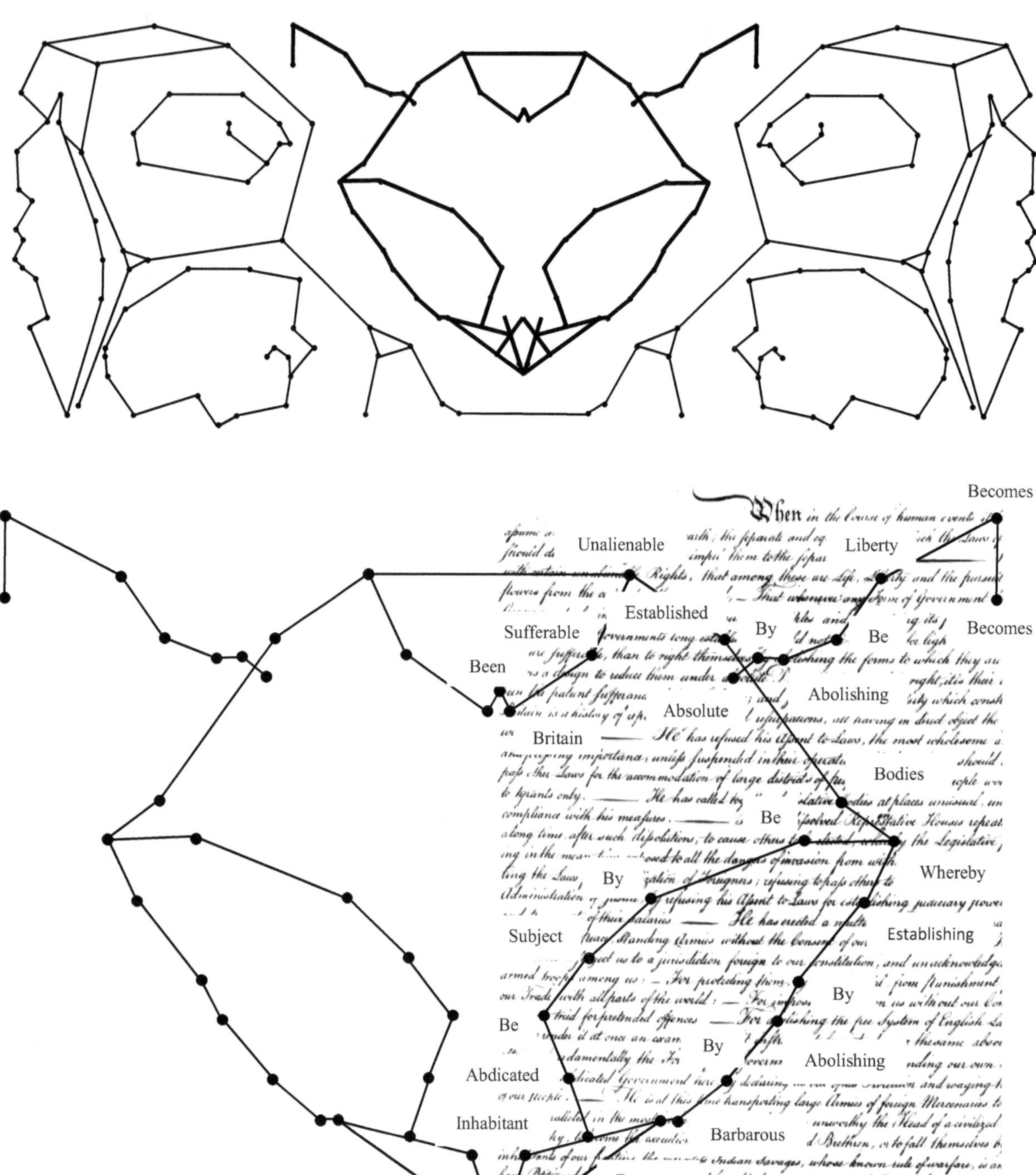

Fig. 113

The Mysterious Queen Bee Goddess

No single ancient culture presents a unified "queen bee goddess," yet bee symbolism permeates the traditions of ancient Greece, Egypt, and the Near East. Artemis of Ephesus incorporates bee motifs and is associated with fertility and stewardship of the natural world. Melissa, the nymph who nursed the infant Zeus, embodies nourishment and care. In Egypt, the goddess Neith, patroness of weaving, war, and creation, sometimes appears with bee symbolism, suggesting protection and strength (Ransome).

Immortality, Rebirth, and Divine Order

Across numerous cultures, bees symbolize immortality, resurrection, and the movement of the soul. Some believed bees guided the dead to the afterlife. Honey symbolized vitality, sweetness, and rebirth. "Melissa," meaning "bee" in Greek, was the title given to priestesses of Artemis, Demeter, Cybele, and even the Delphic oracle. Neoplatonists likewise used the bee as a symbol of purity and illumination. The beehive's structural perfection served as a metaphor for cosmic order and divine intelligence (Cook).

Fertility, Leadership, and Sacred Knowledge

The queen bee's role as the sole fertile female symbolizes abundance and the generative power of divinity. This motif parallels multi-breasted depictions of Artemis or Demeter, signifying fertility and nourishment. "Melissa," meaning "bee," also referred to the priestesses who served these goddesses, linking the queen bee with spiritual leadership.

In several traditions, bees carry lunar symbolism and are associated with the "Word of God" or divine revelation. Their presence across Greek, Egyptian, and Near Eastern traditions, often overlapping with veneration of the Babylonian goddess Ishtar, suggests the bee as a cross-cultural emblem of sacred knowledge and creation (Faber).

Babylonian Connections and Masonic Symbolism

The letter G produces a figure resembling the horned god Baal. Baal's associations with Moloch and the legendary figure Nimrod frame the queen bee as Semiramis. Once Nimrod and Semiramis appeared within the G and B images, their son Tammuz, represented by the monarch butterfly pupa, completed the mythological triad.

"Babylonian religion developed around traditions concerning Nimrod, his wife Semiramis, and her child Tammuz… When Nimrod died… his wife Semiramis claimed he was now the sun god… When she later gave birth to Tammuz, she declared him Nimrod reborn… As they went from Babylon, they took their worship of the mother and child, and the various mystery symbols with them" (Woodrow).

In Freemasonry, the beehive symbolizes a well-ordered lodge. Interestingly, an 1877 report from the Apollo University Lodge at Oxford describes the presiding officer as the lodge's "Queen Bee," who governed "with so much propriety and kindness." This record shows that the queen bee metaphor was consciously used within Masonic tradition (Sherwood, Gilbert, and Piper, Paternoster-Row).

Square and Compasses

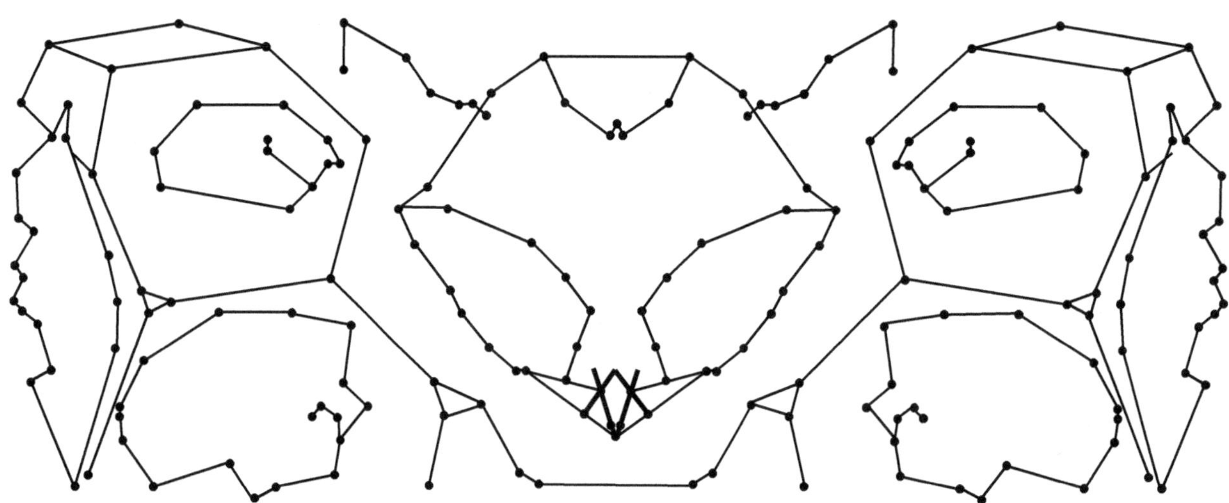

Seven-points are located at the mouth of the bee, arranged in an inverted Freemason square and compasses pattern. The letter B of inha**b**itants, a**b**le, **b**e, and **b**y straddle the centerline. Once the points are mirrored and connected, the form resolves into an inverted square and compasses. As with the lion's head in the W imagery, the presence of Masonic tools initiates rotation. A 180-degree rotation of the bee head triggers a new composite BGP figure, which layers with the pupa and god images to produce additional forms, including a Mesopotamian leopard wearing a miter associated with Nimrod and a hooded hermaphroditic figure identified as the Light Bringer.

This inverted bee–square-and-compasses configuration would likely have gone unnoticed without the earlier analytical framework established through the WVY imagery. At first glance, the arrangement reads simply as the mouth of the bee. However, when the compasses' arc is extended to the central mirror axis, the diamond-shaped geometry resolves clearly (Fig. 114). Throughout this study, geometric interpretations are subjected to a consistent critical standard: constructions are modified only when the underlying framework demonstrably supports the dual functionality of both square and compasses rather than forcing symbolic correspondence.

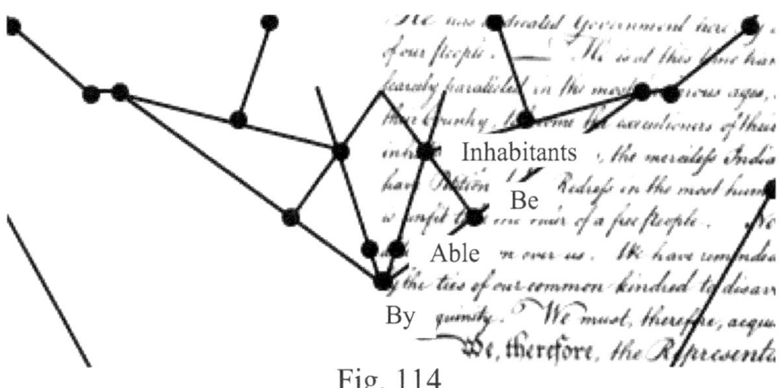

Fig. 114

The appearance of the inverted Masonic tools at the bee's mouth initiates a rotational transformation consistent with prior imagery. When the composite BGP image is rotated 180 degrees, an additional layered configuration emerges. From this transformation, two distinct figures resolve: one resembles a leopard wearing a Mesopotamian-style miter commonly associated in later mythographic traditions with Nimrod; the other takes the form of a hooded, androgynous figure associated in Western esoteric iconography with illumination, transformation, and the transmission of knowledge, often described metaphorically as a "light-bringing" archetype (Fig. 115).

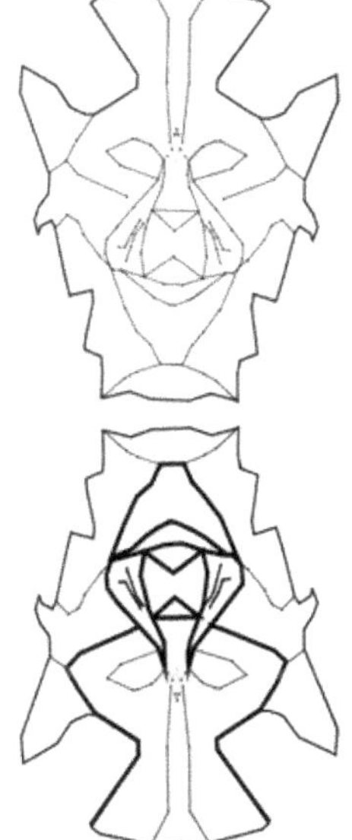
Fig. 115

The placement of the inverted square and compasses at the mouth of the bee invites symbolic interpretation beyond mere form. While the positioning of Masonic tools upon the lion's head in earlier imagery aligns readily with established iconographic conventions, their appearance at the mouth introduces an additional layer of meaning. Within Masonic tradition, the mouth is symbolically linked to secrecy and restraint, reflecting the fraternity's reliance on oral transmission and the safeguarding of initiatory knowledge. In this context, the square and compasses at the mouth may be read as reinforcing the symbolic discipline of silence.

Close-Mouthed

The Mason depicted in the subsequent illustration (Fig. 116), with his hand covering his mouth, serves as a traditional emblem of silence and discretion. As Manly P. Hall and later commentators observed, gestures involving the mouth, eyes, and heart recur throughout Masonic ritual symbolism, forming a complex visual language oriented toward concealment, revelation, and initiation (Buck). The Three Greater Lights, the sacred text, the Square, and the Compasses, and the Three Lesser Lights, the Sun, Moon, and Master of the Lodge, operate together within this symbolic economy to emphasize measured illumination rather than unrestrained disclosure.

(Allyn)

Fig. 116

The association between secrecy and the mouth is linguistically embedded in the term mystical itself. Derived from the Greek mustikos, rooted in mustes, the word literally denotes one who is "close-mouthed," signifying initiation through silence rather than speech (Falconer). Historical descriptions of Masonic signs further reinforce this theme. Early ritual manuals describe gestures involving the hand placed successively upon the heart, mouth, and eyes, accompanied by invocations of secrecy, silence, and darkness, symbolic markers of restraint and guarded knowledge rather than literal concealment (Allyn).

Within this symbolic framework, the placement of the square and compasses at the mouth of the bee may be understood not as evidence of a concealed political conspiracy, but as a visual expression of the longstanding initiatory principle that knowledge is transmitted selectively and progressively. Whether intentional or emergent, the imagery aligns closely with Masonic pedagogical themes centered on discretion, obligation, and the moral governance of speech.

The Masonic obligation, sometimes historically referred to as the "Oath of Nimrod" in later speculative literature, serves as a formalized commitment to secrecy within the lodge. While the dramatic penalties described in early ritual texts reflect symbolic severity rather than literal enforcement, they underscore the cultural importance placed upon silence and fidelity to the fraternity's internal teachings (Churchward).

Honey Bee Cell with Larva

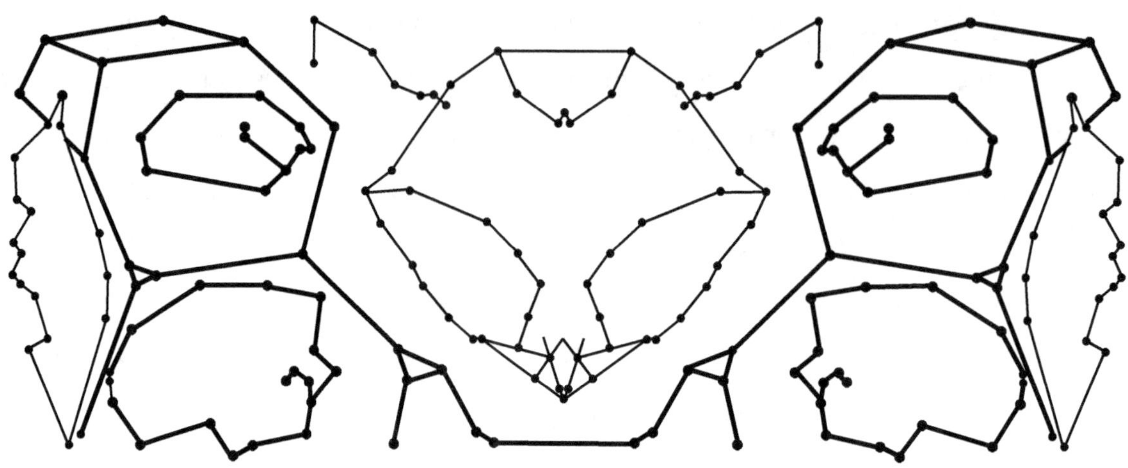

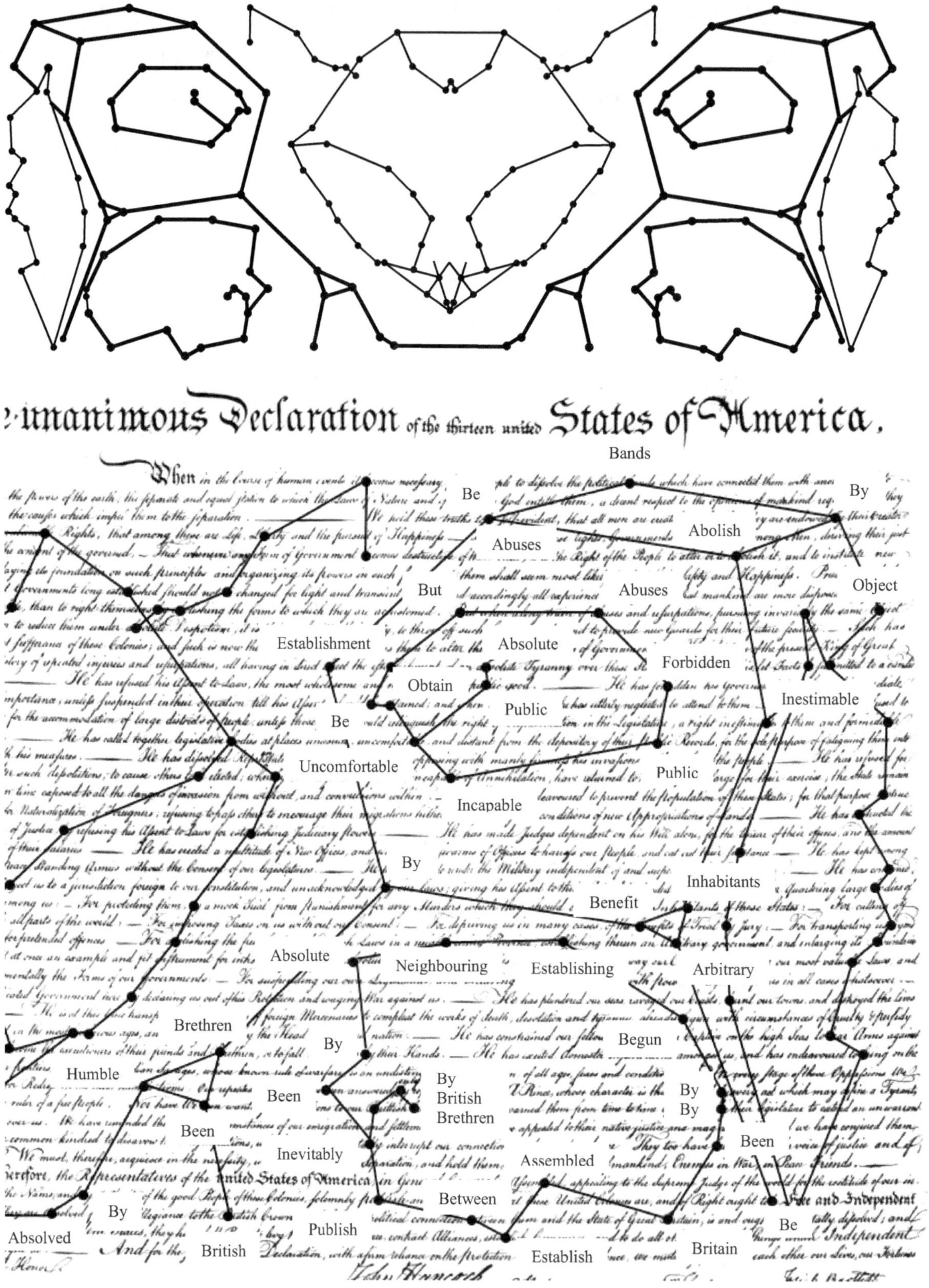

unanimous Declaration of the thirteen united States of America.

Bands
Be
By
Abolish
Abuses
But
Abuses
Object
Establishment
Absolute
Forbidden
Obtain
Inestimable
Public
Be
Uncomfortable
Public
Incapable
By
Inhabitants
Benefit
Absolute
Neighbouring
Establishing
Arbitrary
Brethren
By
Begun
Humble
By
British
Brethren
By
By
Been
Been
Been
Inevitably
Assembled
Between
By
Be
Publish
Absolved
British
Establish
Britain

Fig. 117

The honeybee cell containing a larva is plotted exclusively from occurrences of the letter B in the words: O**b**ject, **b**e, **b**ands, **b**y, a**b**olish, O**b**ject, invaria**b**ly, **b**ut, a**b**uses, esta**b**lishment, a**b**solute, pu**b**lic, for**b**idden, **b**e, o**b**tain, uncomforta**b**le, incapa**b**le, pu**b**lic, **b**e, su**b**mitted, inestima**b**le, formida**b**le, su**b**stance, o**b**structing, o**b**structed, com**b**ined, bo**d**ies, **b**eyond, **b**oundaries, valua**b**le, **b**y, Inha**b**itants, **b**enefit, Ar**b**itrary, esta**b**lishing, neigh**b**ouring, **b**y, a**b**solute, **b**y, **b**urnt, **b**egun, **b**ear, inha**b**itants, **b**y, **b**y, **b**een, **b**e, **b**e, **B**ritain, Assem**b**led, esta**b**lish, **b**etween, pu**b**lish, **B**ritish, inevita**b**ly, **b**een, **b**y, **B**ritish, **b**rethren, **b**rethren, hum**b**le, **b**een, **b**y, and a**b**solved (Fig. 117).

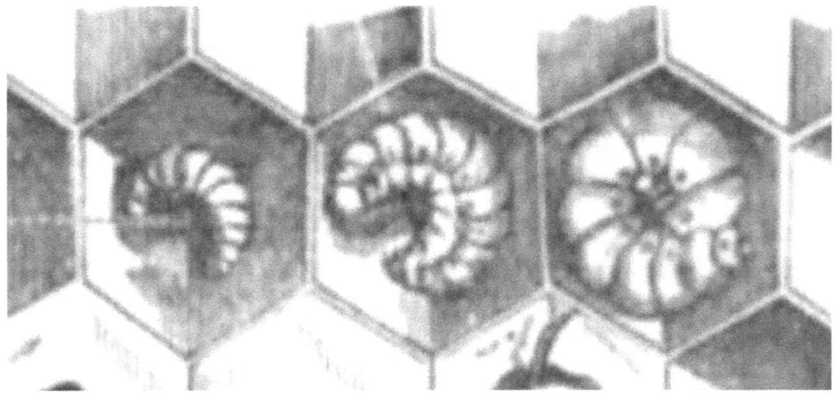

(Harris)

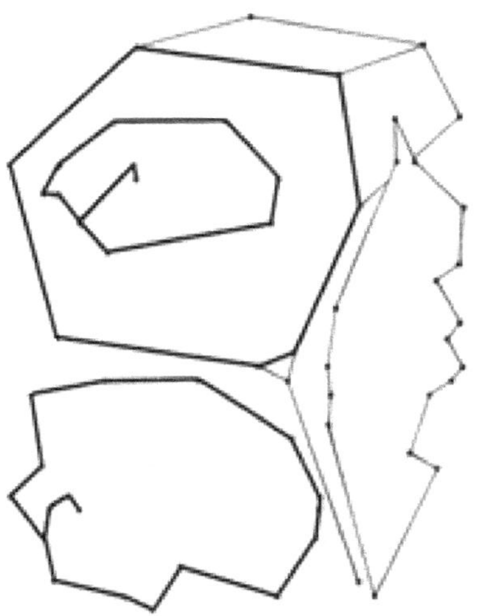

The resulting drawing exhibits an unexpected degree of biological correspondence. Within one cell, a small irregular circle intersects a curved line in a manner closely resembling the terminal ends of an actual larva (Harris). Two adjacent cells converge at a triangular junction, a configuration that occurs naturally in honeycomb structures and reflects precise spatial economy. The emergence of such features, abstracted, miniaturized, and encoded within a line drawing derived solely from plotted letters in the *Declaration of Independence*, is notable. While the geometry arises through a strictly rule-bound process, the outcome nonetheless suggests a level of structural coherence that exceeds what one would ordinarily expect from incidental ornamentation.

Equally striking is the manner in which multiple cells integrate seamlessly within the broader composition. These forms appear while seven distinct images, each derived from different letters, are required to align within a shared geometric framework. That such consistency of proportion and junction appears embedded beneath a document celebrated primarily for its rhetorical achievement continues to challenge conventional assumptions about its purely textual construction.

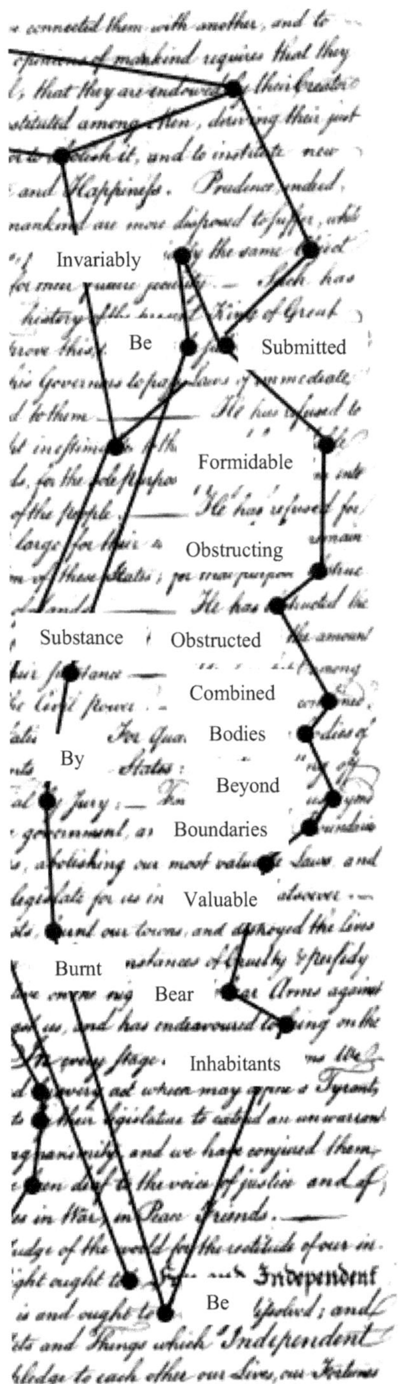

Fig. 118

The Honey Bee Royal Cell

The royal cell is plotted from the letter B in the words invaria**b**ly, **b**e, su**b**mitted, formida**b**le, su**b**stance, o**b**structing, o**b**structed, com**b**ined, bo**d**ies, **b**eyond, **b**oundaries, valua**b**le, **b**y, **b**urnt, **b**ear, inha**b**itants, and **b**e (Fig. 118). In natural beekeeping, a royal queen cell is an elongated structure distinct from the standard hexagonal worker cells. It is within this chamber that a potential queen develops. Under typical conditions, the emerging queen cuts a small, circular opening at the bottom of the cell. If, however, the colony rejects the developing queen, worker bees tear open the side of the cell, killing her before emergence.

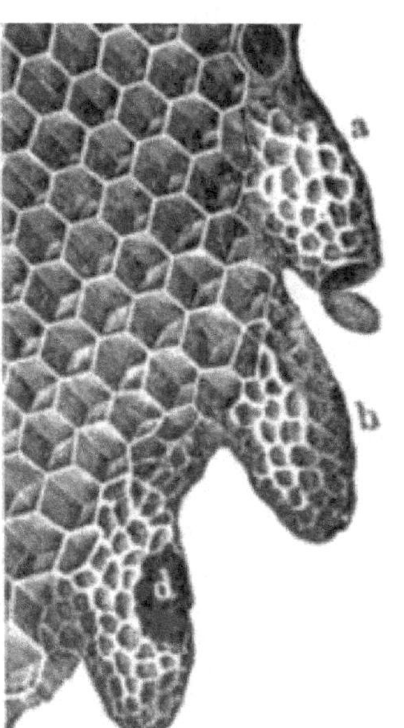

(Lorenzo Langstroth).

In the referenced illustration, three royal-cell conditions are shown: one with a natural bottom opening, one intact and unopened, and one torn open laterally—indicating rejection by the hive. The plotted drawing closely corresponds to the latter form, presenting an elongated cell opened from the side rather than the base.

Within the symbolic framework developed in this chapter, the central bee figure bears strong thematic resonance with later mythographic portrayals of Semiramis, the legendary queen associated in post-classical traditions with authority, fertility, jealousy, and sovereign power. While the image does not assert a literal historical identification, the torn royal cell visually parallels narratives commonly attached to Semiramis in later literary and allegorical sources, particularly those emphasizing rivalry, consolidation of power, and the violent exclusion of challengers.

Contemporary apicultural observations reinforce this symbolic reading. As early writers noted, a reigning queen bee exhibits an instinctive hostility toward potential rivals. When multiple royal cells are present, it is common for only one queen to survive, while others are destroyed before emergence (Bagster). Within an allegorical register, this behavior has long served as a metaphor for absolute sovereignty and the inherent instability it produces.

The Semiramis legend itself evolved over centuries, shaped by Mesopotamian myth, Greek historiography, and later moralized interpretations. Its endurance reflects recurring human preoccupations with authority, legitimacy, maternal symbolism, jealousy, and the fragility of rule. Within this context, the torn royal cell may be read as symbolizing contested sovereignty, authority maintained through exclusion and violence, and perpetually vulnerable to internal rupture. Later traditions even portray Semiramis as ultimately overthrown by her own son, underscoring the cyclical nature of power and succession (Lorenzo Langstroth).

The juxtaposition of two intact worker cells with a torn royal cell introduces a further layer of meaning. In nature, the destruction of a queen cell signals rejection, failed succession, or internal conflict within the hive. Allegorically, the image opens multiple interpretive possibilities: interrupted authority, denied succession, internal fracture, or the violent transition of power. When viewed alongside the broader thematic material of this chapter, the torn cell resonates with narratives of rebellion, rupture, and transformation.

At a political-symbolic level, this imagery invites comparison, without requiring assertion, between the rejection of monarchical authority within the hive and the colonies' historical rupture from British sovereignty. The tearing of the royal cell echoes themes of separation, contested legitimacy, and internal struggle that accompanied the American Revolution.

Chapter Eleven

The Letter G

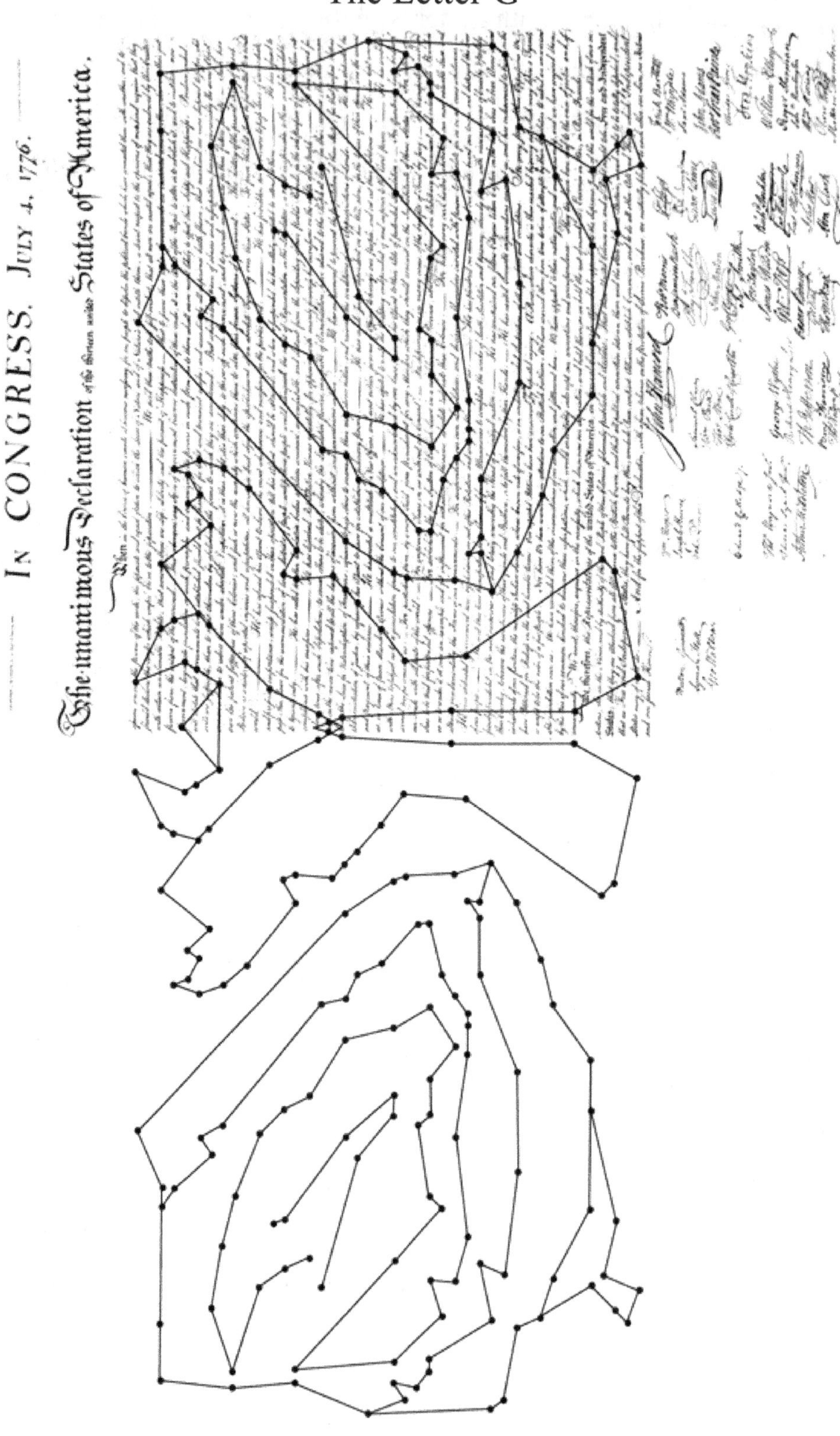

Fig. 119

Mirror Line
Among
Rights/Among
Governed/Government
Government/Layering/Organizing
Governments/Long/Changed/Light
Right/Abolishing
Design/Right
Having
Pressing
Large
Together/Legislative
along
ing/Dangers
ting/Foreigners
Refusing
Standing
Among
Altering
Government
Consanguinity
Good
Allegiance
Right

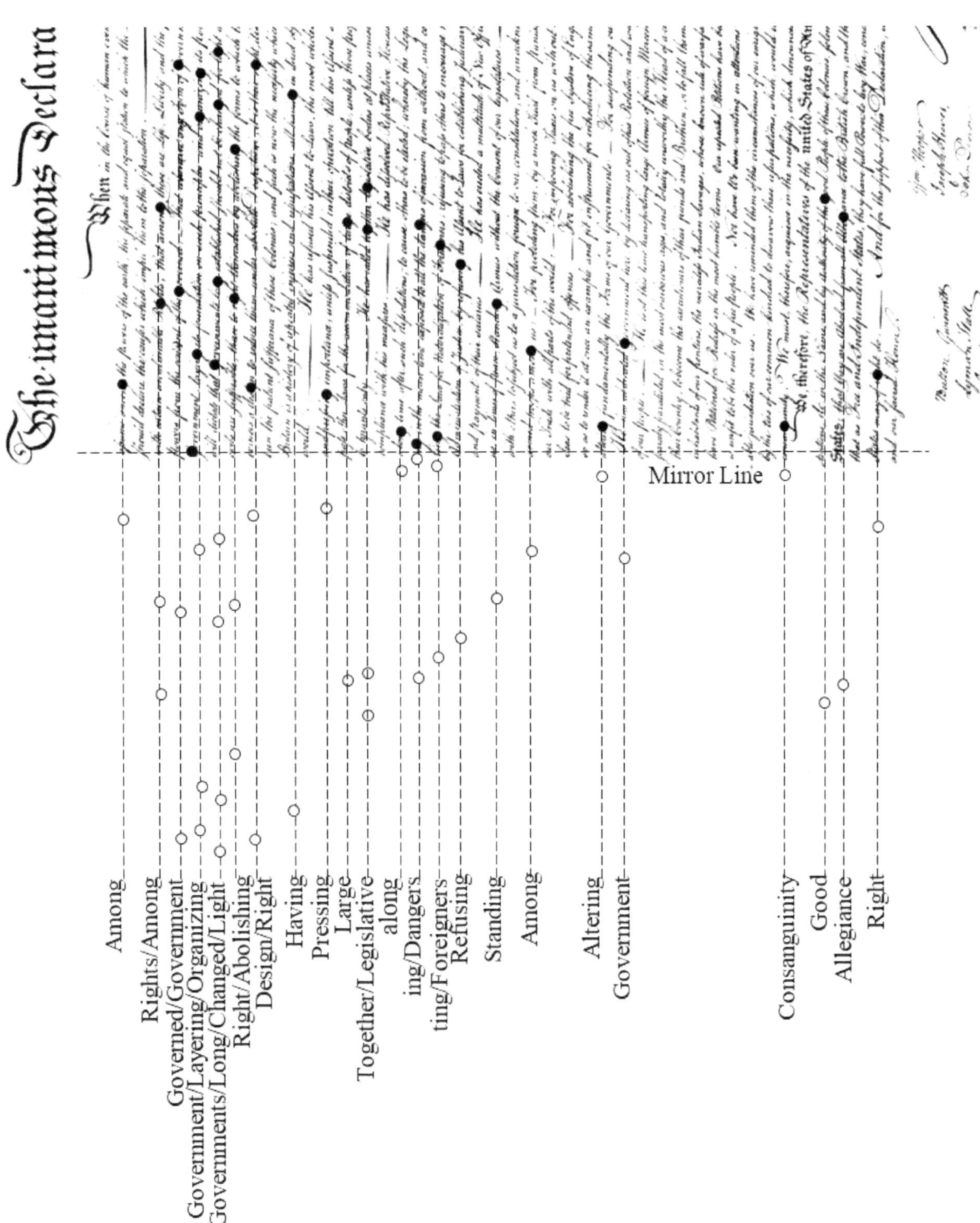

Fig. 120

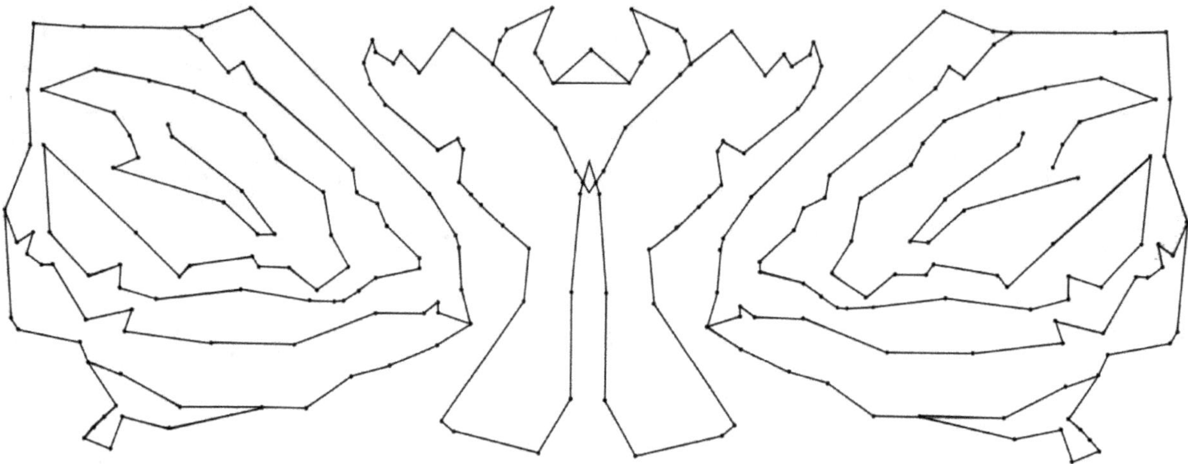

The mirrored G geometry produces a figure that resembles traditional depictions of the Near Eastern deity Baal-Moloch. (Fig. 119). However, we will argue that the deity referenced in the *Declaration of Independence* by the letter G resembles Baal-Moloch, represented explicitly by the likeness of Baal-Moloch. The term Moloch, found in the Hebrew Bible, refers to a Canaanite god associated with child sacrifice by fire. Scholarly debate exists regarding its nature: some refer to Moloch as a distinct god, while others contend the term refers only to the act of child sacrifice performed for the god Baal, who is also associated with the biblical figure Nimrod.

Fig. 121 (Lund)

All points used in this chapter are derived exclusively from occurrences of the letter G in the engrossed *Declaration* of Independence. No letters are added, omitted, substituted, or repositioned. Each G contributes two terminal points, original and mirrored, plotted exactly as they appear within the justified text block, at a fixed scale and orientation. The exception is a single point that lies on the mirror line. Lines are drawn only between corresponding terminal points, using a uniform connection rule applied throughout the chapter. The Mirror plotted G image, a likeness of the god Baal-Moloch, is derived from the placement of every letter 'G' in the *Declaration of Independence* (Fig. 120). This deity is traditionally depicted as a bull, often holding a child or featuring chambers in its midsection where children were placed for sacrifice (Fig. 121) (Lund). Moloch-Baal-Nimrod married the queen bee, Semiramis, and had a son named Tammuz. The image of Moloch in the *Declaration* is derived from amon**g**, **g**overnment, layin**g**, desi**g**n, ri**g**hts, **g**overnments, ri**g**ht, lon**g**, **g**overned, amon**g**, dan**g**ers, abolishin**g**, pressin**g**, lon**g**, remainin**g**, obstructin**g**, alterin**g**, consan**g**uinity, right,

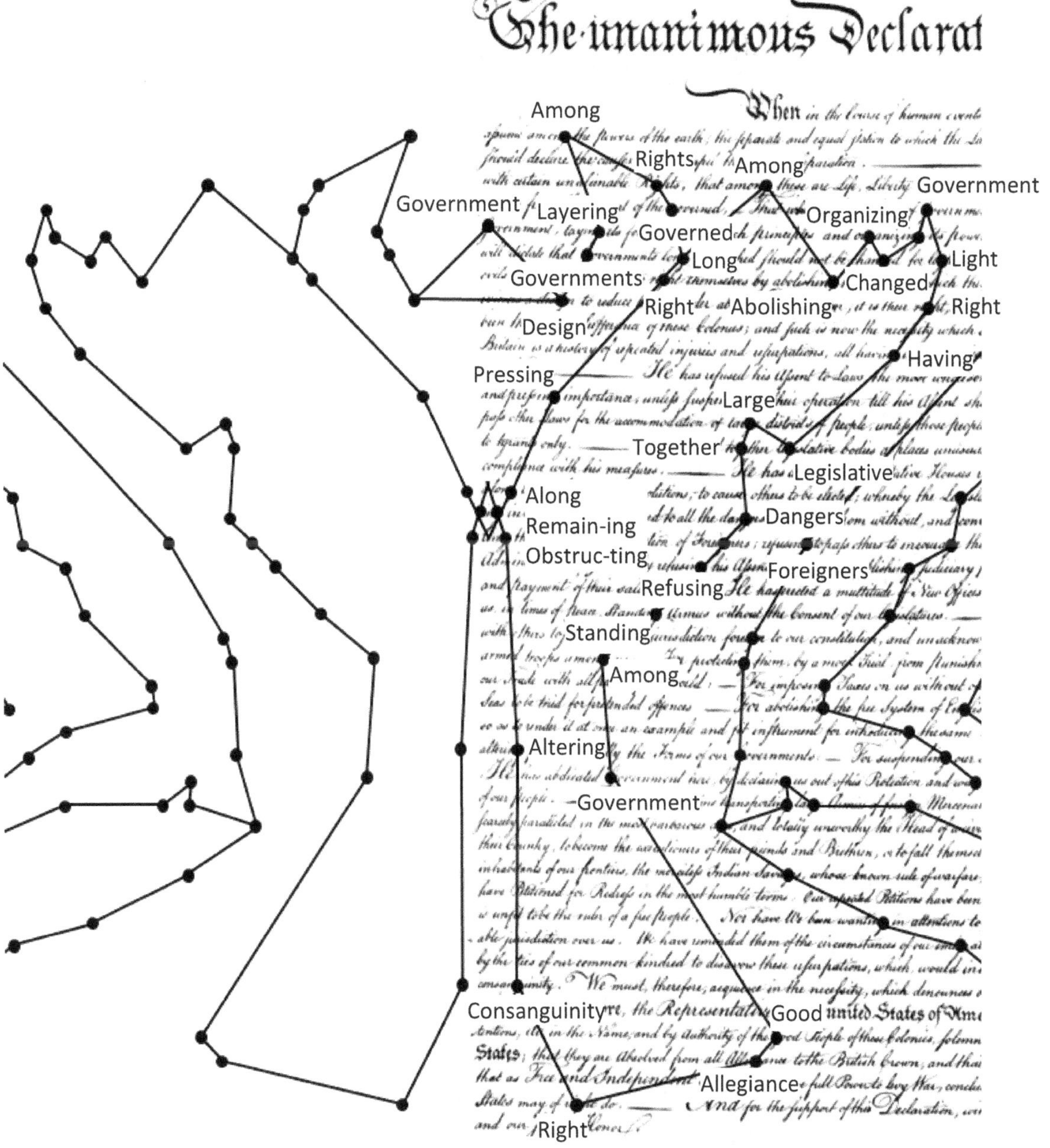

Fig. 122

Alle**g**iance, **g**ood, **g**overnment, amon**g**, standin**g**, refusin**g**, Forei**g**ners, or**g**anizin**g**, **g**overnment, chan**g**ed, li**g**ht, ri**g**ht, havin**g**, lar**g**e, to**g**ether, and le**g**islative (Fig. 122).

Within the *Declaration's* plotted image, note the word 'or**g**anizin**g**' in Moloch's upper right-hand area. Each G is intricately incorporated into the detail, specifically representing rigid fingers.

The triangle on the head of the G-Moloch figure could signify a false godhead, the unholy triad of Nimrod, Semiramis, and Tammuz. This earthly mythological triad represents a hermetic duality, in which darkness mirrors the light of the Father, Son, and Holy Ghost, a theme also depicted in the WVY imagery. "Nimrod became the Canaanite god Molech, the god of fire. Canaanite parents often sacrificed their firstborn to this God by placing the child in the outstretched hands of a large statue of Molech while a blazing fire raged beneath. Infants were considered the most acceptable offerings at the altars of Molech and Baal. This horrible form of idol worship incited God's judgment upon the Canaanite people" (Merrill).

The mouth of Moloch is adorned with a square and compasses, just like the mouth of the queen bee's head is. In Freemasonry, the square and compasses, which cover the mouths of Semiramis and Moloch, signify secrets.

The vertex of the compasses is formed by extending a line from two existing points, just as the vertex was expanded in the B imagery. Crucially, the orientation of the letter G in the square and compasses drawing aligns with the correct reading position of the *Declaration's* text. Thus, when the three BGP drawings (Baal, Queen Bee, and God) are synthesized, Moloch's letter G maintains its displayed position. However, the letter B drawing, representing the Queen Bee, will be rotated 180 degrees toward the Worshipful Master due to the inverted square and compasses positioned at her mouth.

"ing" and "ting"

When using letterpress type (movable type), the purpose of a spacer (Dash) is to align the edge of text at the margins, create openings for images within the body of text, and prevent a word from being unnecessarily hyphenated into two parts, in the case of the *Declaration*, of the three hyphenated words, two are "remaining" and "obstructing." The word "remaining" is separated, reamain--ing, and "obstructing" is separated at obstruc--ting. The hyphenation was generally intended to break the word as close to a pronounceable syllable as possible. The division of a word is emphasized on readability and natural breaks in speech. The syllables of "obstructing": Ob-struct-ing is natural, whereas breaking it as "Obstruc-ting" disrupts the natural "struct" syllable, which is considered less desirable. Separating it as "Obstruct-ing" keeps the more recognizable and pronounceable syllable "struct" intact before the hyphen. The idea of dividing a word due to margin limitations would be understandable if the scrivener of the *Declaration* hadn't incorporated so many dashes, which could have been used to jog the sentences into alignment at the margin. While there might have been some slight variations depending on personal preference, the general tendency would have favored the syllabic division, leading to Obstruct-ing. In addition, the "ing" and "ting" suffixes incorporate the letter G for the god imagery in the complex square-and-compass image. The author's use of the three letters (ing) and the four letters of (ting) at the left margin creates a downward slant connecting the two G's, and, when paired with the word (along) and mirrored on the centerline of the image,

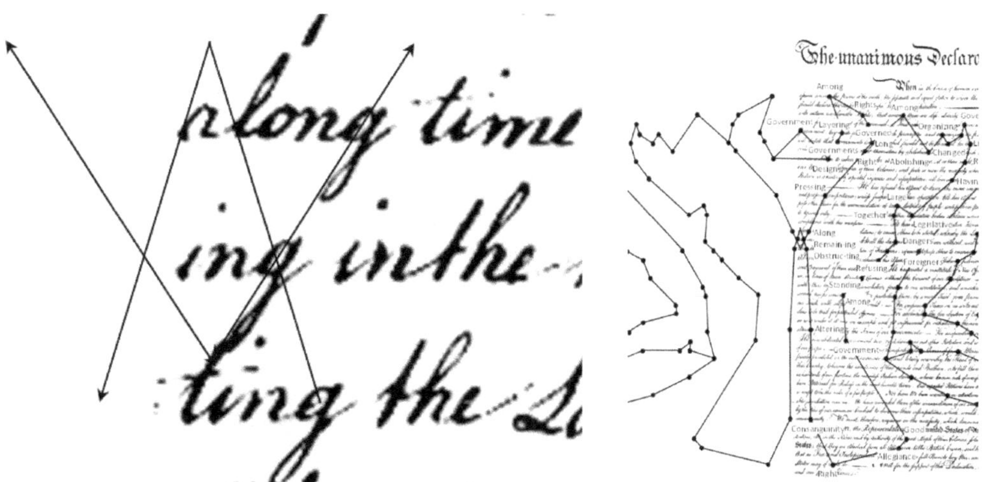

becomes the Freemason square and compasses. The along-ing-ting, square, and compasses are located at the mouth of the figure plotted using the letter G.

Rose

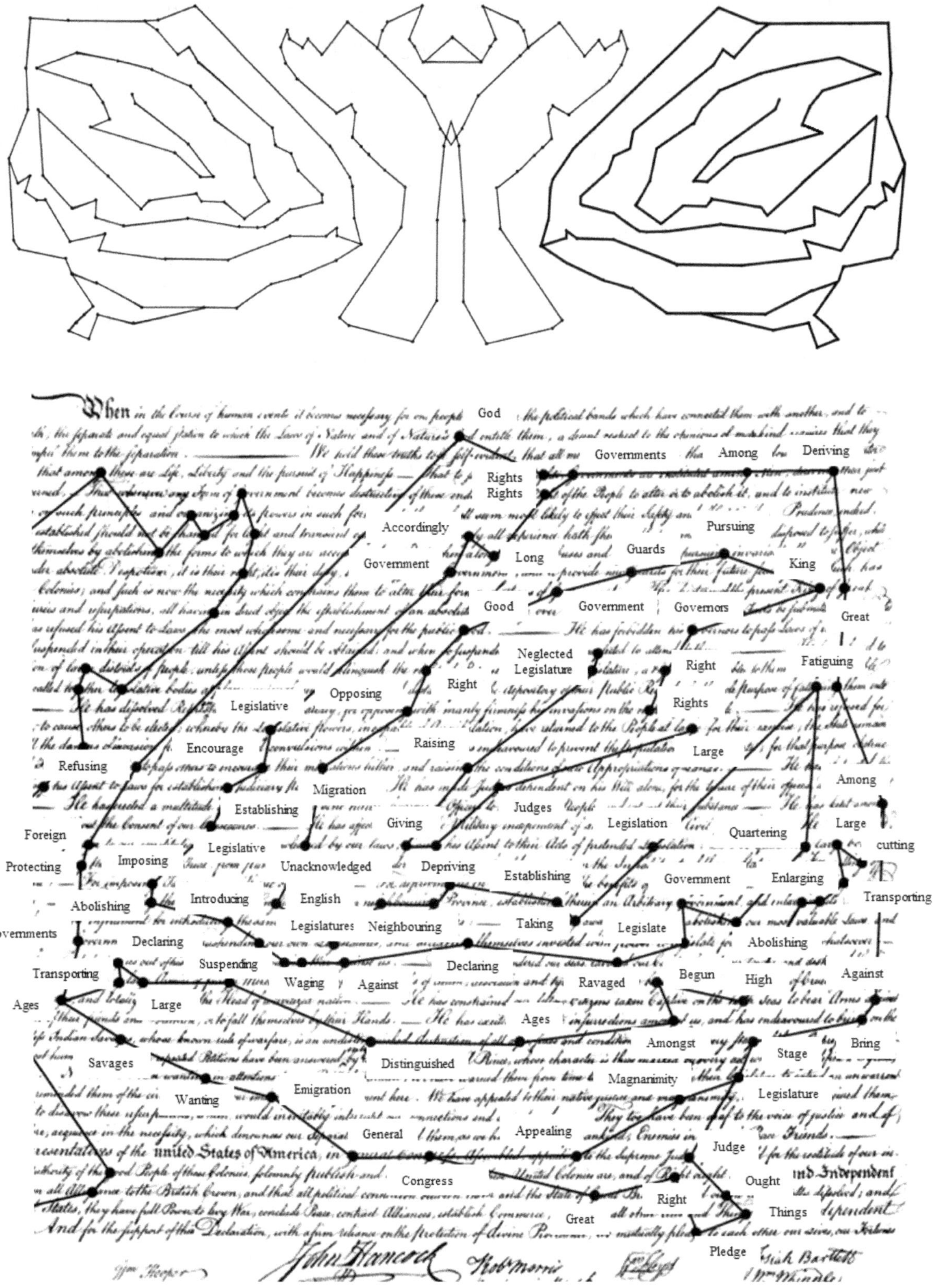

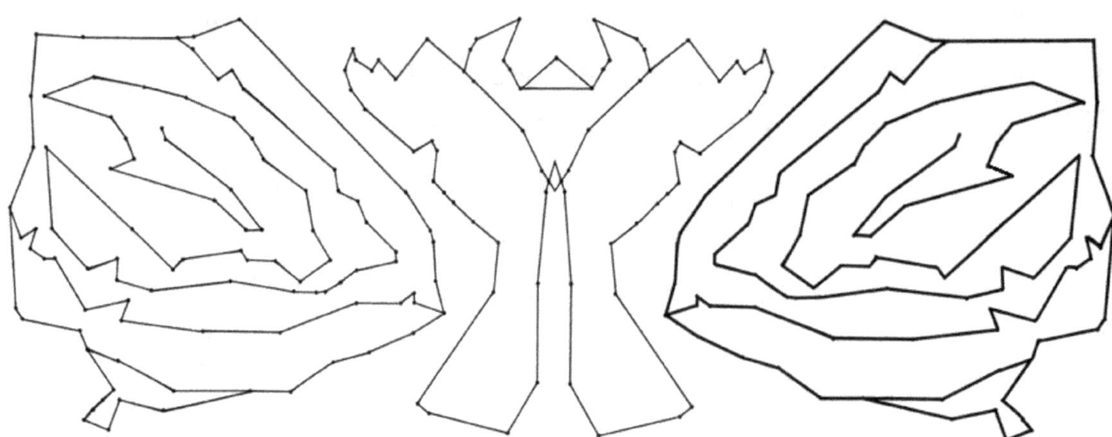

God
Governments Among Deriving
Rights
Rights
Accordingly Pursuing
Long Guards
Government King
Good Government Governors
Great
Neglected
Legislature Right Fatiguing
Opposing Right
Legislative Rights
Raising
Encourage Large
Refusing
Among
Migration
Establishing Judges
Giving Legislation Large
Foreign Quartering
Legislative cutting
Protecting Imposing Unacknowledged Depriving
Establishing Government Enlarging
Abolishing Introducing English Transporting
Legislatures Neighbouring Taking Legislate
Governments Declaring Abolishing
Suspending Declaring
Transporting Waging Against Ravaged Begun High Against
Ages Large
Ages
Amongst Bring
Savages Distinguished Stage
Magnanimity
Emigration Legislature
Wanting
General Appealing
Judge
Congress Ought
Right
Great Things
Pledge

Fig. 123

The rose signifies a god or deity. Similar to the lion letter W image, which features a rose, the Isis letter Y includes a lily; both flowers represent Osiris and Isis as deities. The *Declaration's* consistent identification of a deity with a rose or lily is notable.

The Moloch rose letter G image is plotted from the words savages, ages, wanting, governments, emigration, general, congress, appealing, great, right, pledge, ought, things, ought, judge, magnanimity, legislature, declaring, waging, transporting, large, foreign, undistinguished, ages, amongst, against, begun, declaring, high, stage, bring, against, ravaged, suspending, introducing, abolishing, imposing, English, legislatures, neighbouring, protecting, depriving, establishing, taking, legislate, government, abolishing, foreign, legislatures, unacknowledged, giving, legislation, quartering, large, enlarging, transporting, cutting, among, Judges, raising, encourage, establishing, migrations, legislative, opposing, right, large, rights, right, Legislature, neglected, good, governors, fatiguing, king, great, government, government, accordingly, long, guards, god, rights, rights, governments, among, pursuing, and deriving (Fig 123).

The widespread belief connecting Nimrod, Baal, and Semiramis, often credited solely to Alexander Hislop's 1853 work *The Two Babylons*, actually predates his publication. While Hislop certainly popularized this specific association, he was not its originator. Instead, he skillfully synthesized existing, often speculative, interpretations of ancient history and biblical accounts that had already circulated in various intellectual and theological circles. This is not a new concept introduced by Hislop; it was a theme already woven into the fabric of contemporary thought. Consider Lord Byron's *Sardanapalus*, published in 1821, nearly four decades before Hislop's book. Byron explicitly connects "Baal Nimrod and Semiramis Sole in Assyria," demonstrating a pre-existing cultural familiarity with their purported association. This indicates that the intellectual groundwork for Hislop's thesis was already in place. Hislop's genius lay in assembling and presenting these connections in a compelling framework, solidifying their place in popular consciousness. Recognizing this earlier circulation of ideas is crucial for a nuanced understanding of their true origins, positioning Hislop as a popularizer, not the sole inventor, of this enduring mythological link (Byron).

Nimrod-Baal-Moloch-Semiramis

In the ancient Near East, religious systems often explained natural forces and political authority by elevating human rulers into divine figures. By the early modern period, European scholars were already examining and organizing these pagan traditions. One such example is Richard Brocklesby's 1706 treatise on Christian religion, *An Explication of the Gospel-Theism and the Divinity of the Christian Religion. Containing the True Account of the System of the Universe, and of the Christian Trinity*, written decades before the American Revolution and long before the later work of Alexander Hislop. Brocklesby describes a unified pagan system extending across Assyria, Phoenicia, and Chaldea. In this system, the dominant male deity was Baal. Baal was understood simultaneously as the sun, the planet Jupiter, and elemental fire. In its harshest form, this fiery aspect appeared as Moloch. These were not treated as separate gods, but as related expressions of a single ruling principle.

Crucially, Brocklesby and earlier classical writers also identified Baal as a deified human ruler. This "hero-god" was associated with Mars and ultimately with Nimrod, described in biblical and historical sources as a powerful king and empire builder. After deification, Nimrod was identified as Jupiter Belus, combining royal ancestry with divine authority. This interpretation appears consistently in pre-eighteenth-century scholarship and was not a later invention.

The system was completed by a female counterpart. Brocklesby identifies this figure with Venus among the Greeks and Astarte among the Phoenicians. Like Baal, she was believed to have originated from a historical ruler later deified, Semiramis. Early sources describe Semiramis as a queen associated with the dove, a long-standing symbol of fertility and generation. Over time, her mythology absorbed creation imagery, and she assumed titles equivalent to Juno, the consort of Jupiter.

By the early eighteenth century, scholars were already describing a paired system:

•Nimrod as the deified king, identified with Baal, Moloch, and Jupiter Belus

•Semiramis, as the deified queen, identified with Astarte, Venus, and Juno

together, formed a husband-and-wife model that unified kingship, celestial symbolism, fire, and fertility. Brocklesby treated this structure as ancient and coherent, not as a later corruption.

The importance of Brocklesby's work lies in its date. Written in 1706, it shows that the associations between Baal, Moloch, and Nimrod, and the pairing of Nimrod and Semiramis, were already established in European scholarship well before 1776 and long before nineteenth-century reinterpretations. These ideas were inherited, not invented, and formed part of the intellectual background of the modern era (Brocklesby).

Chapter Twelve

The Letter P

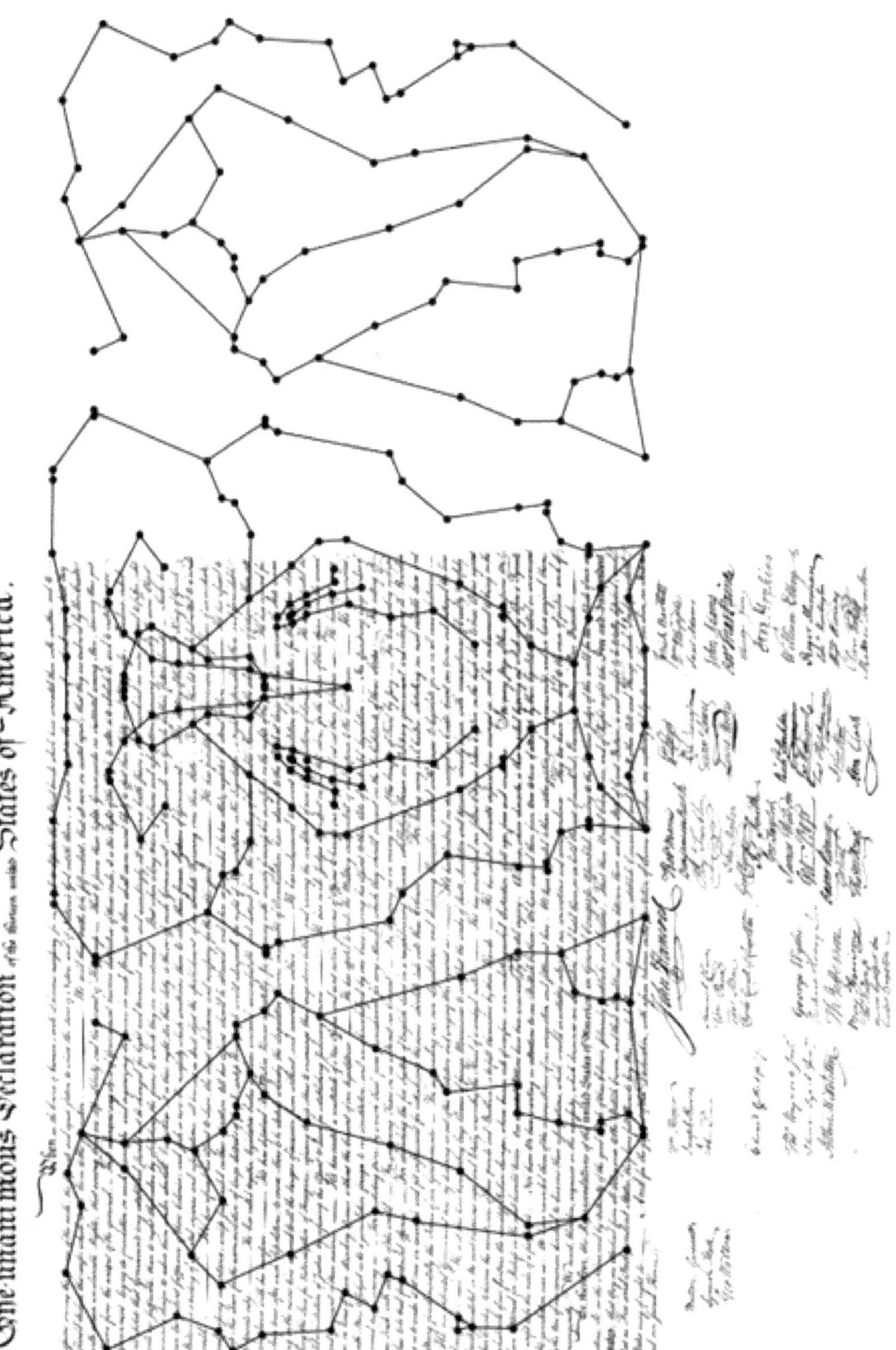

Fig. 124

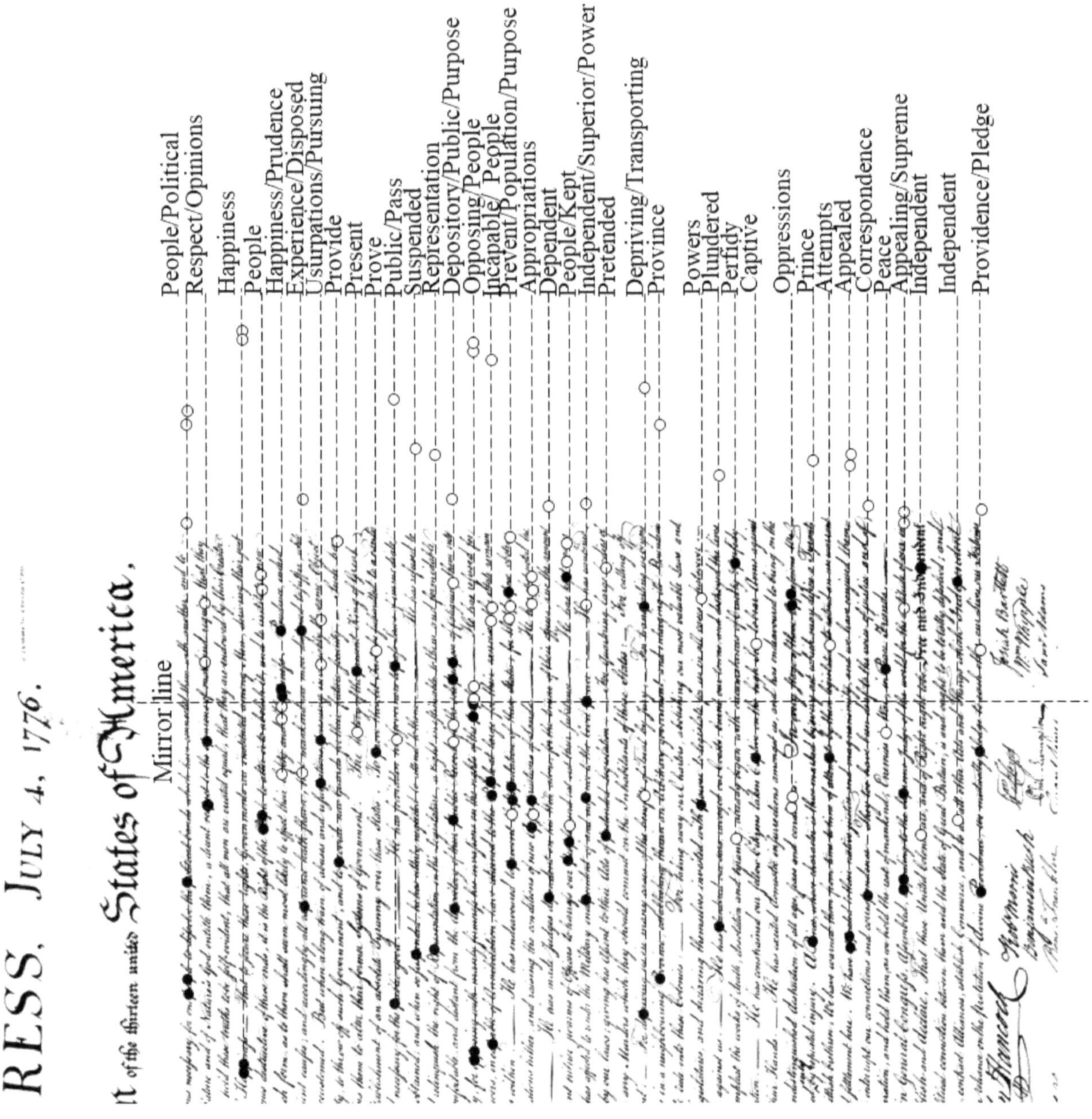
RESS, JULY 4, 1776.
of the thirteen united States of America,
Mirror line
People/Political
Respect/Opinions
Happiness
People
Happiness/Prudence
Experience/Disposed
Usurpations/Pursuing
Provide
Present
Prove
Public/Pass
Suspended
Representation
Depository/Public/Purpose
Opposing/People
Incapable/ People
Prevent/Population/Purpose
Appropriations
Dependent
People/Kept
Independent/Superior/Power
Pretended
Depriving/Transporting
Province
Powers
Plundered
Perfidy
Captive
Oppressions
Prince
Attempts
Appealed
Correspondence
Peace
Appealing/Supreme
Independent
Independent
Providence/Pledge

Fig. 125

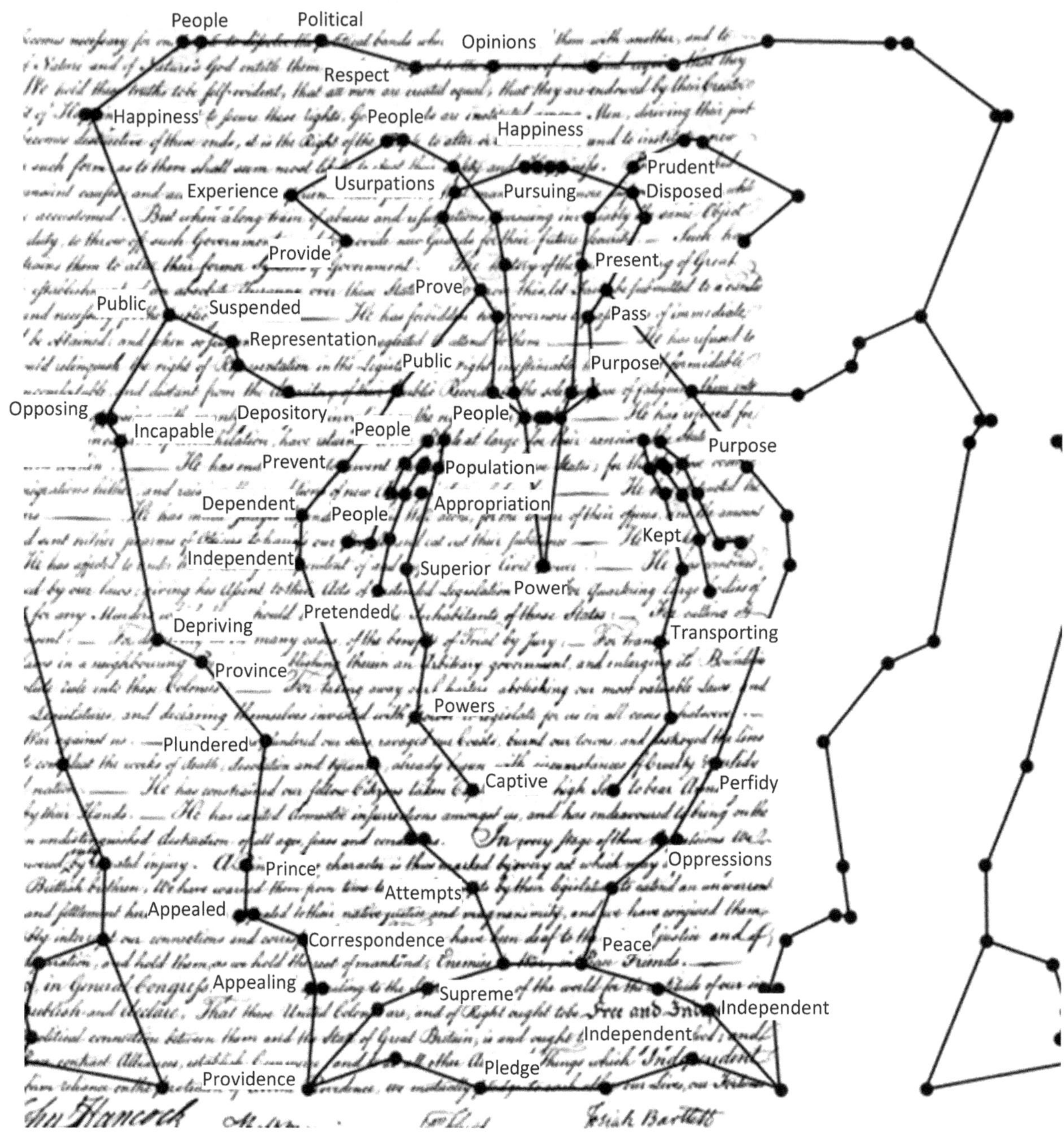

Fig. 126

All points used in this chapter are derived exclusively from occurrences of the letter P in the engrossed *Declaration of Independence*. No letters are added, omitted, substituted, or repositioned. Each P contributes two terminal points, original and mirrored, plotted exactly as they appear within the justified text block, at a fixed scale and orientation. The exception is a single point that lies on the mirror line. The letter P represents pupa. The pupa image depicts a monarch butterfly, mirroring the chrysalis's shape. A butterfly's life cycle includes an egg, larva (caterpillar), pupa (chrysalis), and butterfly. The stage between the caterpillar and butterfly involves cellular death and rebirth, showcasing a marvel of nature and a testament to the incredible complexity of life.

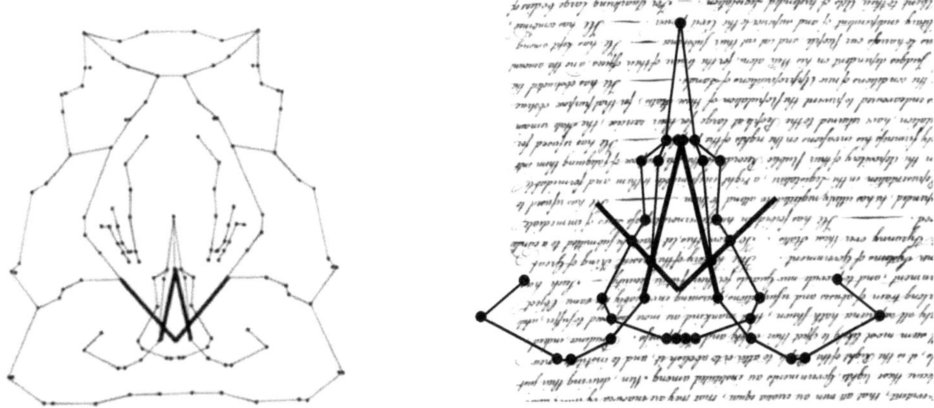

Fig. 127

The transformation from caterpillar to butterfly exemplifies this complexity beautifully. Numerous religious and spiritual societies have woven the metamorphosis from caterpillar to butterfly into their mythology, symbolizing the transition from earthly death to spiritual resurrection. A recurring theme of resurrection within the *Declaration* is represented by the drawing of a two-dimensional coffin entering the unfinished temple. This coffin is later reimagined in three dimensions. The three-dimensional coffin emerging from the temple's upper section symbolizes the soul's transformation into the spiritual realm and enlightenment. The story of Nimrod, Semiramis, and their son Tammuz in the *Declaration* illustrates the concept of reincarnation. Tammuz is depicted as a drawing of a pupa, symbolically resurrected into Nimrod (Fig. 124). The three drawings, Nimrod from the letter G, Semiramis from the letter B, and Tammuz from the mirrored letter P (Fig. 125), when layered together, create a fourth drawing of a Mesopotamian leopard. Rotating the leopard 180 degrees unveils a fifth drawing of a hooded figure, the Light-Bringer. The pupa image is formed for the letter "P" in the following words: a**pp**ealed, a**pp**ealing, corres**p**ondence, **p**rince, su**p**reme, **p**rovidence, **p**ledge, **p**rovince, de**p**riving, **p**lundered, attem**p**ts, o**pp**ressions, inde**p**endent, **p**ur**p**ose, inde**p**endent, **p**eace, **p**owers, ca**p**tive, **p**erfidy, trans**p**orting, **p**ower, **p**retended, inde**p**endent, ke**p**t, de**p**endent, **p**eo**p**le, re**p**resentation, inca**p**able, **p**revent, de**p**ository, su**p**erior, a**pp**ro**p**riations, **p**ublic, **p**o**p**ulation, **p**eo**p**le, o**pp**osing,

public, sus**p**ended, ha**pp**iness, **p**eo**p**le, **p**eo**p**le, ha**pp**iness, **p**olitical, ex**p**erience, usur**p**ations, **p**rovide, **p**ursuing, **p**rove, **p**eo**p**le, dis**p**osed, res**p**ect, **p**ass, **p**resent, **p**ur**p**ose, **p**rudence, and o**p**inions (Fig. 126). The pupa has an inverted square, and compasses drawn from the points at the mouth indicate that it is rotated 180 degrees as it brings the three drawings together (Fig. 127).

Chrysalis

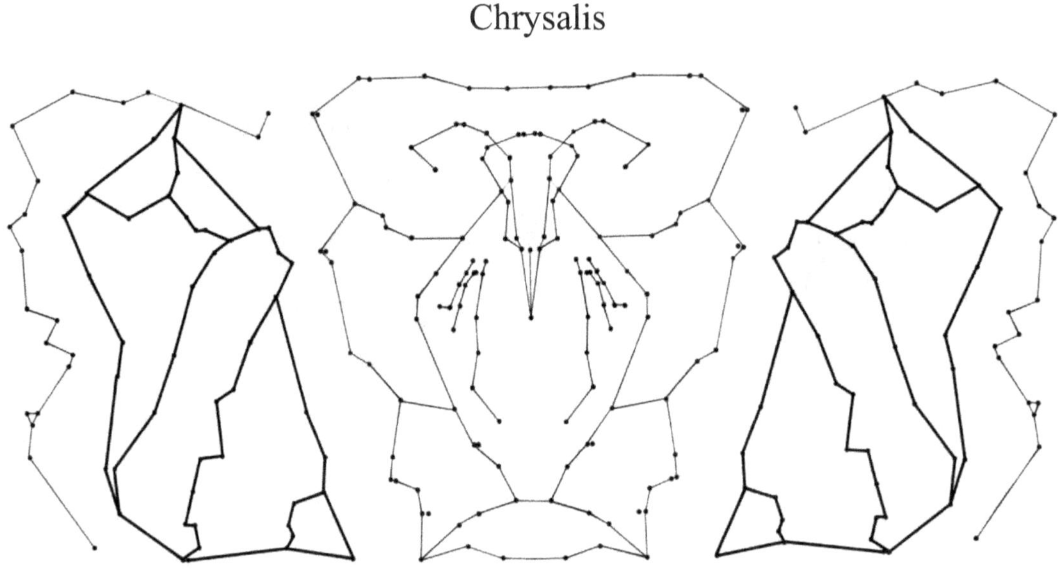

The chrysalis drawing is most closely related to the monarch butterfly's design. It includes the overall shape with a slight indentation along the back. The top of the shell accurately reflects the method of attachment and hanging. The chrysalis drawing of the pointed tip is more pronounced than in a natural Monarch chrysalis example. A smaller pointed tip does occur in the Monarch species, but it is generally not to the extent depicted. Additionally, note that butterfly species can exhibit varying chrysalis shapes due to different environmental conditions. The author could have elongated the pointed tip due to the revision of the Rough Draft of the *Declaration*. The Monarch butterfly is indigenous to North and South America (Weed). If the chrysalis is that of a Monarch butterfly, the drawing's designs may have originated in the American colonies and might not have been imported from Europe. Still, a closely related butterfly species may have similar chrysalis attributes. The Danaus Chrysippus, or Plain Tiger butterfly, from the family Nymphalidae, has a chrysalis that is very similar in design to the Monarch's and lives in Africa, Asia, and southern Europe. Regardless of the origin of the pointed tip, the artist could have taken liberties with it. The open

(Weed)

chrysalis displays the developing pupa on a scale comparable to the chrysalis drawings that frame the open pupa. The pupa and chrysalis drawings exemplify the purposeful scale to which the author crafted all images throughout the *Declaration*, also alluding to the intelligent design of the *Declaration's* drawings. The outer frame, where the chrysalis is attached, appears to be an outline of a butterfly wing. The chrysalis, pupa, and wings, when grouped, create an abstract impression of a butterfly's reanimation. Two lines on the wing form a triangle pointing downward. The downward-facing triangle can contextually be referred to as the hermetic "so below."

The chrysalis and outer wings from which it hangs are formed from the letter "P" in words: **p**owers, se**p**arate, **p**owers, **p**rinci**p**les, **p**atient, re**p**eated, des**p**otism, usur**p**ations, **p**ass, **p**ressing, im**p**ortance, o**p**eration, sus**p**ended, com**p**liance, **p**owers, ex**p**osed, **p**ayment, **p**eace, troo**p**s, **p**arts, **p**retended, **p**etitioned, **p**eo**p**le, **p**ower, **p**aralleled, Inde**p**endent, **p**eo**p**le, re**p**resentatives, **p**eo**p**le, su**pp**ort, **p**etitions, usur**p**ations, trans**p**orting, exam**p**le, re**p**eated, im**p**osing, **p**ass, **p**rotecting, re**p**resentative , **p**owers, com**p**leat, **p**unishment, sus**p**ending, **p**rotection, re**p**eated, interru**p**t, **p**rotection, **p**ublish, **p**eace, **p**olitical, **p**owers, re**p**eatedly, **p**eo**p**le, and **p**ursuit (Fig. 128).

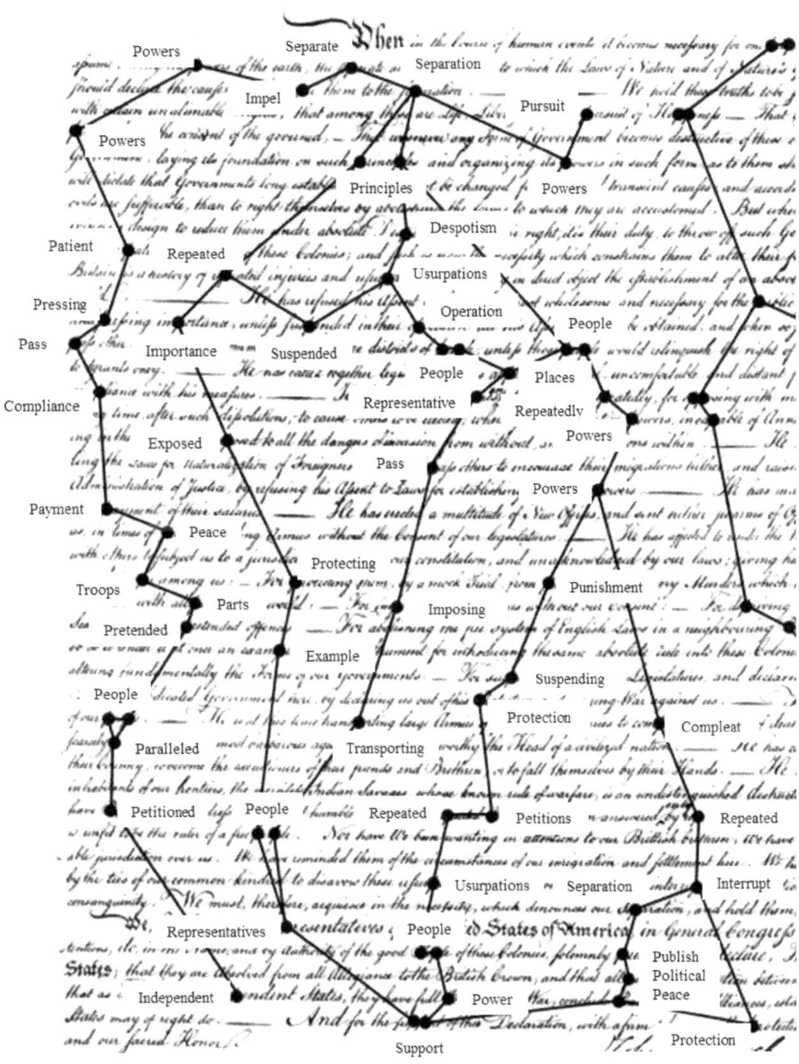

Fig. 128

Chapter Thirteen

BGP

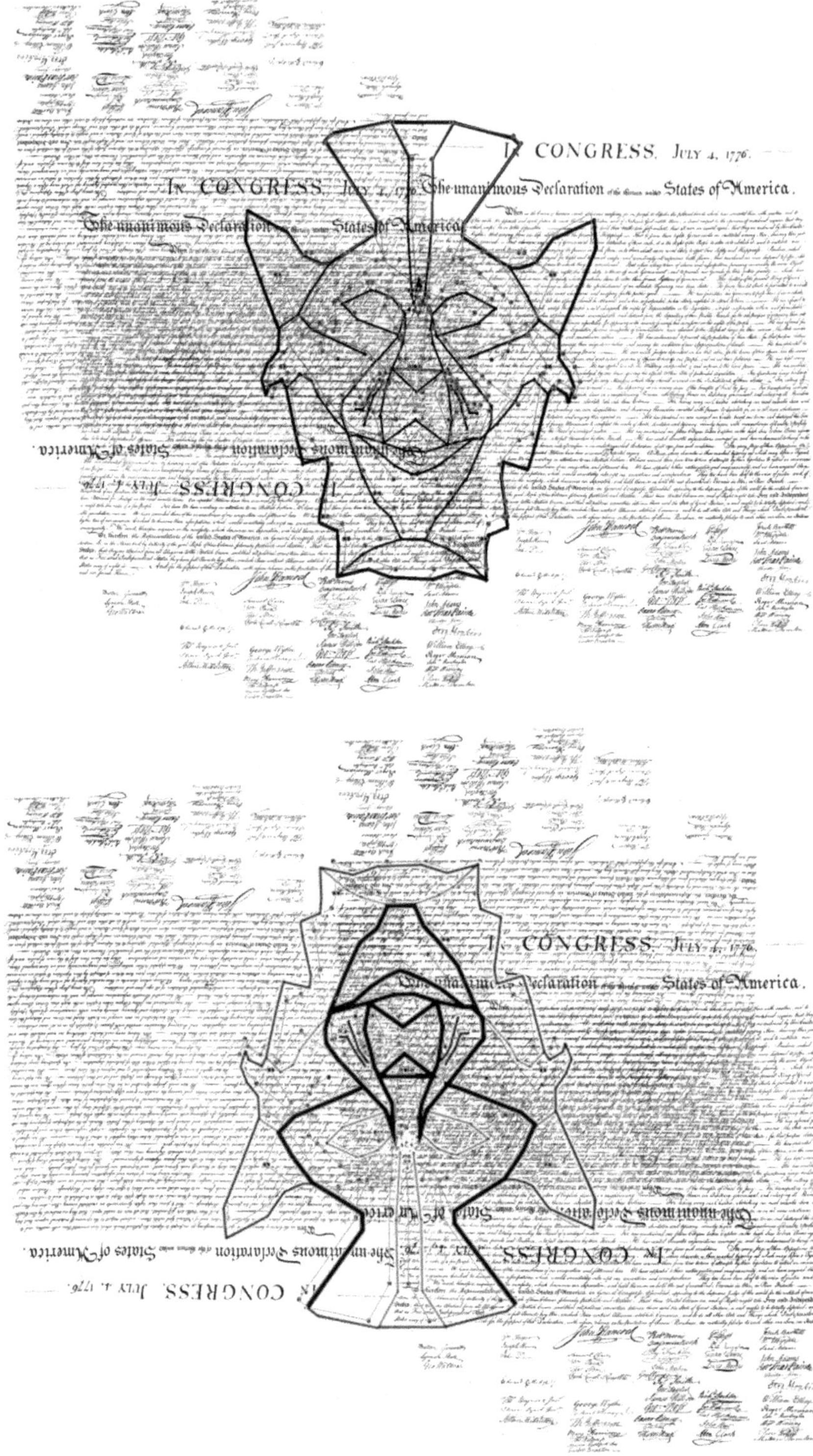

Fig. 129

The example of WVY and the layering of the images suggest that the second set of letters, consisting of the letter P for "pupa," is rotated 180 degrees; the letter B for "bee" is also rotated 180 degrees, while the letter G for the god image remains appropriately oriented (Fig. 129). All three images are combined and layered using the same method as WVY.

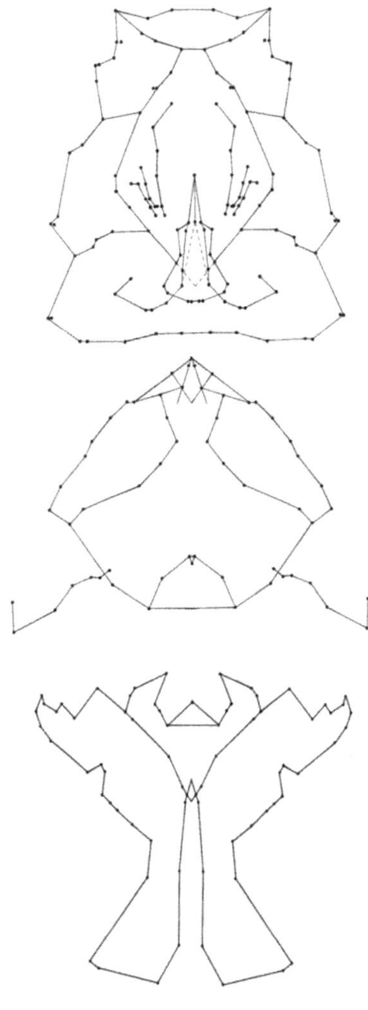

I first looked up the meaning of the letters BGP as either acronyms or initialisms. Focusing on Gnosticism, Rosicrucianism, Hermeticism, Kabbalah, the Old Testament, the New Testament, and esoteric and occult symbology, I found no direct connection. The letters BGP could then represent their symbolic meanings: B for a bee, P for the pupa, and G for the syncretic fusion of three deities: Baal, Moloch, and Nimrod. Layering the queen bee image "Semiramis," generated from the letter B, the horned god image "Nimrod," generated from the letter G, and the pupa image "Tammuz," generated from the letter P together on top of the lightbox and allowing the images to become translucent reveals a larger image of a leopard's head with a Mesopotamian cone-shaped tiara-fez-style hat. The three-layered images admittedly produce an abstract compilation. The finished leopard image is assembled from the original three-layered image. The finished leopard image utilizes only the existing dot patterns from the three BGP drawings. I added no extra dots to the compilation of the three-layered images. On the other hand, I connected new lines to the existing dots to generate the final leopard image.

The leopard image represents Nimrod, "the Leopard-tamer" (Inman). "Now the name Nimrod signifies the subduer of the leopard" (Hislop). "Nimrod tamed leopards so as to make use of them in hunting the other wild beasts in the Persian. In legends collected by Sir William Jones, we find that in primitive times, it was the custom to use leopards in this way. In these legends, it is said that Hoshang, the father of Tahmurs, who built Babylon, was the first who bred dogs and leopards for hunting" (Hislop).

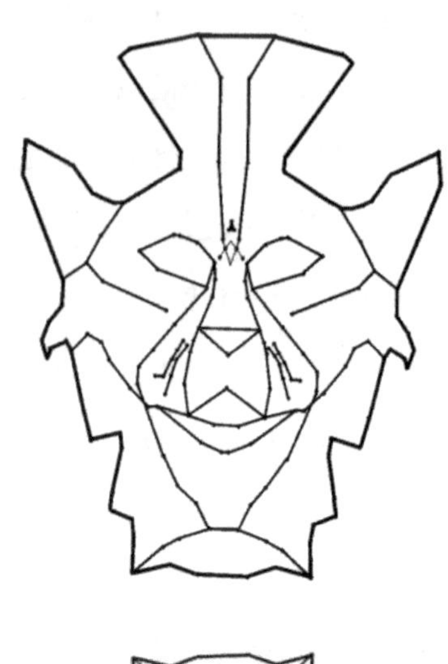

Turning the leopard image 180 degrees on the lightbox reveals an ambiguous picture of the hermaphrodite deity in a hooded ritual cloak. The face is a triangle pointing upward, masculine, and downward, feminine. It signifies the union of opposites, merging masculine and feminine principles. In esoteric traditions, it represents wholeness, self-sufficiency, and the transcendence of duality, representing the hermetic principle of correspondence. The image depicts a complex, multifaceted deity embodying duality, hidden knowledge, and the Hermetic principle of correspondence. It offers a non-traditional interpretation that draws heavily from esoteric and occult traditions. The transformation of the leopard-Nimrod into the hooded Luciferian signifies a descent into darkness.

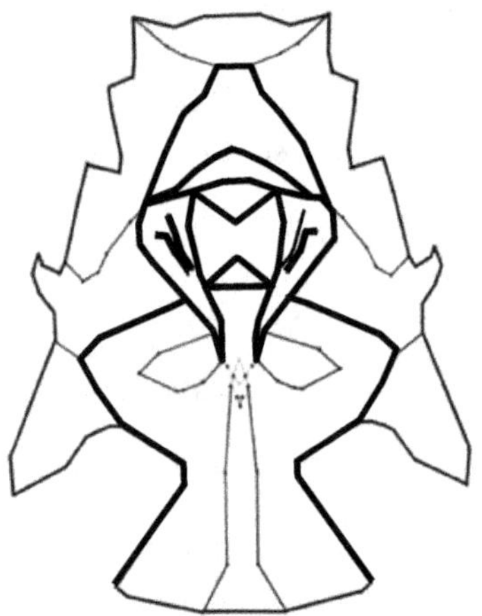

This symbolic metamorphosis echoes the theological shift that reinterpreted the biblical figure of Nimrod (Genesis 10:8-12), the arrogant builder of the Tower of Babel, as the archetypal King of Babylon, as eloquently mocked in Isaiah 14. In this light, the leopard, a symbol of Nimrod's earthly power and mastery, is a prelude to his spiritual inversion, where his defiant pride transforms him into the "light bringer" who boasts of ascending to the heavens (Isaiah 14:13). The final, androgynous form in the hooded cloak serves as a visual representation of this profound spiritual paradox, the ultimate union of opposites, where the defiant earthly king becomes the "fallen star" of esoteric tradition.

Symbolism of WVY and BGP

The WVY imagery represents a pantheon of gods and goddesses associated with virtue and morality. The duality of divine figures pairs deities, representing good and evil. This duality reflects the tension between light and darkness, creation and destruction, and order and chaos. Mythology can be understood as a reflection of human nature mirroring the divine.

In the WVY drawings, God in Christianity is depicted as a benevolent and singular deity. While ancient Egyptian religion features benevolent figures like the father (e.g., Ra, Amun-Ra) or Osiris, these deities belong to a polytheistic system with fundamentally different theological frameworks than the Christian monotheistic one.

The Christian God stands in stark contrast to figures such as Baal and Moloch, who are condemned as false gods and objects of idolatry in the Hebrew Bible, and whose worship was linked to ancient Canaanite and Mesopotamian religions. The placement of Nimrod (letter G), Semiramis (letter B), and Tammuz (letter P) in direct contrast to the Holy Trinity appears mainly in esoteric or alternative religious interpretations. It is not widely accepted in mainstream academic studies of religion or history.

The Hermetic aphorism "as above, so below" describes a correspondence between the divine or cosmic realm and the earthly or human realm. While the sacred, or "as above," represents a benevolent cosmic order, the "so below" refers to the human realm, where actions, including idolatry and the worship of false gods, are often associated with Mesopotamian and Canaanite practices. This understanding of "so below" can thus be seen as reflecting the imperfections and choices of the earthly realm, including those that deviate from monotheistic worship.

The duality of divine figures, such as the Egyptian god Osiris and his wicked brother Seth, who killed Osiris and dismembered his body, spreading his parts throughout the countryside, mirrors the duality of Cain killing Abel with the jawbone of an ass. Although the jawbone of an ass is not mentioned in the *Bible*, it was later included in medieval commentaries and illustrations, as evidenced in images of the letter M. Both examples serve as allegorical lessons on good and evil. The WVY and BGP images create a similar duality, with the letter M images representing the convergence of WVY and BGP.

Chapter Fourteen

The Letter M

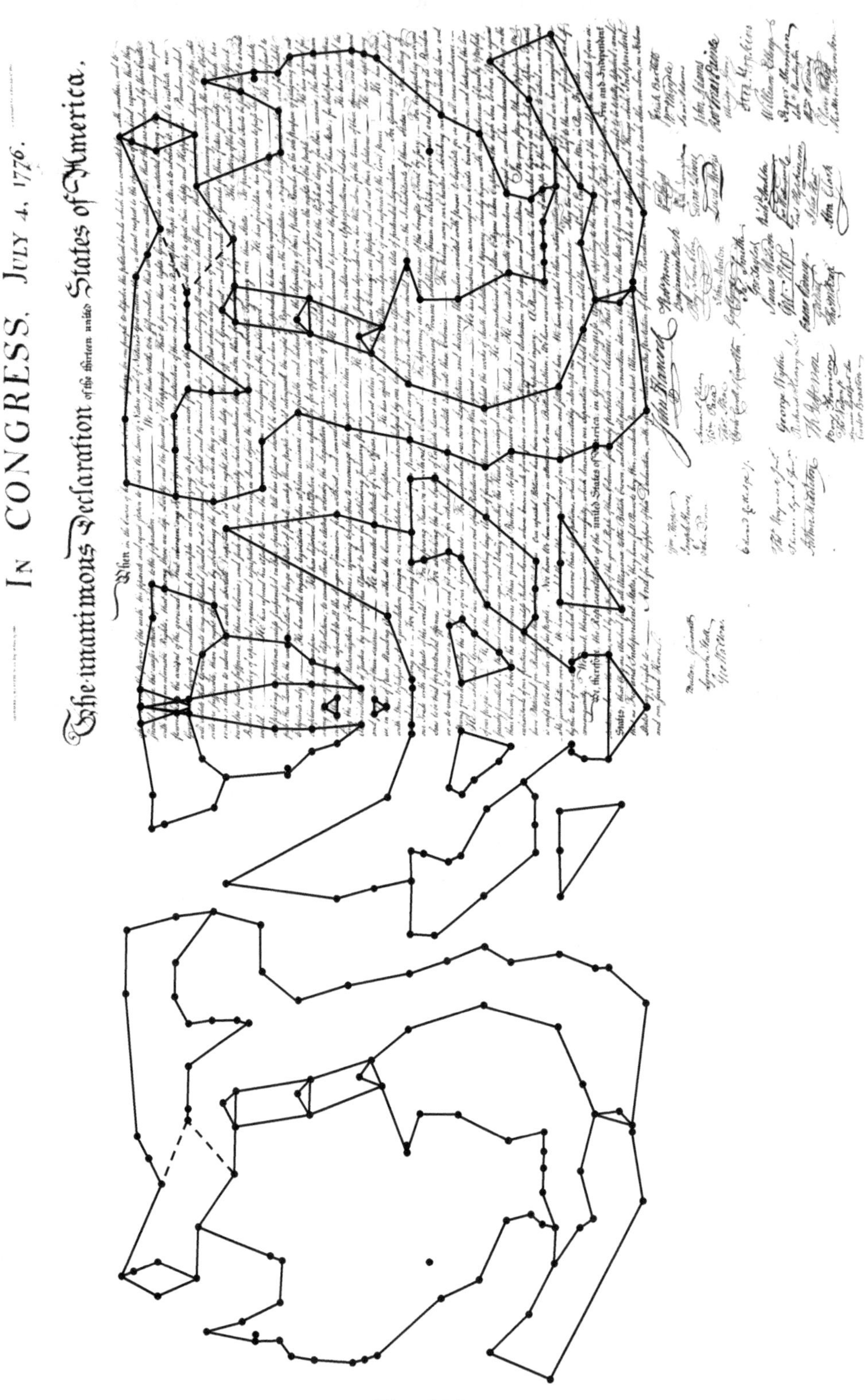

Fig. 130

Mirror Line
Among/Assume
Them/Impel
Among
From
Governments
Government
Themselves
Despotism/Them
Importance
Accommodation
Measure/Compliance
Time
Mean/Time/From
Administration
Multitude/Payment
Armies/Times
From/Mock/Them/Imposing/Among/Armed
Terms
System
Instrument/Example
Governments/Forms/Fundamentally
Government
Armies/Time
Most
Become
Merciless
Terms/Humble/Must
Circumstances/Them/Reminded
Common
Must
Name
From
May

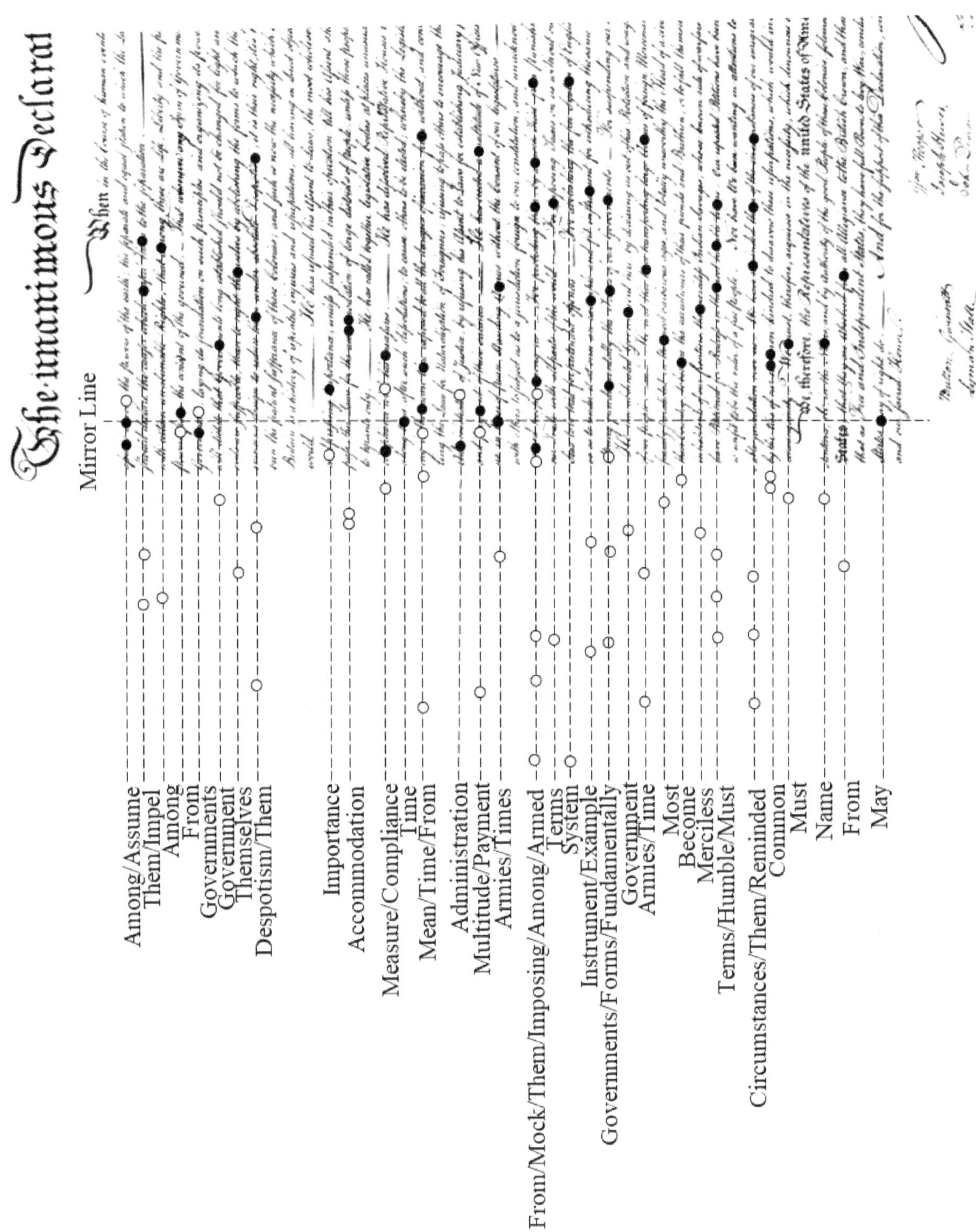

Fig. 131

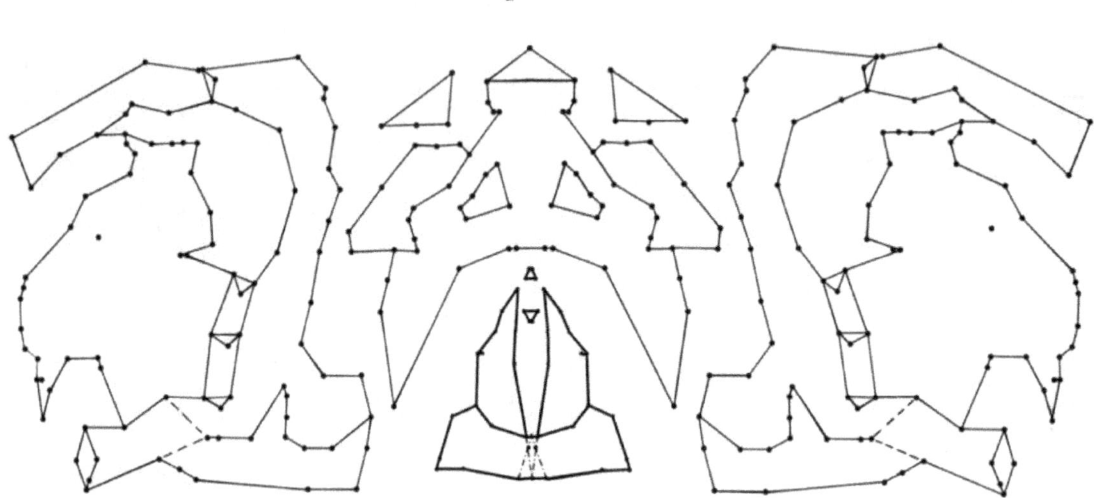

The seventh drawing, created by plotting and mirroring the mirrored letter M within the *Declaration* (Fig. 131), embodies the principle of "as above, so below." It is graphically positioned between the WVY and BGP drawings. The drawings of the letter M illustrate the conflict between light, perfection, and goodness, which respond to darkness, evil, and imperfection.

The seventh image (Fig. 130) plotted from M is labeled "Mysteries." These mysteries convey allegorical lessons about good and evil. The M symbolizes ancient Egyptian mysteries, the Masonic Great Architect, and the gods Thoth, Hermes, Anubis, and the young lion-headed god Osiris. M also includes imagery of the Egyptian Goddess Nut, the jawbone of an ass used to kill Abel, Osiris's interred body, and parallels between Hermeticism and the Catholic Papacy.

The center panel of the triptych depicts Hermes Trismegistus, a syncretic figure combining the Greek Hermes and the Egyptian God Thoth, seated on a throne. An isosceles triangle forms the head of Hermes Trismegistus, representing the triad. The name "Trismegistus" itself means "Thrice-Greatest," which has been defined as referring to his mastery of three parts of the wisdom of the universe (alchemy, astrology, and theurgy) or, in some later interpretations, even as a reference to a type of trinity (Allyn).

In Masonic symbolism, the three triangles within the figure of Hermes Trismegistus enthroned symbolize the unity of wisdom, science, and divine truth. The two outer right-angled triangles, based on the sacred 3-4-5 proportion, represent the operative principles of craftsmanship and moral goodness. In contrast, the central upright triangle, positioned at the top of the head, signifies the speculative achievement of spiritual understanding. When this emblem is rotated, the central triangle aligns with Anubis's nose, revealing a deeper connection between the Hermetic and Egyptian mysteries and their shared goal of illumination. In this union, the Hermes-Anubis synthesis, the Mason sees the eternal reconciliation of the seen and the unseen, of matter shaped by mind. Thus, as the outer operative triangles unite in the central speculative one, the emblem reminds the Brother that all actual building begins within: geometry perfects the soul as surely as it squares the Temple (Brown).

The papal miter, worn by Catholic popes, is centered on the floor at the feet of the great Hermes-Trismegistus (Fig. 124). The picture to the right shows Pope Saint Leo IX (1002-1054) wearing a similar papal miter with a front-facing, V-shaped opening. The image of Pope Saint Leo IX is one of the earliest known examples of this type of miter (Pope Leo IX).

(Pope Leo IX)

In Albrecht Dürer's detailed engraving, *Christ before Caiaphas, The Small Passion* (1511), the viewer's eye is immediately drawn to High Priest Caiaphas, who is seated not only as a judge but also as a figure of exaggerated, worldly power. The most striking part of his attire is his head-dress: a tall, Dagon-style miter that serves as a powerful visual symbol of corrupt authority. It deliberately contrasts with Christ's simplicity, as Christ stands bound and humble before him. The shape of the miter alludes to the Christian bishop's miter, including that of the Pope, which is rooted in the ancient Jewish High Priest's head-covering. By placing an ornate, often symbolically twisted version of this sacred headwear on Caiaphas, Dürer creates a false, blinding contrast between wealth and spiritual emptiness, replacing true divine purpose. This suggests that while the Old Law's authority was passed to the Christian Church, it was first corrupted by the very man who condemned Christ, highlighting a spiritual blindness that fails to recognize the divine. Notice the havelock, also called a neck cape, on both the Dürer print and the letter M image (Fig. 132). In addition, Dürer's 1514 master engraving, *Melencolia I*, is revered by Freemasonry for its

Albrecht Dürer

Masonic symbolism.

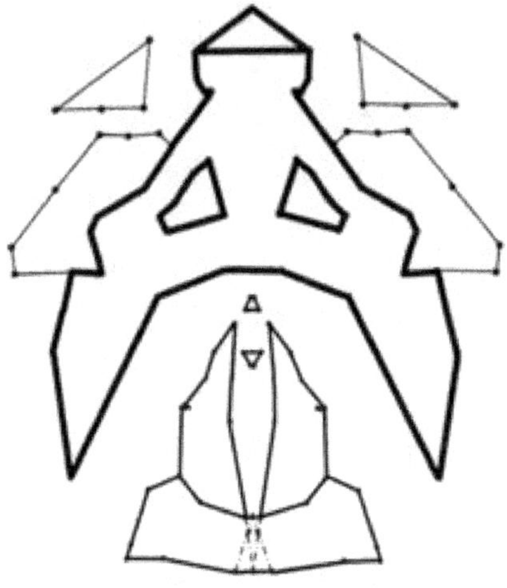

Fig. 132

Inside the image of the miter lie two triangles, one pointing upward, "as above," and one pointing downward, "so below." The papal miter is a powerful symbol of the Papacy and the Catholic Church. The two triangles suggest that Christianity, particularly Catholicism, shares commonalities with ancient Egyptian, Alexandrian, and Gnostic Hermeticism, indicating that reality reflects a heavenly reality. Early Christianity, particularly in the works of Clement of Alexandria, recognized the value in certain aspects of Greek philosophy and Hermeticism.

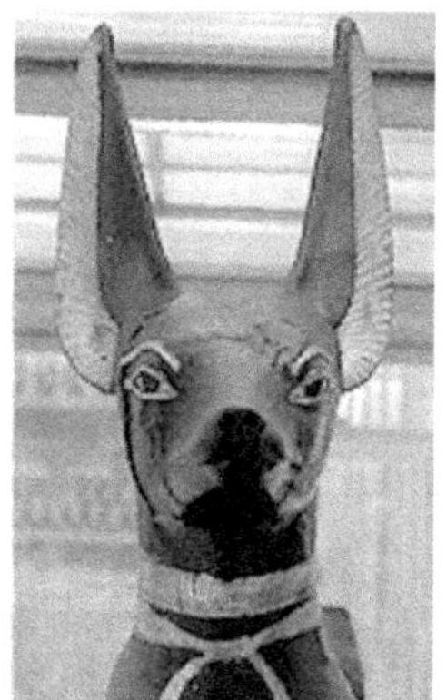

(Thibault)

Fig. 133

During the Medieval Period, the church viewed Hermeticism with suspicion, often associating it with magic and paganism. This led to periods of suppression and persecution of practitioners of Hermeticism. During the Renaissance, a renewed interest in Hermeticism emerged, with some scholars seeking to reconcile it with Christian theology. While not explicitly stated in the same terms, the concept of "as above, so below" has parallels in Catholic theology. For example, in the incarnation, God, the divine, became incarnate in human form (Jesus Christ), mirroring the divine within humanity. Catholic sacraments are seen as outward signs of inward grace, reflecting the divine in the material world. The concept of "Imago Dei" is that humans are created in the image and likeness of God, mirroring the divine within human nature. Christians use the phrase in the Lord's Prayer: "Thy kingdom come, thy will be done, on Earth as it is in Heaven" (Clarke). The base of the Papal Miter consists of points that, when developed, generate an inverted square and compasses that serve as the actuator for spinning the drawing 180 degrees.

Turning Hermes-Trismegistus on the throne (Fig. 132) by 180 degrees transforms him into the face of the Egyptian god Anubis (Fig. 133), the son of Osiris and the Goddess Nephthys. The drawing's rotation initiates the transition from Hermes-Trismegistus to Anubis, symbolically unifying the Greek god Hermes and the Egyptian god Anubis into a syncretic god, Hermanubis (Fig. 134) (Clair). On either side of the great architect, the two mirrored outer panels of the triptych depict images of a young lion's head and face, representing a young Osiris with a pharaoh's beard. At the base of the young lion's neck lies the god Osiris on his back with a golden phallus pointing upward. A curved bill-hook or scythe is drawn at the back of Osiris's head, and wrapped around the young lion's head is a depiction of the Egyptian sky god Nut, who gave birth to Osiris, Isis, Nephthys, and Seth.

(Ménard)
Fig. 134

The letter M is a standalone image; no layering is needed to rotate it or create a new one. The center triptych features Hermes Trismegistus seated on a throne with an isosceles triangle representing the triad of the Godhead, flanked by two right triangles on either side of his head. The irregular shapes alongside the arms and hands are armrests that are part of the throne. The outline of a torso, with arms stretched out and resting on the knees, transitions into the lower body, where the legs are open, culminating in pointed feet reminiscent of bull's horns. These tips transform into the outstretched arms of Jesus, which also end in points, maintaining the same artistic style. The god is depicted as an ambiguous image, an illusory figure that can be perceived in multiple ways. The purpose of such an abstract representation is that when rotated 180 degrees, Hermes Trismegistus on the throne morphs into the face of the god Anubis.

All points used in this chapter are derived exclusively from occurrences of the letter M in the engrossed *Declaration of Independence*. No letters are added, omitted, substituted, or repositioned. Each M contributes two terminal points, original and mirrored, plotted exactly as they appear within the justified text block, at a fixed scale and orientation. The exception is a single point that lies on the mirror line.

The transition from Hermes Trismegistus to Anubis unites the two, forming the god Hermanubis. The compilation of gods, the throne, the triangles, and the papal miter are all formed from the letter M derived from the following words: a**m**ong, assu**m**e, fro**m**, govern**m**ent, co**m**pliance, **m**easures, i**m**portance, ti**m**e, ti**m**e, **m**ean, ad**m**inistration, pay**m**ent, a**m**ong, the**m** , ar**m**ed, funda**m**entally, **m**ay, ter**m**s, **m**erciless, beco**m**e, circu**m**stances, **m**ost, **m**ost, co**mm**on, re**m**inded, hu**m**ble, Na**m**e, **m**ust, the**m**, fro**m**, exa**m**ple, ti**m**e, govern**m**ent, govern**m**ents, for**m**s, ar**m**ies, instru**m**ent, ar**m**ies, the**m**, **m**ock, i**m**posing, fro**m**, syste**m**, **m**ultitude, fro**m**, despotis**m**, , the**m**, govern**m**ents, i**m**pel, the**m**selves, a**m**ong, and ti**m**es (Fig. 135).

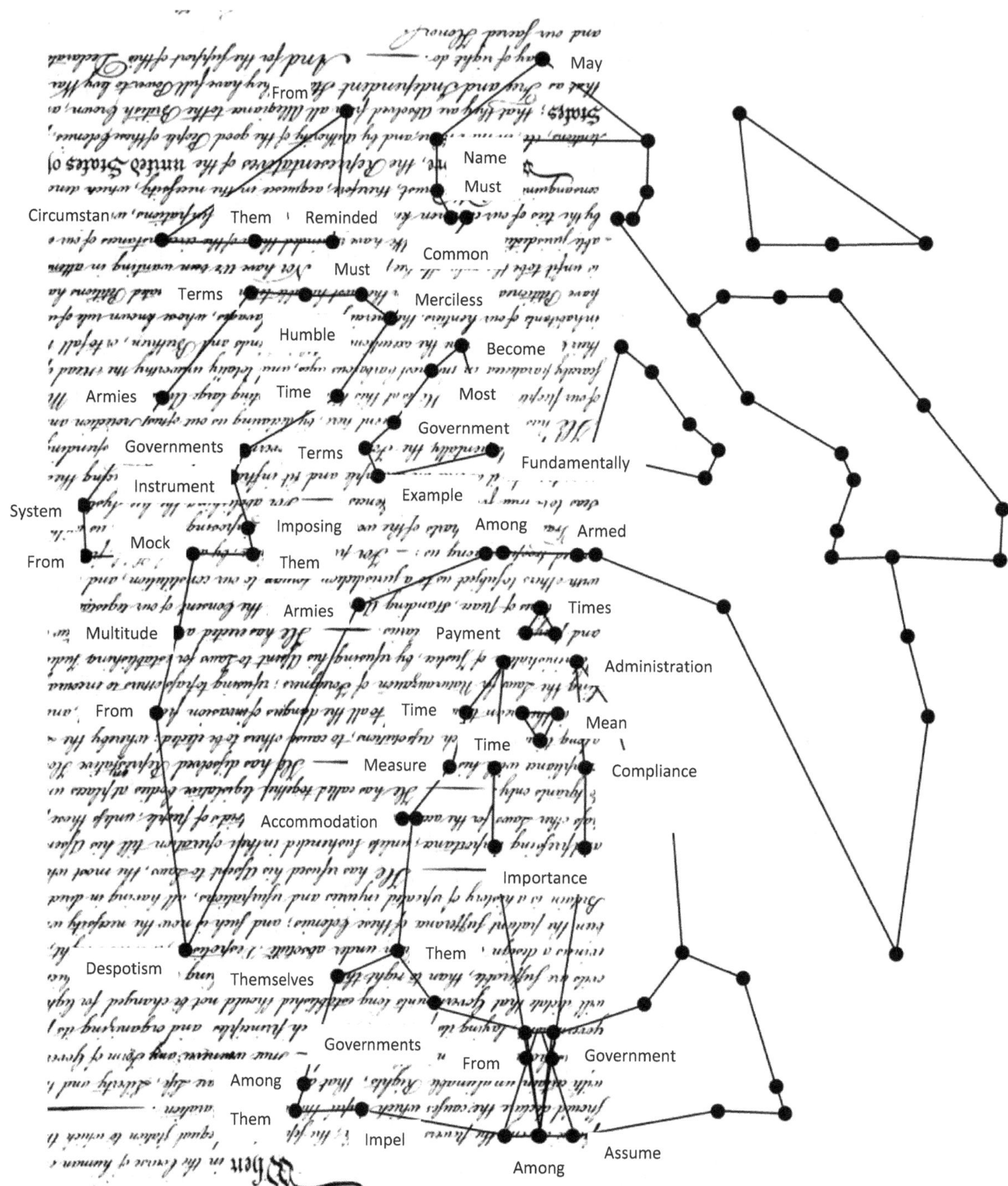

Fig. 135

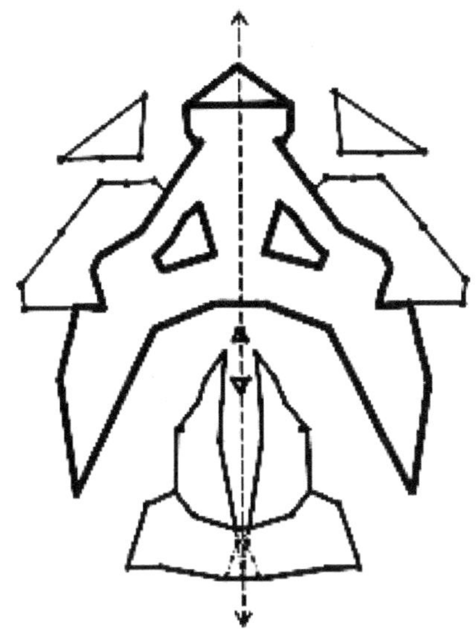

Fig. 136

Of course, the letter M in the drawing of Hermes Trismegistus on the throne has horizontal symmetry due to the center-mirroring line. An interesting aspect of this image is that when the arms of the throne are projected in a perspective-style drawing, the vanishing point above the head, when mirrored down below, also terminates at the square and compasses on the papal miter. The relative proportions of the right triangles, the isosceles triangle, the body of Hermes, the miter, and other triangles create a comparative collection of imagery when arranged in vertical and horizontal symmetry, demonstrating the architect's intelligent design (Fig. 136).

For centuries, master builders have guarded a quiet secret: a perfect diamond formed by four right triangles harmoniously joined. More than decoration, this figure was a hidden law of proportion, guiding the hands that raised England's grandest halls. From Westminster to York Minster, Beverley, and Magdalen College, each façade echoes its geometry. At its heart lies the sacred 3: 4: 5 triangles, the builder's right angle, and the Mason's moral one, a timeless code in stone, ensuring that beauty, order, and truth remain forever aligned (Fig. 137) (Brown).

(Bowes)
Fig. 137

Osiris's youthful face, adorned with a pharaoh's beard, signifies his royal status and role as a king, even in death. The beard is a symbol of power and divinity. The face of young Osiris is derived from the letter M in these words: Ti**m**e, ti**m**e, the**m**, sub**m**itted, fro**m**, **m**arked, govern**m**ent, circu**m**stances, **m**ost, a**m**ongst, do**m**estic, the**m**selves, co**mm**it, **m**any, a**m**ong, co**m**bined, a**m**ount, the**m**, inesti**m**able, i**mm**ediate, the**m**, for**m**idable, re**m**aining, the**m**, sa**m**e, and govern**m**ent.

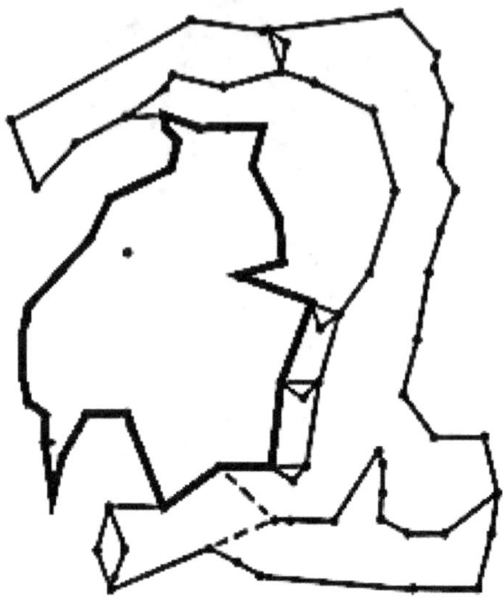

Wrapped around Osiris's head is the Egyptian goddess Nut, the goddess of the sky (Burdge). In Egyptian mythology, she is the mother of Osiris, Set, Isis, and Nephthys. She is often depicted as a woman arching over the Earth. The goddess Nut has a small triangle on her back leg

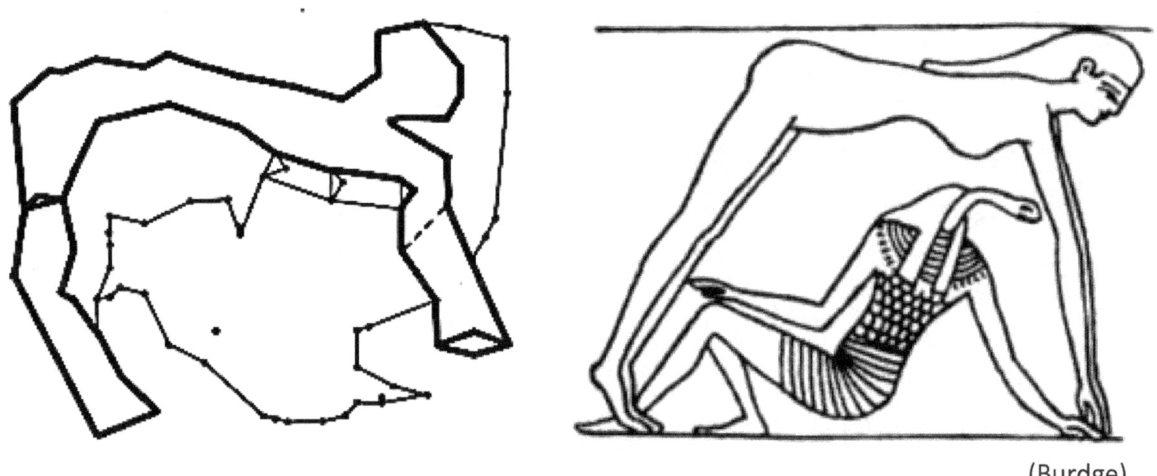

(Burdge)

that reads "as above." Nut, the sky goddess, protects and nurtures Osiris. It symbolizes his rebirth or transition into the afterlife. Nut's embrace is a symbolic womb, representing the renewal of life. Goddess Nut is formed from the letter M from e**m**igration, settle**m**ent, fir**m**, A**m**erica, sole**m**nly, Co**mm**erce, **m**utually, Ene**m**ies, the**m**, Asse**m**bled, the**m**, the**m**, Supre**m**e, **m**ankind, **m**agnani**m**ity, **m**ay, Ar**m**s, the**m**, **m**ercenaries, co**m**pleat, the**m**selves, sa**m**e, **m**urders, punish**m**ent, swar**m**s,

migrations, wholeso**m**e, **m**anly, unco**m**fortable, **m**ost, accusto**m**ed, govern**m**ent, for**m**s, beco**m**es, the**m**, for**m**, for**m**er, syste**m**s, establish**m**ent, and govern**m**ent.

A curved billhook or scythe was used to dismember Osiris's body by his brother Seth. The handle of the scythe is marked with three downward-facing equilateral triangles, indicating "So Below." The curved billhook or scythe has a unique design that resembles the jawbone of an ass that Cain used to kill Abel, the first murderer (Gandolfi). The scythe is derived from the letter M from syste**m**s, settle**m**ent, ene**m**ies, asse**m**bled, the**m**, supre**m**e, **m**ankind, ti**m**e, ti**m**e, the**m**, fro**m**, **m**agnani**m**ity, do**m**estic, co**m**pleat, the**m**selves, **m**urders, co**mm**it, **m**ilitary, **m**any, swar**m**s, **m**ade, fir**m**ness, fro**m**, **m**anly, for**m**er, and govern**m**ent.

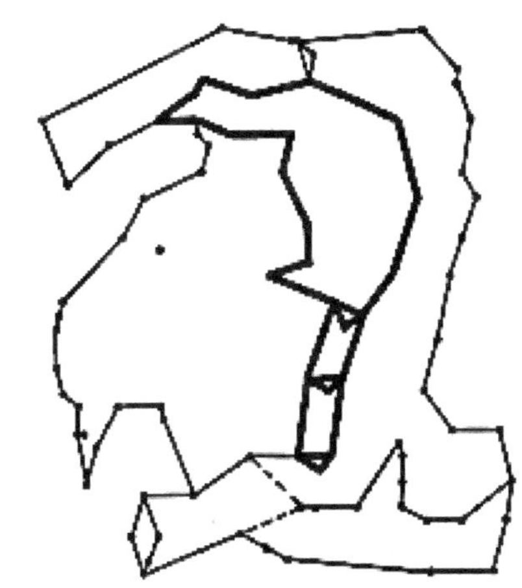

The painting to the right, by Gaetano Gandolfi, 1780, depicts Cain killing Abel with the Jawbone of an ass. The killing of Abel by his brother is a comparative mythology to that of Osiris, who was killed by his brother Seth, and Osiris's body was cut into fourteen pieces. To ensure the body would never be resurrected, Set scattered Osiris's body parts across Egypt. Isis and Anubis recovered thirteen pieces of Osiris's body. The body part that Isis and Anubis could not locate was Osiris's phallus, which had been eaten by a fish in the Nile River. Isis fashioned a replacement phallus out of gold and placed it onto Osiris's body. This allowed Isis and Osiris to pair and have their son, Horus.

(Gandolfi)

The image at the bottom of the triptych depicts Osiris lying on his back after replacing the golden phallus. The image of the mother Goddess Nut wrapped around a young Osiris's face represents the birth of Osiris's life. Osiris's young face, adorned with a pharaoh's beard, represents an ascension to divine status, becoming one with the source of life. The image of Osiris lying on his

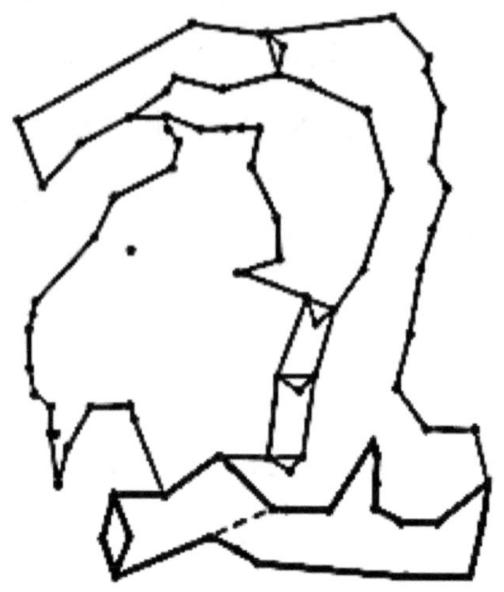

back with a golden phallus symbolizes the dissolution of his physical form, as he returns his energy to the universe and prepares for eventual rebirth. This ties into the cyclical nature of life, death, and resurrection, a central theme in Egyptian mythology. Even in this state of dissolution, the golden phallus hints at the potential for new life to emerge. It represents the return of this energy to the source, the cyclical nature of life and death, or the potential for rebirth from even the most seemingly lifeless state. The imagery isn't just about the birth of Osiris's life but encompasses the entire cycle: life, death (dissolution), and the potential for rebirth. The golden phallus is a powerful symbol of this regenerative power, even in the face of death.

The Osiris image is drawn from M in, accusto**m**ed, govern**m**ent, for**m**, for**m**s, beco**m**es, the**m**, for**m**, establish**m**ent, govern**m**ent, the**m**, **m**ankind, see**m**, **m**ost, a**m**ong, **m**ore, **m**en, **m**ankind, beco**m**es, the**m**, govern**m**ents, the**m**, and hu**m**an.

The letter M is the capstone of this coded document, revealing the Mysteries that underpin the *Declaration of Independence*. The complete triptych, uniting Hermes Trismegistus and the Papal Miter with the cyclical death and rebirth of Osiris, is the *Declaration's* secret Masonic allegorical preamble, linking Cain and Abel to Osiris and Seth to Hiram Abiff (Mackey, *Symbolism of Freemasonry*). It speaks not of politics, but of the eternal reconciliation between heaven and earth, life and death, matter and mind. In this final, geometrically perfect image, the hidden architects codified their highest truth: that the American revolutionary impulse was not merely a political act, but a Sacred design for human regeneration, built upon the ancient wisdom of the thrice-greatest master. The seven letters, thus plotted and exposed, now reveal the complete, esoteric blueprint secretly inscribed at the nation's founding.

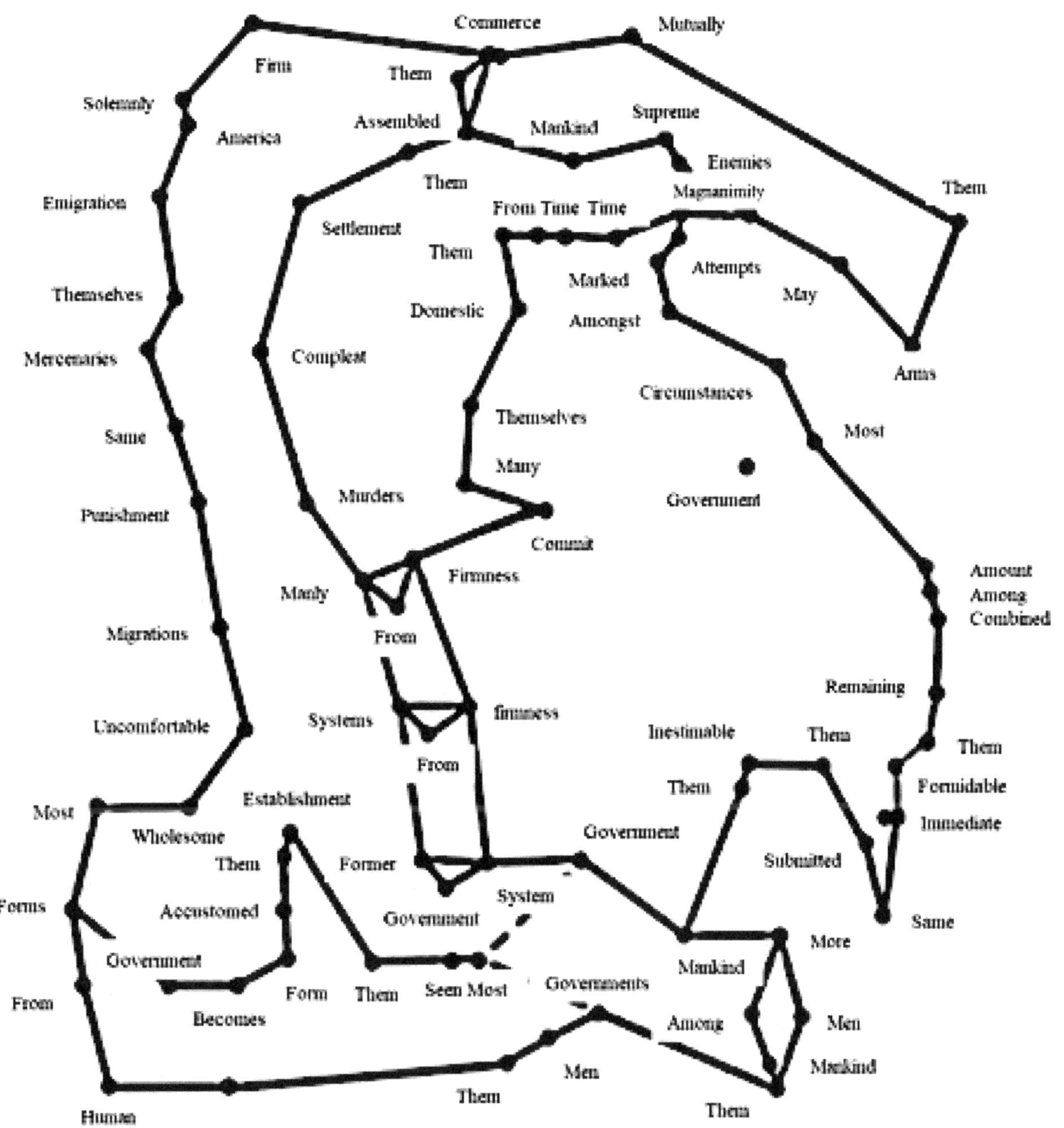
Commerce
Mutually
Firm
Them
Solemnly
America
Assembled
Mankind
Supreme
Enemies
Emigration
Them
Magnanimity
Them
From Time Time
Settlement
Them
Attempts
Marked
May
Themselves
Domestic
Amongst
Mercenaries
Compleat
Arms
Circumstances
Same
Themselves
Most
Many
Government
Punishment
Murders
Commit
Amount
Among
Combined
Manly
Firmness
Migrations
From
Remaining
Systems
firmness
Uncomfortable
Inestimable
Them
Them
From
Formidable
Them
Establishment
Most
Immediate
Government
Wholesome
Them
Former
Submitted
System
Forms
Accustomed
Government
Same
Government
More
Mankind
Governments
Form
Them
Seen Most
From
Becomes
Among
Men
Mankind
Men
Them
Them
Human

Conclusion

This investigation into the *Declaration of Independence*, initiated by the close examination of a single dash, has expanded into a sustained study of geometric patterning across the document's letterforms. What emerges from this process is a coherent seven-figure system generated through consistent plotting and mirroring of the letters W, V, Y, B, G, P, and M. Taken together, these constructions suggest a level of internal order that invites interpretation beyond conventional typographic analysis.

The geometric consistency observed across these seven letters supports the presence of a unified visual framework rather than a series of isolated coincidences. Within that framework, two principal groupings become apparent:

The WVY Triad (As Above): a set of images that can be read as corresponding to themes of divine illumination, resurrection, moral order, and construction, visually aligned with Christian and Osirian symbolism and with the concept of an unfinished temple or work-in-progress.

The BGP Triad (So Below): a contrasting set of images associated with earthly power, transformation, and mythological duality, drawing on Babylonian and syncretic traditions centered on figures such as Nimrod, Semiramis, and Tammuz, and culminating in a "light-bringer" inversion.

These two triads are visually and conceptually linked through the central M figure, which synthesizes Hermetic, Egyptian, and later philosophical traditions. The placement of Hermanubis and the papal miter at this juncture positions the M image as a mediator between opposing symbolic systems. Read allegorically, this mediation reflects long-standing tensions between institutional authority and intellectual or spiritual autonomy, tensions that were very much alive in the intellectual climate of the eighteenth century.

The Question of Intent

The coherence of this system raises a critical question: at what point does coincidence give way to design? A single abstract image might reasonably be dismissed as accidental or as an instance of pareidolia. However, the emergence of two internally consistent triads, governed by mirrored geometry, activated by inverted square-and-compasses constructions, and capable of producing composite figures through rotation and layering, exceeds what is typically attributed to random pattern recognition.

If these images are dismissed as pareidolia, then the phenomenon itself warrants consideration: the human mind would have had to generate, from unrelated letter placements, a geometrically precise and symbolically coherent system that aligns closely with known Masonic, Hermetic, and Enlightenment-era philosophical concerns. Such an outcome would itself be remarkable.

If, on the other hand, the system reflects intentional design, it may be understood not as a hidden manifesto but as an allegorical substructure, a visual counterpart to the *Declaration*'s rhetorical architecture. In this reading, the geometric system functions as a philosophical commentary rather than a directive, using symbolic language familiar to educated initiates of the period.

Exoteric and Esoteric Readings

Under this interpretation, the *Declaration* can be read on two complementary levels:

- The Exoteric Text: the public document, articulating political independence, natural rights, and grievances against imperial authority.
- The Esoteric Framework: a private or initiatory layer, expressed through geometry and symbolic correspondence, suggesting that the principles of liberty, self-governance, and tolerance rest upon deeper philosophical traditions inherited from antiquity rather than from any single religious or political institution.

Such a dual structure would not be unprecedented. Enlightenment thinkers frequently drew upon classical, Hermetic, and natural-law traditions while presenting their arguments in universally accessible language. Geometry, long regarded as a neutral and elevated mode of expression, offered a means of structuring meaning without explicit declaration.

Final Reflection

The significance of this study lies not in proving intent beyond all doubt, but in demonstrating that the *Declaration* of Independence sustains a level of geometric and symbolic coherence that has not previously been examined in full. Whether these patterns are understood as deliberate constructions or as emergent properties of a carefully crafted document, they challenge the assumption that the *Declaration* operates solely as a political text.

The final M image functions as a conceptual capstone: a synthesis of ascent and descent, order and dissolution, authority and renewal. In this sense, the geometric system does not prescribe belief, but stages a dialogue—one concerned with regeneration, responsibility, and the perennial relationship between human law and higher principle.

The reader is therefore left with an unavoidable choice, not of belief, but of interpretation: Are these patterns the accidental byproducts of structure and chance, or do they represent a deliberate experiment in geometry and allegory by minds steeped in the symbolic language of their age?

Note on Sources

This study draws on a combination of primary materials (founding-era documents, period Masonic texts, early editions of Euclid, and historical artworks) and secondary interpretive sources from the nineteenth century to the present. Later symbolic and comparative works are cited not as evidence of intent or transmission, but as records of symbolic traditions used here for visual and geometric comparison.

Bibliography

Allen, Danielle. *Punctuating-Happiness*. UPS Foundation Professor School of Social Science Institute for Advanced Study www.ias.edu, 4 3 2015.

Allyn, Avery. *A Ritual of Freemasonry*. Philadelphia: John Clarke, 1831.

Anderson, James. *The Constitutions of the Free-Masons: Containing the History, Charges, Regulations*. London: William Hunter, 1723.

Andrews, William H. *Collection Made by Committee on Antiquities of the Grand Lodge Free and Accepted Masons, of the State of New York*. New York: Grand Lodge F. & A. M. of the State of New York, 1903.

Arbour, Keith. *Benjamin Franklin's First Government Printing*. Philadelphia: American Philosophical Society, 1999.

Bagster, Samuel. *The Management of Bees*. London: S. Bagster, 1834.

Baring, Anne. *Rosa Mystica: A Symbolic Quest from the West and the East*. 13 December 2024. <https://www.animamundischool.org/voices-of-the-well-blog/symbol-of-the-rose-by-anne-baring#:~:text=In%20the%20Christian%20tradition%2C%20the,earthly%20perfection%2C%20but%20heavenly%20perfection.>.

Bassani, Luigi Marco. *The Real Jefferson*. 5 May 2002. 2 12 2024.

Bauval, Robert. *The Orion Mystery: Unlocking the Secrets of the Pyramids*. New York: Crown Trade Paperbacks, 1994.

Beato, Georgio. *Azoth*. 1605.

Billingsley, Henry. *The Elements of Geometry of the Most Ancient Philosopher Evclide of Megara*. London: Iohn Daye, 1570.

Bles, Major Arthur De. *How to Distinguish the Saints in Art*. New York: Art Culture Publications Inc., 1925.

Bonwick, James. *Egyptian Belief and Modern Thought*. London: C. Kegan Paul & Co., 1878.

Botkin, Dr. Daniel. "The Messiah's Hebrew Name "Yeshua" or "Yahshua"?" *The Eliyah Messenger* May-June 1966.

Bowes, Arthur. "Some Geometrical Canons of Architecture." *Discovery* (1920): 184-187.

Britannica, Domenico Campagnola. *"Domenico Campagnola." Encyclopedia Britannica*. February 2024. 26 December 2024.

Brocklesby, Richard. *An Explication of the Gospel-Theism and the Divinity of the Christian Religion*. London: F. Heptinstall, 1706.

Brown, Vic. *Pythagorean Triangle 3:4:5*. 11 October 2021. 10 October 2025.

Brownell. "Brownell's Oration." *The Freemasons' Monthly Magazine* 20 May 1868: 297-302.

Buck, J. D. *Mystic Masonry or The Symbols of Masonry and the Greater Mysteries of Antiquity*. Cincinnati: The Robert Clarke Company, 1897.

Bunsen, Baron. *Egypt's Place in Universal History*. London: Longman's, Green, and Co., 1867.

Burdge, Wallis. *The Gods Of The Egyptians or Studies In Egyptian Mythology*. London: Methuen & Co., 1904.

Burkle, William Steve. "Musings on the Geometric Properties of the Square and Compasses." 3 October 2008. *Pietre-Stone Review of Freemasonry.* 17 February 2025.

Byron, Lord. *The Works of Lord Byron*. Frankfurt: H. L. Brenner, 1826.

Campagnola, Domenico. *The Descent of the Holy Spirit*. The Cleveland Museum of Art, Gift of Ralph King 1924.215. *The Descent of the Holy Spirit*. Padua, Italy, 1518.

Carlile, Richard. *Manual of Freemasonry*. London: Andrew Vickers, 1855.

Casey, John. *The First Six Books of the Elements of Euclid*. London: Longmans, Green, & Co., 1885.

Castells, P. "The Author's Lodge, No. 345, The Geometry of the Ritual." *The Freemason and Masonic Illustrated. A Weekly Record of ..., Volume 54* 3 April 1915: 552.

Churchward, Albert. *The Arcana of Freemasonry, A History of Masonic Symbolism*. London: George Allen & Unwin Ltd., 1915.

Cino, Alesso d'Andrea and Bonaccorso di. *Hope*. Federico Zeri Foundation, Pistoia, Duomo.

Clair, George St. *Creation Records Discovered in Egypt*. London: Harrison and Sons, 1898.

Clarke, Adam. *The Holy Bible Containing the Old and New Testaments*. New York: N. Bangs and J. Emory, 1825.

Clegg, Robert Ingham. *Mackey's History of Freemasonry*. Chicago, New York, London: The Masonic History Company, 1898.

Cloland, J.K. *The Masonic Trinity and Way of the Cross*. n.d. 5 12 2024.

Compiled by A Member of the Craft. *Text Book of Freemasonry*. London: Reeves and Turner, 1881.

Cook, Keningale. "The Tradition of the Essenes." *The University Magazine* (1880): 146-199.

Cooper, W. R. *The Serpent Myths of Ancient Egypt*. London: Robert Hardwicke, 1873.

Coquerel, Ath. *The Fine Arts in Italy*. London: Edward T. Whitfield, 1859.

Croatti, Mark. *14 American Presidents BEFORE George Washington*. 23 September 2022. 30 11 2024.

Cross, Jeremy L. *The True Masonic Chart, or Hieroglyphic Monitor*. New-Haven: T. G. Woodward and Co., 1826.

—. *True Masonic Chart*. New York: A. S. Barnes & Co., 1857.

Dana, Marvin. "The Sacred Flower." *Lippincott's Monthly Magazine* (1898): 695-697.

Danckert, Cornelius. *De Stadt Ierusalem. The city of Jerusalem*. 1710.

Denslow, William. *10,000 Famous Freemasons*. Charlottesville: Cornerstone Book, 2007.

Dermott, Lau. *Ahiman Rezon, or a Help to All That Are (or Would Be) Free-Accepted Masons, Containing the Quintessence of All That Has Been Published on the Subject of Free-Masonry*. London: Robert Black, 1764.

Drake, Francis. *Dictionary of American Biography*. Boston: Houghton, Osgood & Company, 1879.

Duncan, Malcolm C. *Duncan's Masonic Ritual and Monitor*. New York: Dick & Fitzgerald, 1866.

Dürer, Albrecht. *Christ before Caiaphas*.

Ernst, Jacob. *The Craftsman and Freemason's Guide*. Cincinnati: Jacob Ernst Company, 1859.

Eyer, Shawn E. *This Divine Science: Architecture and Speculative Freemasonry*. 23 May 2015. 1 12 2024.

Faber, George Stanley. *The Origin of Pagan Idolatry Ascertained From Historical Testimony and Circumstantial Evidence*. London: A.J. Valpy, Tooke's Court, Chancery Lane, 1816.

Falconer, Don. *The Square and Compasses in Search of Freemasonry*. St. Ives, NSW: Don Falconer, 1999.

Fallaner. *Collection of Vatican Museums (Museo Gregoriano Egizio): Lions of Nectanebo I from Heliopolis*. Fallaner, CC BY-SA 4.0 <https://creativecommons.org/licenses/by-sa/4.0>, via Wikimedia Commons. *Own Work*. Vatican, 2020.

Ferguson, George. *Signs and Symbols*. London, Oxford, New York: Oxford University Press, 1954.

Finlayson, J. Finlay. *The Symbols And Legends Of Freemasonry*. London: George Kenning & Son, 1910.

Fludd, Robert. *Clavis Philosophiae Et Alchymiae Fluddanae. Sive Roberti Fluddi Armigeri, Et.* Francofurti: Prostat apud Guilhelmum Fitzerum, 1633.

Franklin, Benjamin. "Image 114 of Benjamin Franklin Papers: Series III, 1728-1841; Miscellaneous material; 1728-1783 (vol. 31)." 5 April 1775. *Library of Congress*. 30 December 2025.

—. *Poor Richard*. Philadelphia: B. Franklin, 1735. Digital.

FreeCEN. *FreeCEN. Free UK Genealogy*. n.d. 6 June 2025.

Freemasonry, wiki. *Orion's Belt*. 4 February 2024. 10 12 2024.

Gandolfi, Gaetano. *Cain Killing Abel*. Honolulu Museum of Art (formerly Academy). *Cain Killing Abel*. Bologna, 1760-1780.

Genchi, Daniel. *A Brief Introduction into Sacred Geometry*. 7 Oct 2021. 1 December 2024.

Grand Lodge of Maine. *Chapter 1*. 2025. 26 2 2025.

Great seal of the U.S." reverse side. Retrieved from the Library of Congress. *Great seal of the U.S.* n.d.

Hall, Manly P. *The Secret Teachings of All Ages*. San Francisco: Philosophical Research Society, 1928.

Hall, Manly. *The Lost Keys of Masonry: The Legend of Hiram Abiff*. Los Angeles: Hall Publishing Company, 1924.

Hambridge, Jay. *Dynamic Symmetry, The Greek Vase*. New Haven: Yale University Press, 1920.

Harris, William Hetherington. *The honey-bee: its nature, homes, and products*. London: R. Clay, Sons, and Taylor, Printers, 1884.

Hislop, Alexander. *The Two Babylons: The Papal Worship Proved to be The Worship of Nimrod and his Wife*. London: S.W. Partridge and Co., 1853-1919.

Hodson, John et al. *Masonic History of the Northwest*. San Francisco: The History Publishing Company, 1902.

Hogan, Timothy. *The Alchemical Keys to Masonic Ritual*. Timothy W. Hogan, 2007. .

Hogan, Timothy W. *Gnostic Reflections in Freemasonry*. 9 July 2009. 17 July 2023.

Holy Bible. *The Holy Bible Containing The Old and New Testaments*. Oxford: The University Press, 1854.

Hulme, Edward. *The History, Principles, and Practices of Symbolism in Christian Art*. London: Swan Sonnenschein & CO., 1892.

Hunt, John. *Altar's horns*. 2016. 09 12 2024.

Inman, Thomas. *Ancient Faiths Embodied in Ancient Names*. London: Trubner & Co.,, 1868.

Jameson, Mrs. *Sacred and Legendary Art Vol. I.* London: Longmans, Green, and Co., 1879.
Jefferson, Thomas. *The Life and Morals of Jesus of Nazareth.* New York: N. D. Thompson Publishing Co., 1902.
—. *The Works of Thomas Jefferson.* New York: Townsend, 1884.
—. *The Writings of Thomas Jefferson.* Washington: Taylor & Maury, 1854.
Jeremias, Alfred. *The Old Testament in the Light of the Ancient East.* New York: Williams & Norgate, 1911.
Julian Boyd, Gerald Gawalt. *The Declaration Of Independence: The Evolution of the Text.* Washington: . Library of Congress in association with the Thomas Jefferson Memorial Foundation ; Distributed by University Press of New England, 1999.
Kalian, Robert. *The Hidden Power of Freemasonry.* New York: Page Publishing Inc., 2018.
Kopel, Jonathan. *A fellowcraft's application of the plumb, the square, and the level in medical practice.* 13 January 2020. 1 12 2024.
Ladner, Gerhart B. *Images and Ideas in the Middle Ages.* Roma: Edizioni Di Storia E Letteratura, 1983.
L'EDIFICE. *Three small steps... to the Master's March.* n.d. https://www.ledifice.net/7310-J.html. 4 12 2024.
Lemaire, André. "Burial Box of James, the Brother of Jesus. Earliest archaeological evidence of Jesus found in Jerusalem." *Biblical Archaeology Society* (2002).
Littlefield, Gary A. "Grand historian's Corner." *Connecticut Freemasons* (2019): 9.
Lorenzo Langstroth, Charles Dadant, Camille Pierre Dadant. *Langstroth on the Hive and Honey Bee.* Hamilton: Dadant & Sons, 1907.
Lossing, Benson J. *Harper's Popular Cyclopedia of the United States History.* New York: Harper & Brothers, 1889.
Lucas, Stephen E. "The Stylistic Artistry of the Declaration of Independence." *Prologue: Quarterly of the National Archives and Records Administration* Spring 1990.
Lund, Johann. *Die Alten Jüdischen Heiligthümer.* Hamburg: Johann Wolfgang Fickweiler, 1722.
Mackey, Albert G. *An Encyclopedia of Freemasonry and its Kindred Sciences.* Philadelphia: Moss & Company, 1874.
—. *An Encyclopedia of Freemasonry and its Kindred Sciences.* Philadelphia: L. H. Everts & Co., 1894.
—. *An Encyclopedia of Freemasonry and Its Kindred Sciences.* Philadelphia: Moss & Company, 1874.
—. *Symbolism of Freemasonry.* New York: Clark and Maynard, 1869.
—. *The Symbolism of Freemasonry: The Sprig of Acacia.* New York: Clark and Maynard, 1882.
Masonic Encyclopedia. *Lion of the Tribe of Judah.* 2024. 12 12 2024.
Masonic Mirror. "Masonic Mirror." *Masonic Mirror and Mechanic's Intelligencer* (1826): 278.
McCabe, James D. *The Illustrated History of the Centennial Exhibition.* Philadelphia: The National Publishing Co., 1876.
McCoy, Drew R. "An Old Fashioned Nationalism: Lincoln, Jefferson, and the Classical Tradition." *Journal of The Abraham Lincoln Association* (2002): 55-67.
Ménard, René. *La Vie Privée des Anciens, The Private Life of the Ancients.* Paris: V. A. Morel and C. publishers, 1883.
Merrill, Steven. *Nimrod Darkness in the Cradle of Civilization.* United States: Xulon Press, 2004.

Moore, Charles W. "Masonic Portrait Gallery, The Living and the Dead No.3." *The Freemasons Monthly Magazine* (1872): 325-326.

NASA/JPL-Caltech. "Geologic 'Face on Mars' Formation (PIA01141)." *JPL Photojournal.* Pasadena: NASA, 25 July 1976.

Observatory, Chandra X-Ray. *Orion.* 10 12 2024. <https://chandra.si.edu/photo/constellations/orion.html#:~:text=Ancient%20Egyptians%20thought%20the%20stars,soul%20of%20the%20god%20Osiris.>.

Okorafor, Chris Aniche. *Readily Identifiable Footprint of the Cabala in Craft Freemasonry.* 3 October 2008. 27 12 2024.

Parenti, Daniela. *The Baptism of Christ.* n.d. 26 12 2024.

Pennsylvania, Grand Lodge of. *The Square and Compass.* 11 March 2016. 17 12 2024.

Person, A. *The Computation of 666 and Its Relation to Antichristian Systems.* London: James Nisbet & Co., 1891.

Peterson, Merrill D. *Thomas Jefferson: Writings.* New York: The Library of America, 1984.

Pike, Albert. *Morals and Dogma.* Charleston: Supreme Council of the Southern Jurisdiction of the Scottish Rite of Freemasonry, 1872.

Pope Leo IX. Illuminated Manuscript. *Pope Leo IX.* 1049-1054.

Portal, Frédéric baron de. *An Essay on Symbolic Colours in Antiquity, The Middle Ages and Modern Times.* London: John Weale, 1845.

Potter, T. Chalmers. *Queenie.* New York: Moffat, Yard and Company, 1911.

Preston, Willian. *Illustrations of Masonry.* London: R. Spencer, 1861.

Raddato, Carole. *Apis Bull.* Attribution-ShareAlike (CC BY-SA 2.0). *Lifesize basalt statue of the Apis Bull dedicated by Hadrian to Serapis in Alexandria (Egypt), Osiris, Sunken Mysteries of Egypt exhibition, Paris.* Paris, 2016.

Ransome, Hilda M. *The Sacred Bee in Ancient Times and Folklore.* London: George Allen &Unwin, 1937.

Roberts. *The Sacred Heart of Jesus.* Library of Congress. *The Sacred Heart of Jesus.* New York, 1866. Digital.

Robinson, Ray. *Pietre-Stones Review of Freemasonry, Collection of Masonic Tracing Boards,3rd Degree, England 1780.* 9 5 2012. 5 1 2025.

Robson, Clive. *The Square Magazine, The Theosophical Society.* 2024. 5 12 2024.

Sherwood, Gilbert, and Piper, Paternoster-Row. *The Freemason's Quarterly Review.* London: Madden and Co., 1847.

Short Talk Bulletin - Vol. X November, 1932 No.11. *Sprig of Acacia.* November 1932. 11 12 2024.

Simson, Robert. *The Elements of Euclid.* Glasgow: Robert and Andrew Foulis Printers to the University, 1751.

Stevenson, David. *The Origins of Freemasonry: Scotland's Century 1590-1710.* New York: Cambridge University Press, 1988.

Stone, E. *Euclid's Elements of Geometry.* London: Tho. Payne, 1752.

Tangopaso. *Sarcophagus of Ramses III. Width on the southern side. (Louvre Museum, Paris, France).* Tangopaso. *Self-photographed.* Paris, 2018.

The Ankh Cross and Freemasonry. *The Ankh Cross and Freemasonry.* 07 2 2024. 5 12 2024.

The Asiatic Quarterly Review. "Mythology and Psychology of the Ancient Egyptians." *The Asiatic Quarterly Review Volume 3* January-April 1892: 377-413.

The Library of Congress. *Catalogue of the Library of Thomas Jefferson Volume IV*. Washington: United States Government Printing Office, 1955.

The U.S. National Archives and Records. *Lee Resolution (1776)*. 8 February 2022. 30 November 2024.

Thibault, Marie Thérèse Hébert & Jean Robert. *Egypt, Cairo, Museum of Egyptian Antiquities, Anubis*. cc-by-sa-2.0. *Egypt, Cairo, Museum of Egyptian Antiquities, Anubis, the jackal god, found in the tomb of Tutankhamun. Cairo*. Cairo, 2020.

Unknown. "Sprig of Acacia." *Short Talk Bulletin - Vol. X No.11* (1932).

Vinci, Andrea del Verrocchio e Leonardo da Vinci. *Baptism of Christ*. Uffizi Gallery. *Baptism of Christ*. Florence, 1472–1475. Digital, Photographer Livioandronico2013.

Warren, Henry George. *The Freemasons' Magazine and Masonic Mirror Vol. V.* London: Ford and Tilt, 1858.

Weed, Clarence Moore. *Life Histories of American Insects*. London, New York: The Macmillan Company, 1897.

Wehle, F.W. *Ascension of Christ. Ascension of Christ*. Milwaukee, 1884.

Wheeler, Ken L. *Pythagoras, Plato and the Golden Ratio. The Golden Ratio and the Pentagram in the philosophy of the Pythagoreans*. Lexington: Darkstar Publications, 2005.

Woodrow, Ralph. *Babylon Mystery Religion Ancient and Modern*. Riverside, California: Evangelistic Association, Inc., 1966.

XIII, Catholic Church. Pope 1878-1903: Leo. *Humanum Genus*. Charleston: GR Orient of Charleston, 1884.

Author's Note on Artificial Intelligence Assistance

During the preparation of this manuscript, generative artificial intelligence tools, including versions of ChatGPT, Google Gemini, and Grammarly, were employed to refine grammar, phrasing, and structural clarity. Crucially, these tools acted only as linguistic aids; they did not generate the core ideas, speculative frameworks, or interpretive analysis presented here. The intellectual substance and creative vision of this work are entirely my own.

www.ingramcontent.com/pod-product-compliance
Lightning Source LLC
LaVergne TN
LVHW081633120826
845149LV00025B/1885
9780999639764